Facts, Artifacts and Counterfacts

Theory and Method for a Reading and Writing Course

DAVID BARTHOLOMAE
and
ANTHONY R. PETROSKY

University of Pittsburgh

BOYNTON/COOK PUBLISHERS, INC.
UPPER MONTCLAIR, NEW JERSEY 07043

Library of Congress Cataloging-in-Publication Data

Facts, artifacts and counterfacts.

　　1. English language—Rhetoric—Study and
teaching. 2. Reading (Higher education)
I. Bartholomae, David. II. Petrosky, Anthony.
PE404.F33　　　808'.042'0711　　　86-4235
ISBN 0-86709-135-5

For information address Boynton/Cook Publishers, Inc.
52 Upper Montclair Plaza, P.O. Box 860, Upper Montclair, NJ 07043

Printed in the United States of America.

86　87　88　89　10　9　8　7　6　5　4　3　2　1

Facts, Artifacts and Counterfacts

Theory and Method for a Reading and Writing Course

To Robert D. Marshall

Preface

    This is a book about reading, writing and teaching and the ways each can be imagined, variously, as acts of composition. It offers materials from a course we have been teaching for several years, and it offers accounts of the course and its students by ourselves and our colleagues. We speak most immediately, then, about reading, writing and teaching through our work with "basic writers," students whose performance when asked to use or produce written texts has placed them outside the conventional boundaries of the undergraduate curriculum. This is a book to serve those who teach similar courses (or who would like to experiment with ours) or those who have a more general interest in basic problems of advanced literacy (the problems of students who, while they can read and write, fail to read and write in ways that serve the ends or meet the expectations of university education). The book offers abundant examples of their work and argues a way of reading them.

    The point of reference, however, can shift the other way. The course we describe could easily be imagined as an honors course and not a remedial or developmental one. This is deliberately so. The earliest argument we made when our college was debating whether to include this course in the curriculum (and whether to include it for credit) was that there was no reason to prohibit students from doing serious work because they could not do it correctly. In a sense, all courses in the curriculum ask students to do what they cannot yet do well. There was no good reason to take students who were not fluent readers and writers and consign them to trivial or mechanical work in the belief that it would somehow prepare them for a college education. It would make more sense, rather, to enroll these students in an exemplary course — a small seminar where students met to read, write and talk about a single problem or subject — and to provide the additional time and support they needed to work on reading and writing while they were, in fact, doing the kinds of reading and writing that characterize college study.

If, as we believe, the course presented here can stand as an example of any first- or second-year course in the liberal arts, then our book offers also the opportunity for educators generally to see how those acts of reading, writing and thinking that characterize work in the academy appear to those students whose preparation has not made those activities "natural" or "normal" or habitual. These "marginal" students offer their approximations of our world and our work. It is a dramatic and sometimes difficult experience to see our world through their eyes. If nothing else, it has changed what we take for granted when we talk about how or why a person should read or write.

Our work on the course began several years ago when Bob Marshall, the dean of our college, asked if we could design a course for the increasing number of students who were unprepared to do the work of the standard curriculum. This was not, however, to be a course outside the curriculum — an annex where certain students would be assigned to learn what they had failed to learn in high school. It should be rooted in an existing department. It should be taught by regular faculty. It should be the sort of course for which students could receive full academic credit. Even if the students did not yet have the skills they were supposed to have, the dean was unwilling to have the college define its students in this way, believing that to do so would be destructive not only to the students but to the college itself (in the latter case by allowing the faculty to assume that the only measure of quality work was that which they took for granted on the basis of what they saw in themselves, or in young people who were, more or less, versions of themselves). The dean who prepared the way for this course taught a section in our first semester, when there were many looking on to see if we could do what we said we could do; and he continues to teach a section each semester, including today, when there is no one but the students looking on. His example as a teacher and his commitment to liberal education remain exemplary for us. We are pleased to offer this book in his name.

The book is divided into three parts. The "Introduction" is a fairly long essay presenting an overview of the course and the versions of reading and writing that hold it together. The second part, "Teaching Reading and Writing," presents the course materials and a short chapter on how they are used. The course materials are presented in the exact form that they are distributed to our students. It isn't necessary to read through them all in order to understand the essays that follow in the third part. It would be helpful, however, to skim through the assignments to get a general sense of the rhythm and texture of the course. The final part, "Discerning Principles," brings together some of the research and writing that has been done in the course. The purpose of these essays is not to defend or explain a curriculum. They all examine basic issues or problems in composition: revision, editing, invention, reading and interpretation. They locate these issues, however, in a single setting — the charged situation of a classroom in which novices are asked to perform as experts.

One of the pleasures of this book for us is that it stands as the record of a collaborative project. The course is shaped and revised year in and year out by the staff who meet regularly to share student papers, to revise assignments and to talk about the truly perplexing business of representing reading and writing in a college classroom. We have, then, many people to thank, particularly those of our colleagues who are not represented here as authors: Bob Marshall, again; Karen Hjelmervik and Susan Merriman, who helped early on to shape the course materials; Elaine Lees, Tina Calabro, Dan Morrow, Sue Gelburd, Paul Kameen, Fred Koloc, Lynn Buncher Shelley. All have helped to keep the course alive for us and for our students. We owe thanks to Harry Sartain, Bob Hinman and Mary Louise Briscoe — department chairs who have helped to preserve and foster a course which makes peculiar demands on the staff and the curriculum. Bob Glaser and the Learning Research Development Center at the University of Pittsburgh gave us valuable support in the preparation of this manuscript. Whatever we have learned about writing assignments and using them to define a sequence of instruction began with the rich and compelling example of our colleague, William E. Coles, Jr. The profession generally owes a debt to Bob Boynton, who has helped make it possible for us to talk to each other in public about teaching. We are grateful for his long-standing support and encouragement. The two of us also owe a debt to his colleague, Peter Stillman, who helped to push, shove and guide our project into print. And, finally, we would like to thank our colleagues who are featured here as writers: Mariolina Salvatori, Nick Coles, Susan Wall, Marilyn DeMario and Glynda Hull. Their scholarly interest in the course and its students has done much to improve our teaching.

Contents

3. Teaching the Course
Marilyn B. DeMario

I.

Introduction

1.
Facts, Artifacts and Counterfacts

A Basic Reading and Writing Course for the College Curriculum

DAVID BARTHOLOMAE
ANTHONY R. PETROSKY

> I believe that the communication of information, of ostensive and verifiable "facts," constitutes only one part, and perhaps a secondary part, of human discourse. The potentials of fiction, of counterfactuality, of undecidable futurity profoundly characterize both the origins and the nature of speech. . . . They determine the unique, often ambiguous tenor of human consciousness and make the relations of that consciousness to "reality" creative. Through language, so much of which is focused inward to our private selves, we reject the empirical inevitability of the world. Through language, we construct what I have called "alternities of being." To the extent that every individual speaker uses an idiolect, the problem of Babel is, quite simply, that of human individuation. But different tongues give to the mechanism of "alternity" a dynamic, transferable enactment. They realize needs of privacy and territoriality vital to our identity. To a greater or lesser degree, every language offers its own reading of life. To move between languages, to translate, . . . is to experience the almost bewildering bias of the human spirit towards freedom.
>
> George Steiner, *After Babel*[1]

The Course — A Beginning

Nine years ago (1977), at the request of the Dean of the College
of Arts and Sciences at the University of Pittsburgh, we designed
a course to teach young adults how to read and write. Ours were
students outside the mainstream, students unprepared for the
textual demands of a college education. Most of them were
minority or special-admission students. With our colleagues, we
have taught the course every year since then, making changes as
we better understood what we were doing and who we were
doing it to.[2] This book is not only a description of the course
as we are teaching it now, but it is also an extended presentation
of the metaphors we have chosen to represent our subject.

The opening passage from *After Babel* is offered not so
much as a credo (our staff does not regularly recite "I believe
that the communication of information is only a secondary part
of human discourse"), but as a way of initiating a discussion of
reading and writing. Steiner's language allows us grand and tempt-
ing claims: we offer, then, the enactment of "alternities," the
possibility of "freedom," the assertion of personal and territorial
rights. But the impulse can be translated into a more everyday
setting. Ours is not a course in study skills. We don't teach students how to find information in a textbook — to skim and scan
and read topic sentences. We don't use workbooks; we use real
books. Our assignments ask for something other than reports
and summaries. Our students write drafts and revisions, not exercises; they work on semester-long projects, not the usual set
pieces defined by discrete weekly themes.

We intend, in other words, to reclaim reading and writing
from those (including our students) who would choose to limit
these activities to the retrieval and transmission of information.
We don't have students shuttling information from texts to
teachers and back again, but shuttling, themselves, between languages — theirs and ours — between their understanding of what
they have read and their understanding of what they must say
to us about what they have read. (Our language is the language
of written academic discourse, including the peculiar spoken
version that passes as "talk" in disciplined classroom discussion.
Their language, when they speak or write for us, cannot simply
be characterized as the language of the streets or the language
of home or the language of the neighborhood. It is something
in the margin, belonging neither here nor there and preventing
their participation as speakers with place, privilege or authority.)[3] We want students to learn to compose a response to their

reading (and, in doing so, to learn to compose a reading) within the conventions of the highly conventional language of the university classroom. We are, then, teaching the language of the university and, if our course is a polemic, it is so because we believe that the language of the university can be shown to value "counterfactuality," "individuation," "potentiality," and "freedom."

Let's imagine one of our students sitting down to write the first assignment, an essay in response to a chapter from Margaret Mead's autobiography, *Blackberry Winter*, a chapter about her experience as a student at DePauw. The student is writing this essay before she has heard or participated in any discussion of that chapter in class, so this is a situation that dramatically calls into question her relationship to her material (that text) and her situation (one where she must bring into play whatever language she can muster to cast that text into our terms). She has read the chapter, but it is still there, on her desk, with whatever marginal notations or underlinings she has made (probably none), and it is there, in her head, with whatever memory she has of words, characters and events. But with all of this, the chapter remains stiff, obdurate — silent. The student has nothing to say (or so she would say if we stepped in and asked her). She is unable to speak, and the text is silent, unable to speak for her and fill up her page. (Unless, that is, she begins to literally copy Mead's page onto her own, word for word. This is a telling gesture and, most likely, a desperate one. It is also one we have frequently observed.)

The question for a teacher is how to phrase the problem here. One could say that it is conceptual. The student, we've found, would be quick to say that she doesn't remember what she read, and that this frustrates her. And yet no reader, of course, remembers everything in a text. The problem for this student, more likely, is that she doesn't trust the selective contours of her memory. She remembers this and that (most likely some of the moments from the anecdotal sections of Mead's chapter), but she takes those bits and pieces as fragments without a context (again, since she can't remember the whole chapter) or as evidence that her wavering attention is arbitrary or perverse. (She remembers things from the text, but they are not what she is *supposed* to remember.) This is a student, we could say, who lacks easy access to procedures for organizing and presenting what she does remember (or for organizing and presenting what she could find were she to go back into the text and look again at its pages).

One could also say, however, that the problems are those of status and authority. The student does not feel empowered to create the context within which the bits and pieces of the chapter could be organized (by articulating, for example, her account of why it might make sense to think of the chapter through those episodes she recalls). She does not feel that she has the authority to turn her wavering attention into a *reading* of Margaret Mead, into a translation of that chapter that could stand as a successful reading. She faces the essential dilemma of any reader: to write about the text she must displace it, cast it into her terms, turn it into something that it is not. She must do more than copy Mead's words down on her sheet of paper. She has to misread, and she has to take that misreading as a sign of her place as a reader and not as a sign of her failure. Reading is misreading. This is one of the commonplace paradoxes of those accounts of the reading process that dominate recent critical theory. As Jonathan Culler says:

> The claim that all readings are misreadings can also be justified by the most familiar aspects of critical and interpretive practice. Given the complexities of texts, the reversibility of tropes, the extendability of context, and the necessity for a reading to select and organize, every reading can be shown to be partial. Interpreters are able to discover features and implications of a text that previous interpreters neglected or distorted. They can use the text to show that previous readings are in fact misreadings, but their own readings will be found wanting by later interpreters, who may astutely identify the dubious presuppositions or particular forms of blindness to which they testify.[4]

The question is not, then, whether some students' readings miss the mark. All readings are misses. The key question, as Culler says, is "whose misses matter," and *these* decisions depend upon a "host of complex and contingent factors," factors that help "one to question the institutional forces and practices that institute the normal by marking or excluding the deviant."[5]

For our hypothetical student to have something to say, she must replace Margaret Mead's words with her own. This is a bold and difficult act. She is, as she knows, in a "remedial course," a course for poor readers and poor writers. And Margaret Mead is not only a writer, someone represented to her in a published text, she is a writer whose work has been assigned in a course where the student is a student. The student, in other words, must assume an authority that, in a very real sense, she does not have. If her teachers would tell her what to say, if we would give her an authorized translation, then she would not be in such a bind. But her teachers, in this case, have remained silent, too. This silence is, we believe, the only proper beginning. If she lacks the key words and interpretive schemes of a reader or writer in the mainstream, she also lacks a place to begin, a position that would authorize her as a reader and a writer. A course in reading and writing whose goal is to empower students must begin with silence, a silence students must fill. It cannot begin by telling students what to say. And it must provide a method to enable students to see what they have said — to see and characterize the acts of reading and writing represented by their discourse. The purpose of this reflection is to enable revision, to enable students to reimagine the roles they might play as readers and writers. A course in reading and writing must, then, provide students with a place to begin, and it must do this in the first week of class. It fails if it assumes that it need only provide the preliminary skills, some groundwork that will enable students to begin later, perhaps after the basic writing course or the freshman English course or the introductory course — when, for the first time, they will sit down with the responsibility of having something to say.

As we read Steiner's opening passage, it argues that the conceptual ability to transform that which is given to a writer (what he calls "reality") cannot be imagined separately from the rhetorical ability to transform an historical situation (to negotiate territory, to "move between languages"). Steiner insists that to move between languages is "to translate." It is not like shedding skin or changing clothes or replacing one tape with another in a cassette player. It is neither a matter of taking "native" abilities and refining them nor a matter of replacing ignorance with wisdom. Both of these designs imply pedagogies that we felt the need to push against when we began thinking about our course. There are liberation pedagogies to restore to students their "natural" voices and there are, to use Freire's terms, "banking pedagogies," which deposit true knowledge in minds that are otherwise empty. Our experience with basic readers and writers has taught us that the change that takes place can never be so complete or total, and the process can never be so easy, since, as Steiner suggests, it calls into play "needs of privacy and territoriality vital to our identity." And if this is generally true for all language users, it is dramatically and sometimes violently true for our students. As Steiner demonstrates in the opening passage, it is not just a "subject" that is changed when one turns it into an artifact, but a writers's relationship to those around him that is changed as well.

Our students begin, then, with a hesitant and tenuous relationship to the materials we put before them, to the terms and imaginative structures that could make that material available, and to the institutional context within which they are required to speak and to write. These are the "facts" that students face, the facts that must be transformed or translated into the artifacts — the student papers and performances — that provide the real subject matter of a course in reading and writing. The subject our students study, then, is their own discourse — their representations of the class's common material, the key terms and structures of their discussion and essays, the context they represent and imagine. And the pedagogy of the course, the mechanism of instruction, is represented by our representations of the motive to "counterfactuality," the motive to alter those artifacts, to reject their apparent inevitability. The assignments we provide offer the occasion for our students to reimagine and reapproximate the classroom materials, the terms and structures that make those materials available for thought and discussion, and the situation that places these students outside of the mainstream work of the academy. The purpose of the course is to bring forward the image of the reader and writer represented in our students' textual performances (what some would take as their inevitable roles) so that they can reimagine themselves as readers and writers. This is the way we read (and, as some would say, domesticate or qualify) Steiner's assertion that "Through language, we construct . . . 'alternities of being'."

In the course, and in this book, we are presenting reading and writing as a struggle within and against the languages of academic life. A classroom performance represents a moment in which, by speaking or writing, a student must enter a closed community, with its secrets, codes and rituals. And this is, we argue, an historical as well as a conceptual drama. The student has to appropriate or be appropriated by a specialized discourse, and he has to do this as though he were easily and comfortably one with his audience, as though he were a member of the academy. And, of course, he is not. He has to invent himself as a reader and he has to invent an act of reading by assembling a language to make a reader and a reading possible, finding some compromise between idiosyncracy, a personal history, and the requirements of convention, the history of an institution.

Culler says that "To read is to play the role of a reader and to posit an experience of reading." [6] The difference between our students and the students Culler imagines ("successful" students in a college literature course) is not that our students are unaware that reading requires this complex act of imagining but that they do not have such easy access to the structures of reading that English teachers take for granted, those structures that provide access to the "normal" curriculum. For these students, then, the stakes are higher. When they present a "reading" of a text, their misreadings do not serve as predictable responses in a standard classroom drama — where a teacher takes delight in "naive" readings, since those readings are the very cues that enable his performance as a teacher. For our students, the misses are precisely those misses that matter — those that, because of principles of inclusion and exclusion that go largely unquestioned, deny some students participation in the play of reading that goes on within the boundaries of the academic community.

"To move between languages, to translate . . . is to experience the almost bewildering bias of the human spirit towards freedom." As we are reading Steiner now, we are putting particular pressure on this sentence, since we are arguing (and, we believe, in the same spirit of generosity) that the experience of translation is simultaneously the experience of "the bewildering bias of the human spirit" towards captivity, towards participation in an established discourse community, one represented by our classrooms. A translation, then, is also a loss, a displacement of the original, a definition of oneself in terms of another or in another's terms.[7] The course described in this book is designed to give students access to the language and methods of the academy. It is not a course designed to make the academy — or its students — disappear.

Reading and Writing

Behind this course are certain assumptions about what successful reading and writing are and about the procedures that make them possible. What follows attempts to bring these assumptions forward. After reading and reviewing a quarter century's research and theory on reading and writing, we are well aware of the dangers of portraying mental processes as schemes or set routines. Still, to paraphrase I. A. Richards, it is better to make a mistake that can be exposed than to do nothing; it is better for a teacher or a researcher to have an account of reading and writing than to have none, provided, that is, "that we do not suppose that our account really tells us what happens — provided, that is, we do not mistake our theories for our skill, or our descriptive apparatus for what it describes."[8] This is why we were quick to say, earlier in this chapter, that we are offering metaphors for reading and writing, not descriptions of the processes themselves.

The failure to recognize the metaphorical nature of such descriptions has haunted research and pedagogy in language learning. Because writers, for instance, can be said to proceed systematically, teachers have offered as holy writ that writers begin with a "controlling idea." The work of writing, then, is to illustrate and amplify the truth of that controlling idea. This version of writing locates control outside of language or its use by a writer (in an "idea" that stands before writing) and serves a rhetoric where the greatest good is the celebration of the given, one of the generally available cultural commonplaces that students can quickly bring forward in a topic sentence: "Hard work leads to success." "Sports are valuable because they teach us sportsmanship." "Rules stifle the imagination." A writer's job, at best, is only to illustrate and extend the commonplace, not to question it or to qualify its truth through the exemplary material a writer might bring forward. As a consequence, it frustrates students who either do not feel the "controlling" force of an idea or who are dissatisfied with it. And it frustrates teachers, who complain of well-formed essays that "do nothing" or "go nowhere."

The appeal of this pedagogy most likely resides in the very image of control it takes for granted, one that defines a writer's authority as his ability to locate himself within the givens of our culture (including our academic culture) and that defines the work of the writer as the job of using set routines (examples, transitions and conclusions) to extend and justify the "truth" of what he has been given to say. This is the writer's version of a classroom task often set for readers — where a reader finds a topic sentence or a controlling idea in a given text (like a chapter from *Blackberry Winter*) and presents it in its own terms. For the writer, however, the "text" is the text of our common culture. The rhetoric of the controlling idea requires writers who are not only able, but also willing to work with common examples or to take common truths as their own. It presents special problems, then, for marginal students, students outside what we take to be our "common" culture, students without easy access to that stock of commonplaces or routines for their presentation. An alternative pedagogy would locate "control" in readers or writers and in what they can do with the material before them. The pedagogy of the "controlling idea," in other words, is not a neutral technology. It offers a view of public life that excludes some and includes others. And it defines writing in a way that serves specific social and intellectual purposes.

The rhetoric of the "controlling idea," a rhetoric whose model of the good citizen is at the center of most writing instruction, has its reading counterpart. The reading textbooks say, "Find the author's main idea, look to see how he supports it, and shape your reading accordingly." There is no reason to assume that this describes or should describe a student's experience of a text or the best possible use she can make of it. Because readers need to distinguish between the possible translations of a text and what the text might signify to a particular community of readers, it is useful to talk about a "main idea," where the main idea represents a guess at the consensus comprehension of a particular group reading for a particular purpose. Teachers, for example, may not want students to talk about what they did over the weekend in an essay on *Coming of Age in Samoa*, at least if the purpose for writing about that book is to summarize what would generally be taken as Mead's appraisal of key elements in Samoan culture (or if the purpose is to imagine what a specific group of readers — readers in the academy, for example — would notice, recall and have to say about that book).

One could imagine a context, however, in which a discussion of "what I did last weekend" could demonstrate a powerful understanding of that book. As soon as a "main idea" is taken to be a *thing* residing fixed in a text, to be guessed at or located by following clues in paragraph structure, anything useful in the metaphor of the main idea is lost altogether. More importantly, however, meaning becomes something external, something contained in a text (the way a can of peas contains peas) or something that exists out in the world (like a chair or a desk), rather than something that results when a reader or writer finds a language to make the presentation of meaning possible, a process that is at once an individual's concession to the beliefs of the community and an assertion of his own vision of possibility, of her territorial rights.

There is a strong textual bias in this approach to reading, one that ignores the rhetorical nature of reading, where a "main idea" is as much a function of a reader's prior experience with a subject (his way of speaking about that subject and representing it to himself) and his reason for reading as it is a function of anything "coded" in the text. When Bartholomae reads an essay by Walker Percy, for example, his account of the main ideas (or of the key terms or the interesting examples) is different from Petrosky's, although Petrosky is not wrong about the essay and it is not useful to assume that he is a poorer reader. The difference is not an index to the quality of the reading. And the meaning a book (like *The Message in the Bottle*) has for us the first time we read it is very different from the meaning we would say that we "found" in it when we reread it two or three years later.

The overriding pedagogical problem with the concept of a single, identifiable main idea that all readers can agree upon is that it denies readers their own transaction with a text, and it denies them the understanding that reading is such a transaction rather than an attempt to guess at a meaning that belongs to someone else. In fact, the exercises used in traditional reading skills instruction are set up as if these factors did not exist, or as if they were static, mere annoyances. When we first started thinking about the course, we visited the only existing reading courses on our campus, those offered in a learning skills center. What we found was instruction that gave students a way of looking at sample paragraphs in an exercise book but not a way of looking at readers or reading. We also found teachers who took the inevitable hassles over what a paragraph "means" as signs of student failure or perversity and not as signs of vigorous, successful reading. We certainly don't intend to say that *all* student readings are vigorous and successful. We do feel, however, that there are strong pedagogical reasons why a teacher might be more generous.

When reading is defined as something other than the activity of working one's way through a long, complex text and imposing order and meaning on the information acquired from the text, it is easy to see literacy as the sum of constituent skills. This distortion is most pronounced in a reading lab where a specialist teaches students to read without, in effect, having them do any reading. Students read isolated paragraphs in workbooks and choose sentences that could be said to stand for the main idea in the passage. They then wait to be told whether they are correct or not. The skills approach, common in high schools and universities, makes among other mistakes the simple one of failing to see that comprehending a paragraph in isolation is so very different from comprehending a whole text — in the amount and nature of textual material to be processed and in the nature of a reader's involvement with that material — to make it virtually impossible for one to stand for the other.

Our review of our students' reading problems led us to agree with Thomas Farrell that the alarm about college students' low reading ability is misdirected if those problems are taken to be problems with the "mechanics" of reading.[9] The skills that need to be developed, for students at this age and level of development, can't be separated from specific texts and specific academic tasks. Or, to put it another way, if a chapter from *Blackberry Winter* presented difficulties to our students, those difficulties can't be adequately represented as difficulties with vocabulary, syntax or structure. Workbook exercises in vocabulary, sentence structure or paragraph patterns would not improve our students' ability to reconstruct the chapter in a meaningful way, since the grammar of that elaboration is not defined by the grammar of the sentence or the structure of the paragraph. Even if our students could literally remember and understand every word or sentence in that text (and, of course, this would be madness), they'd be no better able to reassemble that text in an essay of their own. The unsatisfactory responses in our students' essays, might, then, best be seen as approximations of a hypothetical, "standard" academic response rather than as evidence of the failure of the reading mechanism. If we see those responses as approximations of conventional responses, as attempts at translating a "reading" of the chapter into the language of classroom discourse, where each failure is evidence of possibilities incompletely imagined, then a different course of instruction is implied. Rather than leading students through exercises aimed at the mastery of constituent skills, we might allow students regular attempts at imagining what a reader might say and do in response to a full and demanding text.

In the arguments we had to make to convince a university administration that reading could be taught in an English department (English teachers, we were told, don't know how to teach reading), we did not get very far arguing that the available skills instruction was theoretically naive. In fact, we had little success until we turned the reading skills model against itself and asked the faculty if the only use they could imagine for reading in the college curriculum was the reading of introductory textbooks. If the textbook was the central text of the liberal arts curriculum, then skimming and scanning and searching for topic sentences perhaps was sufficient. If not, then something else was required.

It is easier, however, to say that students, as readers, should be at the center of a course on reading and writing than it is to imagine such a course or to teach one. If, for example, a teacher cannot — or should not — tell students what Mead says in *Blackberry Winter* (or if she cannot — or should not — tell students whether they have found the "right" meaning), then what does a teacher do and what is it that a teacher teaches? How, for example, does she distinguish between one student reading and another? The quick answer is that she teaches writing (ways of composing a reading of *Blackberry Winter* and ways of reading what a student has composed) and that she distinguishes between students' responses on the quality of the demonstration they offer. (And there is, of course, no quick answer to the question of how it is that a teacher is to do this. We could say that a good reading is one that is interesting or useful or coherent or self-conscious or authoritative or generous or disciplined, but all of these words are empty — mere bluff — unless you can see how we use them to distinguish one student performance from another and, in doing so, demonstrate our beliefs about the value and purpose of intellectual life. Most of the chapters that follow base their discussions on examples from students' essays. The very fact that we talk about teaching through examples of our students' work is one sign of what we value. As you read those essays, you'll have a chance to see us — that is, the group of us who teach the course and who write about it — demonstrating our beliefs in our practice.)

To those who would say that the problem with a course that turns meaning over to students is that "anything goes," we would answer that the problem with ones that don't is that nothing happens — or nothing that seems to us to be intellectually or educationally interesting.[10] A course of instruction that directly or indirectly tells students where to "find" meanings — by giving meanings to them in lectures or through leading questions (where meaning can be found in the words of experts) or by providing techniques for finding the topic sentences (where meaning can be found through an accurate map of the text) — does not enable students to imagine a reader who makes meanings and who finds herself caught between individual responses and public responsibilities. It is not, in other words, a course in reading.

Our course offers reading as an activity and centers itself on a general inquiry into the possible relations between a reader and a text, something that can be represented by studying the specific written responses of specific readers. This is where we begin each term. Our goal is to develop a way of talking about a reader or a reading that can make sense to students. We want to develop, through dialogue, an enabling language, one that can give students a view of themselves as readers and writers so that they may begin to transform the roles that they play. A text in our class, then, becomes an occasion for meaning, not a meaning in itself, and the possibilities for meaning in any given text remain open until, as a class, we see what we have done and begin to imagine what else might be done. Any reading necessarily reduces the text, makes it less than it is, so that the appropriate question is not whether a reading is correct but whether, on the one hand, it is rich, convincing, useful or interesting, and whether, on the other, it is conscious of its own governing shape, disciplined, coherent. In evaluating any individual reading, we are evaluating a reader, or the image of a reader defined in the language of a response. As Richards argues in *How To Read A Page*, texts

> have many meanings because they touch us at points at which each of us is himself many-minded. Understanding them is very much more than picking a possible reasonable interpretation, clarifying that, and sticking to it. Understanding them is seeing how the varied possible meanings hang together, which of them depends on what else, how and why the meanings which matter most to us form part of our world — seeing thereby more clearly what our world is and what we are who are building it to live in.[11]

By studying our readings, Richards says, we can see more clearly what our world is and who we are that are building it — building it, that is, the way a reader could be said to construct (or reconstruct) a text out of the languages available to him. While it may be possible to imagine a world that exists independently of our ways of talking about it, while it may be possible to imagine a text that exists separately from a reading of it, the world that we know and the texts that we know are compositions that we write, languages about languages, stories we write based on stories we recall, stories buried in and making up our consciousness. It is for this reason that we choose to represent our student readers as composers rather than decoders. And it is for this reason that our course begins, rather than ends, with the texts our students write. From the second meeting on, we reproduce sample essays written for the class and put them on the table for the group to study. We want them to see readings of *Blackberry Winter* that represent readers (perhaps confused, perhaps many-minded), in order to begin to talk about the stories those readings tell.

For students to begin to write, they must assume that the chapter we have given them is meaningful (often the first failure of the readers we encounter). This means more than that they must *hope* that meaning can emerge from their encounter with the text; it means that they must act as if it can and that the meaning can be spun from their words rather than Mead's. (We think of I. A. Richards' response to a student who felt stymied by a difficult text: "Read it as though it made sense and perhaps it will.")[12]

The history of classroom instruction contains many stories of reading.[13] One of them goes something like this. A reader is a person who imagines that the text embodies certain intentions — meanings put there by a writer saying something to a reader. This is not a necessary structure for reading, but it is a familiar one. For example, the structure "When Margaret Mead says X, she is saying Y" is a translation based upon a fiction a reader may create to justify a reading by performing it in the name of someone more powerful than he, in this case in the name of Margaret Mead. He can create a line of argument and attribute it to Mead (and years of schooling may demonstrate that this can be done convincingly), but he has no immediate access to what could be called Mead's actual intentions. In other words, the "Margaret Mead" who has written, the "reader" who has read her, the situation that gives shape and authority to this reading — all are part of a narrative the reader invents, one he is hypothetically free to invent in a variety of ways, depending on his willingness to subvert conventional expectations. He could, for example, use his reading as the occasion to reveal what Mead had intended to keep secret, to speak of secret rather than manifest intentions. He could argue that the details Mead presents as insignificant are, "in fact," the most significant details, "keys" to the text. Or he could talk about the text as though he had no responsibility to anyone called "Margaret Mead" at all.

The varieties of readings a class actually produces, in other words, can be presented as evidence that reading is a constructive act, not that some students are good readers and some bad. And they can be offered as evidence that a written reading — an essay written about a text — is both retrospective and recuperative. At their best, these essays speak of a control that the writer has the leisure to imagine and to invent in an act of writing. This "reading" comes after a reader has read over the pages or "finished" the book. This seems obvious — that you write a reading after you read a text — and yet it is more common to hear teachers and students talk as though a reader "had" a reading, an understanding of what is "in" the text, before he sits down to write. The act of writing serves to justify, to repair or to speak into coherence an experience that, while it occurred, felt more like loss and confusion. "I kept forgetting what she was saying," our students tell us. "I didn't know where she was going or what she was saying." "I don't remember what I read." "I didn't get it."

Our students, perhaps because of lessons they have learned in the classroom, equate comprehension with certain memory, and they are haunted by the fact that they cannot remember all that they have read, whether it be a passage or a chapter or a book of 300 pages. And what they do remember, they suspect, is the very stuff they should have forgotten — material remembered arbitrarily, by chance, or perversely, because they were paying attention to the wrong things. When they finish a book, they feel they don't "have" it and they don't, therefore, know where to begin when they sit down to write.

Frank Kermode, in *The Genesis of Secrecy*, speaks of forgetfulness, but he speaks of it as an inevitable element in a successful reading — inevitable in that we all must forget, and successful in that it puts the burden of coherence (of accounting for the appropriateness of what we remember) where it belongs, on the person who is recomposing the text, who is inventing a past that will enable him to say, "I have understood." [14] The desire to remember everything is not only obsessive, if achieved it would be madness: "A text with all its wits about it would see and hear and remember too much." [15] And a reader "with all his dull wits about him," the reader who would literally recall a text, would never be able to misread and would, therefore, be able to speak only the same text back to itself (like our student, rewriting the text of Mead's chapter on her page). The concern for getting the right meaning, for memory, a concern that dominates our students' sense of the "good" reader, puts our students in an impossible position. The very gap between a text and a reader's version of a text, the gap that makes reading possible, stands for our students as a sign that they cannot read.

We have been speaking in broad terms about our students' inability to imagine a working model of the reader. Their most basic assumptions about who readers are and what readers do make it vitually impossible for them to act like readers. There are small, local manifestations of this. Because our students feel that they should "have" a book once they've finished reading it, they have not developed procedures to make a book available to them once they've read through all the pages. They need to learn, in other words, to create the kind of index that a more experienced reader creates by putting checks in the margin or circling page numbers or in some way indicating sections or phrases that seem interesting or puzzling or significant, sections or phrases that they can turn to later when they need to work up an account of what they've read. They leave their books blank and so a rereading stands only as the act of going back again to empty text — to read it again; this time, they hope, to get it right.

They believe that difficulty in reading is a sign of a problem, either theirs or the book's, and not a sign that there is some work for a reader to do. They are unable, that is, to see difficulty as a condition of adult reading, as a gift that makes reading possible. (This problem is accentuated in most of the "readers" available for use in composition courses. These anthologies contain short, straightforward, simple essays — the sort of essays that announce their own meanings and seem to solve all the problems they raise. They contain essays that invite students to believe that all a reader need do is sit back and admire the wit and wisdom of an author. All the work seems to be done, and a reader is led to believe that all he need say in return is "Yes," or "My, that was well said." When students of these "readers" are placed before essays of substance and texture, complicated essays, they are, in a real sense, unprepared to read.) When they are faced with a difficult passage, our students' intuitions lead them to the worst possible response. They slow down and focus on smaller and smaller units. They dwell on individual sentences or words rather than postponing their need for closure and clarity and pressing ahead, trusting that context, example, repetition or explanation will give them the material they need to translate confusion into other terms. A student, for example, who had trouble with the phrase "inner custodian" (one of the italicized phrases in Gail Sheehy's *Passages*) spent his time with a dictionary looking up first "inner" and then "custodian," and with predictable results.

Our students are bound by the model of reading they carry to the act of reading. These stories of reading are what a teacher must attend to, not isolated reading "skills." Our students' obsessive concern over the fact that they don't remember everything they read, their concern to dig out the right answers, their despair over passages that seem difficult or ambiguous are symptoms of a misunderstanding of the nature of texts and the nature of reading that must be overcome if students are to begin to take charge of the roles they might play in the classroom. And yet the language of reading instruction, like the language of writing instruction, is loaded with images of mastery and control. A writer begins with a controlling idea. A reader finds a main idea and follows it. The practice of reading and writing, however, is nothing like this. Mastery and control, at least as we can speak of them in positive terms, come late in the game. We never know what we've read until we are forced to perform as readers — as though we know what we've read — and we face all those occasions (lectures, tests, papers) with that sense of anxiety, that doubt whether we can pull it off, which is evidence that comprehension is not something we possess but something we perform.

When we began studying the problem of student reading by looking at students' writing, we were concerned with two things: (1) the ways students textually established their authority as readers — their right to speak — and (2) the ways they located, then arranged and accounted for the points they were willing to call "significant" in what they read. By beginning here, with what they did, a course could move to what they might do next. The story of reading that undergirds our course, then, has a necessarily simple structure. It has a reader noticing something and then accounting for the significance of what he notices. What is it that a reader notices? For our purposes, it could be anything, but it is, initially, what a reader did in fact notice: an event, a phrase, a moment of confusion, something Margaret Mead said or did, or something she failed to say or do. A student recalls, for example, three events from Mead's first year at DePauw University and then presents those events as somehow "keys" to an understanding of Mead or DePauw or "the first year of college." Or a student goes back to the sections in a longer text that are indicated by checks placed in the margin and works out a way that these can be connected — perhaps with "and," perhaps with "x, but on the other hand, y."

Students work together in class and prepare a consensus list of "significant" moments and "insignificant" moments in the experience of Maya Angelou and they write about the process of change or "development" indicated in her account of her life. They prepare lists of passages that indicate the differences between the way Maya Angelou understood her experience when she was a child and the way she understands it now, as an adult writing about her childhood. From this they write about how her understanding of her own experience has changed and about what, then, they can say about the process of "change."

This activity becomes complicated as students return to the papers they have written, imagining who these readers are, what they can and cannot see and do, and how those readings might be transformed. And their work is put to another test. The positions they have taken are applied and revised through the ongoing work of the seminar. After a student has written about "change" as it is represented in the experience of Margaret Mead, Maya Angelou, and in the class's own personal experience essays, he is asked to look at *Hunger of Memory* and to see how Richard Rodriguez's experience can be understood in the context of the theory of change he has been developing. What, given that frame, can a reader see in a new text? What does he fail to see? What use, now, can he make of the work he has begun?

Students study and revise the readings they propose over the course of a semester, but they need a place to begin. And so, in simplest terms, we present reading to them as a process through which the moments they notice or recall in a text become the significant moments in that text. Their job, then, is to find a way of using those moments to talk about a text's meaning. The assigning of significance is, in a sense, an act of naming, perhaps the most basic act of naming for any reader, since it precedes any attempt to describe, categorize, elaborate or generalize.

Significance may be attributed to a text ("What would you say is the central point in this chapter?" or "What point is the author making?"), to an individual reader ("What strikes you as significant in what you've read?"), or to a situation or a project ("You've read Margaret Mead's account of her experience in her first year of college. You've read the account of your colleagues in this class of their first experiences here at the university. You've proposed a theory of adolescent development. What, then, strikes you as significant in Gail Sheehy's account of life's early 'passages'?"). Each act defines a context and a reader and organizes the given text in a different way. Each causes passages that were silent to suddenly speak, or passages that spoke loudly to move into the general undersound of a text.

Each allows a reader's wavering attention to be renamed and to be given priority as an act of attention. And when a student moves to account for the significance of what she has noticed, the competing demands of convention and idiosyncracy are, perhaps, most dramatically and illustratively felt.

When we talk about locating significance, then, we are not talking about a student's ability to find a topic sentence or to remember what the text said. It is perhaps more accurate to say that the student is remembering a past that he is busily in the process of reconstructing, a past which will allow him to say, "I have understood." This is partly a matter of recovering one's status as a reader and partly a process of covering one's tracks. This is one of the lessons a reader must learn: that reading, like writing, begins in confusion, anxiety and uncertainty; that it is driven by chance and intuition as well as by deliberate strategy and conscious intent; that certainty and authority are postures, features of a performance that is achieved through an act of writing, not qualities of vision that precede such a performance.

One could also say that this act of reading (which is also an act of writing) is partly a matter of bringing forward an agenda that belongs not to the student or to the text but to conventional structures of reading that the student is approximating — usually classroom structures of reading, but sometimes structures derived from the church or from the home or from any of the cultures outside our classrooms. This is certainly part of the hidden agenda that both accounts for and is revealed by the check marks she put on the page or the passage she recalled from *Blackberry Winter.* And this is another of the lessons that a reader must learn: that a reader carries a project that belongs to others and that it is useful to know what it is about and where it is going.

Student Readers

We're aware that the course we've been describing doesn't sound anything at all like a conventional remedial reading or composition course. The students who have been taking it (and passing it), however, are like those students channeled into basic skills courses at large universities across the country. We identify an average of 90 students each year on the basis of a writing sample and the Nelson-Denny Reading Test.[16] These are students whose test scores place them in the bottom five percent of the freshman class.

In 1977, the first year the course was offered, we conducted an extensive study of both the course and the students.[17] The mean SAT verbal score of the students in the course was 360, with scores going as low as 220, and with fifteen percent of the total below 300. The mean vocabulary and comprehension scores on the Nelson-Denny Reading Text fell at the 28th and 35th percentile with norms set at grade 13.

We found these students to be hesitant, unsuccessful readers. Many, we found from a survey, had never read a book. They had crammed from books for tests or strip-mined books for term papers or class reports, but they had never sat down on their own and read a book from beginning to end. Most of the students were apprehensive about reading, and this was often linked to someone telling them, at some point in high school, that they had a "reading problem." When asked to describe the problems they had with reading, most responded that they couldn't remember, couldn't concentrate or had a poor vocabulary.

From our own diagnostic testing, we found these students to be powerless when faced with a text of even moderate difficulty for their age level — powerless, that is, when asked to *do* something with what they read. Their written responses to a chapter from *Blackberry Winter* were at best lists of Mead's observations and comments. They had no access to strategies for elaborating, commenting, connecting or drawing conclusions from what they read, even though the essay had immediate bearing on their own situations as first-term college freshmen. Their problems, we concluded, were due partly to their limited knowledge of how to read (as evidenced, for example, by their preoccupation with remembering rather than understanding), but those problems were due, to a greater degree, to their limited knowledge of academic discourse, of what it is a reader looks for and says when asked to read and respond in an academic setting. In this sense, their failures as readers and writers are part of a general inability to imagine the language, conventions and purposes of academic discourse. It was not that these students were unable to encode or decode, but that they needed to better imagine the work of a reader or writer.

Our preliminary research on our own students convinced us to build a curriculum around reading as a conceptual act, one that could only be represented by written responses to whole texts. Our convictions were supported by later research on the course. When we administered a series of Cloze Tests (tests of "literal" comprehension, of students' abilities to process syntax and predict words left blank in a sample text), we found that all of our students, even those with the lowest test scores at the beginning of the term, scored above the level indicating adequate literal comprehension on passages whose readability was scaled at grade 13. We concluded that the low reading speeds and the general failure to comprehend or to give adequate response must be attributed to something other than difficulty processing sentences. Their problems, we concluded, were not intrinsically reading problems but problems of composition, of the ability to "compose" a reading.

We want to look for a moment at some examples of students' readings of two chapters from *Blackberry Winter*. One chapter is an account of Margaret Mead's experience as a freshman at DePauw; the second is an account of her experience as a student at Barnard.[18] These essays were written early and late in the term — with the DePauw chapter first and the Barnard chapter second. In both instances, the writer was given two hours to read the passage and to write a response. The question set for the students read as follows:

> We'd like you to describe as carefully and as completely as you can the important point or points you see Ms. Mead making about her experience at DePauw/Barnard.
>
> Would you go on, after that, to talk about whatever in the chapter seems most important or most significant to you? And would you be sure to explain why you choose what you do?

Here is one of the DePauw essays:

> In the nineteen hundreds the word discrimination classifies the moral issue which was very concerting to people like Ms. Mead's family, which were in a sequestered minority group. The society which Ms. Mead belonged contained a highly intellectual status, which exemplifies the idea that everyone was meant to go to college and be happy, successfully. Her brother was a doctor along with a very intelligent sister who could strive and obtain any role she desired, she didn't really have a planned path having to do with a career.
>
> Ms. Mead's first impression of DePauw was focused on the fact that everybody that was going to college was more interested in football games and meeting and knowing people who belonged to their equal status in peer group. The discrimination which she was exposed to was no great shock for her, being how her family was anti discriminate.

She was hurt, however she wasn't going to stop trying to be accepted by her "superiors." She one day she received a bid to join a sorority for helping the two sororities become against each other. In college she was disconcerted by the rejection of women in sports. She later felt she wanted to go to an all girls school. De Paul cleared her picture of the kind of school she wanted to attend — a school where one goes to learn and expand the intelligence in many areas.

She learned by being rejected that humankind is demorally defected. However today the ammendment that all men are equal has over-powered any unequality.

We can't help but admire what the student is trying to do here, even though the essay is often quite funny, almost a parody of a certain style of academic writing. The student has accurately sized up the situation he faces. He has been asked to write for university professors, and so he writes in the language he assumes to be ours. There are problems with what he does with the Mead chapter, as well as problems with the writing. But his problems are also his virtues. He is trying to do what he cannot do, trying to write himself into a role that is not his but that he would take as his own. He is writing for his professors and he knows that he must cast his reading in their terms (in his best approximation of our terms). This was, in fact, a student who was told that he had a "vocabulary problem"; and he had spent the summer working with a "vocabulary builder." He is correct in imagining that his job as a reader is to translate the text into a language that is neither the text's nor immediately his own. The language he brings forward, however, is not one that can simultaneously structure a reading. It has a lot of fancy words, but no corresponding agenda or purpose.

There is more to his version of an academic reading than the big words, however. There is an emerging structure to what he has written. The paper is framed, for example, by a characteristic gesture of authority. If he is to establish his position as a reader, it must be within the context of specialized knowledge or expertise. He begins and ends the paper by proclaiming a general legal-historical expertise that seems appropriate for the occasion but that, in fact, he cannot carry off. He assumes the knowledge to speak about discrimination in the 1900s and concludes by saying that "today the ammendment that all men are equal has over-powered any unequality." A knowledgeable reader, in other words, is one who can place the text in some broad historical perspective. A reader is a person who can speak through a perspective that is not the same as the perspective of the text he has read.

This student was on the verge of a different kind of conclusion in the sentence, "De Paul cleared her picture of the kind of school she wanted to attend." But that sentence seems unconnected with anything that comes before or after. (He did not forget that sentence, however. In his final essay, he places himself in a role he can carry off, defining himself as an authority on Margaret Mead's college years and drawing, as no other student did, on his memory of the chapter he had read at the beginning of the term. He wrote, "Margaret Mead's experiences at DePauw made her realize that she could do anything she had a desire to do. By the time she graduated from college she knew what she could do in life.")

In the essay above, the chapter from *Blackberry Winter* is represented as a string of bits of information from the text: discrimination was disconcerting to Mead and her family, Mead's family belonged to an intellectual elite, Mead's brother was a doctor, Mead didn't have a plan for a career, Mead's first impressions of DePauw led her to conclude that students were more interested in status than study, Mead wanted to be accepted, Mead was disconcerted that there were no organized sports for women, Mead learned about discrimination. These bits and pieces, however, never come together in any coherent statement. The essay ends with a statement about humankind and equality that draws its power, we suppose, from the fact that it is upbeat and bold. The general argument — the structure that controls this reading — is that if things are bad they are going to get better (that a "student can't stop trying to be accepted by her superiors"). There is a way of arguing, however, that this reading pays little attention to the text. It draws on a way of talking about a student and her situation that is both present and powerful for this, as for many student writers. If this student "misreads" the text of Mead's essay, he has not completely misread his situation, his position in relation to that text and to the classroom within which he reads and writes.

Here is another DePauw essay:

> Ms. Mead makes very important points about her experiences at De Pauw colleage, which can probable be looked apond as something we can use today. She tells of her experience as a person that is rejected by her peers for reason of sex and even religion. She tells of the pressure she had to endure and how she felt hurt, but she also had

her mind set to complete what she came for a education
and she didn't let any of the pressures disturb that.

During the beginning of school she was very disappointed not only because the kids didn't seem colleage
enough but she was also held back because of the lack of
communication with her piers because she didn't belong
in a sorority so she was considered a out-cast.

I think that what she wrote about her family and
people she know who went to colleage was very significant
she proved that everyond was a intellect and how you can
be different and get more out of being your own self.

There is no real misinformation here. (The chapter is
"about" Mead's exclusion from the sorority system — an
experience, she says, which enabled her to better understand
racial discrimination — and about her expectations of college
life and how they were frustrated by the students she met.)
The student has not said anything wrong, a fact he would be
quick to defend, but he has not been able to imagine an appropriate context for the information he brings forward to represent the chapter, Mead's point of view and his own.

The "points" Mead makes are, he says, "important" because they can be looked upon as "something we can use today."
If they have value, they have value as words to live by rather
than as objects for study, as statements or attitudes the reader
could represent to himself, think about, translate or consider.
He turns her story into a conventional account of perserverance
against great odds, a version of her experience that is not inaccurate, although it is inappropriate for an audience that wants
Mead to be considered as a subject rather than as an oracle or a
figure of allegory. There is a buried but telling "because" in the
center of that last paragraph. "I think," he says, that what she
wrote about her family and friends is significant *because* she
"proved that everyone was a intellect and how you can be different and get more out of being your own self." The link between the story she tells and its significance is that it can be
subsumed into a story of "making the best of things" and "being
true to yourself," a story the student has been told and, more
likely, that he tells himself to account for his position in the
world. When the student read the chapter, he composed it according to the code of *that* conventional narrative, a narrative
that "proves" what he says Mead proves in her chapter. The
story that he attributes to Mead, in other words, is a story that
precedes his reading of the chapter. It is something he "had" in

advance. There is, then, a double edge to this sense of a "proof."
A "proof" is what a text offers; it is something a reader finds
there. It is also, however, that which a reader brings to a text,
the truth that enables this reading. This reader can see neither
the text, nor his relation to it, in such a way that these truths
become problematic.

What this text contains for this reader are the things that
Mead "tells" a reader. It does not, in other words, consist of
passages that might be cited and discussed or examples that
could be read with (or against) Mead's reading of them. Mead
"tells" of this and that. This is the repeated refrain in the opening paragraph, where the reader accounts for what he sees in
the chapter. He sees Mead telling things, and it is more important
for him to tell *that* Mead tells of her experience of rejection or
of the pressures she endures than it is for him to bring forward
what she says or the narrative detail that grounds, for her, a discussion of pressure and rejection. There is no distance, then,
between the event and the utterance that explains the event. There
is no requirement to see Mead "reading" her own account of her
experience. (And there is no occasion, then, to question her
family's assumptions about college life or Mead's understanding
of those assumptions. There is no reason to ask whether the
people who counseled her were "right" or whether Mead was
"right" in listening to them or whether, as a writer, she is
presenting their advice to show that they prepared her for
college or to show that they failed to prepare her.) A reader, in
other words, is not a person who tells what he sees as he studies
the words on the page, but one who tells what he is told. As a
consequence, he has little motive to say much at all, which is
one way of accounting for the length of this essay.

As this writer represents Mead's chapter, it is not a collection of words or a textual performance — something he can
"look at." It is, rather, something he can hear, as he would hear
a familiar conversation, understanding the flow of words as they
fit comfortably into his expectations of what the people he
knows and talks to would say. David Olson and his colleagues,
in fact, say that this failure to "see" a text as a text is a central
problem of schooling for students whose understanding of language is based on their experience in an oral (rather than a literate or academic) culture. Olson says that the "cognitive and
social competencies involved in coping with authoritative writing, particularly those involved in learning to read and write
textbook prose . . . are distinctive and important and require
detailed analysis."

Although processes involved in dealing with oral utterances and written texts differ in many ways, including modality of input, degree of interaction, role of extralinguistic cues, spatial and temporal commonality of participants, specificity of audience and the like . . . one factor seems to us to be central to all of the others, the one mentioned at the outset, the relation between the speaker/writer and the speech/text. Writing provides the occasion for the radicial differentiation of a writer from his text. This differentiation is critical in that it may lead the linguistic form to be seen as autonomous, of having an authority different from the authority of the writer, and as having a meaning different from the meaning intended by the writer. Both of these factors, the authority and the meaning, may help to explain why school text is difficult to read, especially to read critically, and more importantly, why particular forms of writing such as expository prose are so difficult to master.[19]

Let us turn, now, to the concluding paragraph of this student's later essay on the second Mead chapter. It is preceded by a rather full and detailed account of three sections in the Barnard chapter: Mead's sense of the place and the women she lived with, her friendship with Leonie Adams, and her decision to go into anthropology. The essay is three times the length of the first essay, although both were written in a two-hour sitting. The amount of detail the student brings forward is, we believe, evidence that he sees this chapter in a way that he did not see the first — as a text with parts, some of them examples, some of them general statements, all held together by an author's performance and all "material" for a writer to bring forward and shape into a reading. (Note, for example, in the section included below, the way the student includes a section of Mead's text in quotation marks. He brings forward the words of the chapter and defines himself in relation to those words as words, as Mead's way of talking about what he, too, will talk about.)

The impressive thing about the conclusion of the essay is the way it pulls together the account of the sections of the chapter that stood out as significant for this writing. He organizes them within a context that he provides, one that is not represented in the chapter as a "main idea." In addition, the student locates and brings forward a section of the text that would be overlooked by a "naive" reader. He brings it forward and makes it a key element in his understanding of the text. In this case, it is the student's performance that is powerful and convincing, not Mead's.

The most impactive thing said in the piece was, "finding the focus in your life." It show that you must do something in your life to work from. Margaret Mead attended college to find this focus point. When she first attended school she might of never knew she was in search for this focus point. Then her friends told her to search and strictly concentrate on her subject of interest. Then Ruth told her that "anthropology is something that matters." Each said that you must do some thing in life that will count for yu. I concluded from what I have read that a friend is an important thing to have. Not only as someone to talk and relate to, but a person who can help you make decision by showing the focus points of your life.

The student has translated this chapter into terms that are partly his own, partly the text's. He begins by bringing forward Mead's metaphor of "focus." It is worth repeating that this metaphor is not signaled by the text as a "key" metaphor. In fact, the passage is one that any "naive" reader might miss (that is, any reader not reading through this reader's account of the text). It is this act of attention that initially defines his authority as a reader. He takes the metaphor and translates it into a key word, a working term, "focus point," and then puts the term to work. He both examines and demonstrates its usefulness through application. And by the end of the essay he is able to say more than that it is good to have friends (a general commonplace, something he was prepared to say before he ever read this chapter). He says, rather, that a friend is a person who can help you make a decision by showing the focus points of your life. There is a dialectical action represented by the appropriation and use of this term that enables us to say that the student is the author of this reading of Mead. This is not to deny that his authorship is in service of a familiar academic project. It is to say, however, that he has defined a role for himself as reader and writer that empowers him to participate in such a project.

The Course — Basic Reading and Writing

The course is taught as a freshman seminar. It's worth six credits, however, which makes it the equivalent of two regular freshman year courses. Most classes are team taught and meet in a seminar room (a small room with a big table) for six hours a week (three two-hour sessions). In the term students study a single problem, one easily located within the immediate experience and knowledge of beginning students, and they study it using the basic methods of university inquiry: reading and writing, discussion and debate, research and inquiry, report and commentary. The course has been organized around subjects like "Work" (for adults in the evening college) and "Growth and Change in Adolescence" (for freshmen in the College of Arts and Sciences). We will talk about the course on adolescent development in this chapter, although the two courses have similar structures. In both cases, we have tried to identify subjects that would bring forward powerful and pressing themes from our students' experience. We want students to see quickly that they have a stake in the transformations they can perform on the ways they see and, thereby, participate in the world.

There are two strands to the course, each represented by a set of linked assignments. There is a sequence of writing assignments involving about 12 sets of assignments and revisions. (We teach writing primarily by teaching revision and editing.) And there is a corresponding sequence of reading assignments. (The texts move from first-person and fictional accounts of adolescent experience to works by psychologists, sociologists and anthropologists.) Students are also reading from a reading list of their own design. The written work in the reading strand is represented by drafts and revisions but also by work in a reader's journal. All of this is in the context of regular seminar meetings — meetings, that is, that center on the discussion and analysis of papers presented by the students. The situation is this, then: students who have been identified as poor readers and writers spend six hours a week for 15 weeks in a discussion class that centers on a single subject. They read, on the average, 12 books and write 25 drafts and revisions.

Each week two or three student papers are reproduced (often the first and second drafts of a single paper) and these papers, kept by each student in a folder, provide an additional text for the course. Class discussion generally centers around a piece of student writing. There are no lectures or general discussions. We don't discuss "the family," in other words, but what X has said about families, and the seminar meetings as a result become workshops or proving grounds, where students learn to read and write in an academic setting. They begin to make decisions about what is interesting and what is banal, what passes as an idea and what does not, what forms of argument work and what don't. The phrase makers and the idea people soon become centers of interest in each class.

By means of these classes, students learn how to become (and imagine) both audience and participants in such a discussion. They learn, for example, to talk in sentences and they learn to take notes on what their colleagues say and write. Anyone who has taught a course like this will understand what patience and violence underlie the teaching and learning of such skills as talking in elaborated turns (not "yeah," but "yeah" with reasons or explanations or examples) or paying attention to the words of classmates and participating in a developing discussion. On reflection, this seems like such a simple matter, but every semester classes and participants have been poised on the verge of collapse because of the weight of responsibility for speaking, writing, and listening in a discussion where the instructor does not fill the silence with right answers or final explanations. The key point here, however, is that students learn about reading and writing by learning to imagine and participate in a semester-long inquiry into a single subject. They are not "given" a subject (the way "American History" is given in a course on American History), but they develop a freshman's version of an academic discipline, one that constitutes a subject and makes its understanding possible (as though they were members of the Center for the Study of Growth and Change in Adolescence). The specialized vocabulary, the jargon, the key terms, the central concepts, the major figures, the central interpretive schemes — all of these emerge from the students' efforts to find a way of talking about and understanding their common material. The instructors serve to keep notes, to record phrases and ideas on the board, to rerepresent the terms of a day's discussion, to ask pivotal questions, to hold students to rules and requirements and, generally, to keep the group and its work together.

The students' papers are used for discussion. They are also, however, used as "cases" in the seminar's study of adolescence. The stories they tell are used both as evidence of "adolescent development" and as evidence of readers or writers at work. This distinction (between the figure in a paper on playing basketball and the figure of the writer writing a paper on playing basketball) is, in fact, one of the difficult first lessons of the course. The seminar begins by developing its own terms and frames of reference for a discussion of its subject but moves, about two-thirds of the way into the term, to test those terms and schemes against those in professional academic texts.

The sequence of assignments proceeds along these lines.[20] Students begin by writing a series of papers about their own experience, describing moments when they changed or didn't change or tried to change, and then, on the basis of this work, they are asked to draw conclusions about what change is as it is represented in the stories they have told. These papers are revised and reviewed and serve as the primary materials, for each student, for a series of papers that build to a theory of adolescent development. While students are working on these papers, they are also writing about the fictional and autobiographical accounts of the experience of young adults.

The first writing assignment reads as follows:

> For this writing assignment, we'd like you to recall an experience from the last two years or so that strikes you as particularly significant, one that has changed the way you are or the way you think about things. We want you to describe this experience as completely as you can, providing us with all the details we need to understand what happened. Then, when you've finished telling us what happened, go on to explain why this experience was a "significant" one. That is, go on to explain how and why it affected you as it did.

The problems the first writing assignment creates for students can be illustrated by the following paper.

> When I went to South Catholic I became friends with my spanish teacher, his name was Brother Larwarance Dempsey. He was a great teacher and was also assistant Coach to the wrestling team. One day he invited me down to the weight-training room, he showed me a few of the machines and how to use them. Since he was just starting to lift weights I wanted to start to. That October he wanted me to go out for the wrestling team. I was scared to death a little puggy kid like me.
>
> He had such a spirit and drive that I stuck with it. He always boaste me by saying "fire up." I really got into weights after the season and running. I became more confident. As fast as it went the next year came I was down a weight class and ready to go I beat out 5 kids for the position and went first string varsity the rest of my junior year. At the end of the year we all got word that brother Larry was to go to Jersey City. I was very dissappointed because I know I'd miss him. I was losing my cofidence and almost gave up the sport. I then had to decide what to do. I was determined now more than

before but this time make it on my own the next year I became team Captian.

    If you work hard and follow the rules things will get better and better.

This essay has a clearly discernible structure, but the structure does not represent an act of inquiry as inquiry is defined by the conventions of classroom discourse. The writer can turn his experience with wrestling and Brother Lawrence into a subject and he can provide commentary on that subject, but neither subject nor commentary stand within the language and methods of the university. The subject is consumed by the conventional *Boy's Life* narrative of struggle and success. And Brother Lawrence, who comes forward as a key figure in the narrative, disappears in the concluding commentary. The student's discussion of how and why the experience was significant, a discussion that provides a "reading" of the narrative, offers a reading that turns most of what he has said into insignificant detail. Freire would say that the student has not learned to "problematize" his "existential situation."[21]

    There is reason to question just what this situation is that has not been made problematic. We are not prepared to argue that this student has not seen the truth of his relationship to Brother Lawrence or wrestling. We are, however, prepared to argue that, as a writer, he fails to see his relation to a way of talking, a discourse. For our pruposes, it is not the student's situation in relation to wrestling or Brother Lawrence or his disappointment or his confidence that is the subject of the course but his situation in relation to a way of talking about wrestling or Brother Lawrence or "disappointment" or "confidence." He turns an event from his past into a narrative of Boy Makes Good, and it is the structure controlling this presentation that is inappropriate for our purposes.

    The single sentence conclusion to this essay has a resounding finality: "If you work hard and follow the rules things will get better and better." It's upbeat, "true" and passes as the voice of authority for a student suddenly forced to speak as an author (and not only as a wrestler who was made team captain). The conclusions we receive in these early papers are generally phrased as single-sentence aphorisms or Lessons on Life:

- I feel that you should always go out in school and give it your best shot to learn no matter how hard the teacher may be teaching the subject.

- Through good or bad changes there is always improvement if you know how to learn to make these changes for your benefit.

When called upon to speak the language of insight and authority, our students generally speak the language of parents, coaches or other powerful adults: "Give it your best shot." And, of course, they speak in service of axioms that promise success: "Things will get better." They draw on those structures of understanding. This is the way of speaking and these are the terms that our students bring forward to constitute their authority as speakers, to both frame and justify the stories they have to tell. They need to learn, then, to try on other forms of authority (to speak with intellectual rather than moral authority), including that form of critical authority that establishes itself by calling attention to and pushing against the voices and structures that enable a writer to write. It takes a remarkable muscularity of mind, however, for a student to move from the mode of presentation in an essay like this one to one where a writer comes forward in the text and pushes against the emerging structure of his own discourse. There are intermediate steps.

These begin as students imagine other interpretive frames and then read their experience through them. To the student who wrote the paper above, we can say only, "No, that's not it," and then do what we can to characterize what it is that he has done that we cannot accept. (We can ask him, for example, where he has heard a sentence like the last one in that paper, who speaks such words and why it is that he would want to talk to the rest of us in those terms.) The interpretive schemes our classes develop are quite predictable, even though they emerge "spontaneously" from the work of each seminar. The experience of adolescence is sorted by students into categories, usually binary oppositions, like the following:

- the need to conform/the need to be an individual
- the pressure to follow rules/the pressure to rebel
- a sense of confusion/a sense of direction
- the family/independence
- school/independence
- friends and enemies/independence
- who I am/what they want me to be
- who I am/what I want to be
- my past/my future
- reality/dreams

These are used to frame narratives where things happen to teenagers as if by magic and where the terms of transformation are total and absolute: "I used to be shy, but now I am popular." "I used to fight with my father, but now he is my best friend." But the effect of these new terms is to make the stories less easy for students to tell, where fights with parents are seen as signs of *both* a sense of direction, for example, and a sense of confusion. These interpretive schemes, as predictable as they may be, have incredible heuristic power for a class fascinated with the slopes and valleys of their own lives and drawn to the power of the theory or the generalization.

In working out their analyses of individual cases, the classes develop a specialized vocabulary. It is often equally predictable: "peer pressure," "family pressure," "risk," "crisis," and so on. These tags, however, often lead to the development of new and (for the group) powerful terms. One class coined the term "Thomson Syndrome" to describe a specific kind of family conflict. The term came from a paper in which a student wrote about her position as the youngest in a family of five star basketball players. In response to everyone's expectation that she follow suit, she took up field hockey. Another class refined the concept of "peer pressure" by adopting as common terms "running alone" and "rebounding." A student who was a serious runner had written about how his running isolated him, since his friends spent most of their time partying and hanging out. He would move back and forth, he said, between "running alone," when for long periods of time he would drift away from his friends and be serious about diet, exercise and training. Then he would become frightened about having no friends (his mother would say, "Why don't you go out and have some fun?"), so he would give up running, exercise and diet completely. He was, the class decided, "rebounding." By identifying the two terms, the class could talk about his experience not as it was presented but as it could be reimagined — where both "running alone" and "rebounding" were seen as choices this student made, not as the inevitable consequences of his life. Both running alone and rebounding, in other words, could be characterized as foolish or excessive. Or both could be called sensible strategies, providing the twin poles of a life that refused to stick to a single track. The terms, in other words, made a discussion possible that wouldn't have been possible otherwise. And they are terms that could be applied to other cases, demonstrating the way intellectual activity can connect material that seems otherwise random or disparate. In each seminar, in fact, groups have formed around sets of key terms, terms that would serve different lines of inquiry.

The purpose of the opening assignments, then, is to engage students in a process whereby they discover academic discourse from the inside. They have to learn to define a subject, to make decisions about significance, utility and authority, and to assume the burden of developing working concepts and a specialized vocabulary. In this sense, they are given the task of inventing an academic discipline: a department for the study of growth and change in adolescence. For the midterm assignment, students are asked to draw upon all the writing they have done to that point and produce a long autobiographical essay, one that deals with the events of the last three years that best represent change or development. These are, on the average, 12–15 pages long and they provide tremendously exciting reading.

Students, by this time, are no longer writing variations on "Boy Makes Good," although the papers are characteristically (and properly) hopeful. They deal with major experiences: family crises, problems at school, problems with the law, problems with friends, major moments of transformation (often involving decisions about going to college, taking a big step in school or sports, and deciding to change what seemed to be the inevitable patterns of their lives). Whatever else they've learned, the students have learned from the earlier discussions to write about things that matter to them.

These autobiographies are sent down to central printing, reproduced, bound, and sold back to the class as the next assigned text. Students are directed to read the autobiographies as "case studies" and to report, in writing, on what they see to be the significant patterns — common or contradictory themes, for example — and to provide names and labels for these patterns. They do this in order to go on, in a later assignment, to develop a theory about the way adolescents change and the kinds of change that occur. The first set of assignments had students generalizing from their own individual experience; this set asks them to generalize from a set of case studies. The last set of assignments in the semester directs students to published, academic studies.[22]

The first assignment after the papers on the autobiographies directs students to the opening third of Gail Sheehy's *Passages* (the section on young adults), where they see her involved with an identical process of inquiry, report, labeling, generalizing and theorizing. She describes herself, in the introduction, reading through hundreds of case studies and trying to make sense out of them, and the sense she makes out of them is defined by a set of recognizable terms: she divides personality into *merger self, seeker self* and *inner custodian*. Students are prepared to read these italicized terms because they have spent half a semester, in a sense, producing their own. As writers, in fact, they are directed by the next assignment to go back and reconsider the autobiographies, this time using Sheehy's labels and interpretative schemes as well as their own. The assignment asks, essentially: "What does Sheehy see that you didn't see?" "What did you see that Sheehy doesn't see?" and "What use can you make of what she does with her case studies when you look, now, at your own?"

The course moves on, then, to books like Edgar Friedenberg's *Vanishing Adolescent* and Mead's *Coming of Age in Samoa*. Again, the writing assignments direct students back to reconsider the autobiographies using the language and methods of these professional studies. If the Sheehy assignment asks students to think about their material through the frame of Sheehy's book, these assignments ask them to do the same thing with the work of a sociologist and an anthropologist. In doing so they learn not only a lesson about writing, but they learn a way of reading academic prose. To put it simply, students learn that the italicized words and the long sections of abstract discussion serve a purpose; they are conventions that represent a strategy, a way of thinking and speaking; they are not simply traps for the unwary.

The point of the final set of assignments is to place students' work in the context of the work of professionals. There are immediate, curricular justifications for this. We are, in the final third of the semester, preparing our students to carry out that complex negotiation where a reader or writer uses the work of others, neither his equals' nor his colleagues', to enable work that he can present as his own. There is an immediate, practical lesson here as well, for it is at this point that we can begin to help students sort out the mysteries of quotation, paraphrase, citation and plagiarism. At this point, however, the lines are in a sense cleaner, since students are prepared to see how someone else's ideas fit into a project they themselves have begun.

They are not, now, left with nothing to write about but what they can pull out of books in the library. And they are in a position to see how the words of another can function in their own arguments: providing key terms; providing examples of statements that help authorize what they, too, would say; providing examples of statements that can be shown to be limited or inadequate.

Having come from a project that they took to be their own, they are also prepared to be more critically aggressive in reading the work of others. (Our students generally take exception to Sheehy, who, they feel, is too mechanical in charting the stages of adult development and in defining the process of change.) They don't, that is, see these more official texts as speaking with an oracular authority — speaking a truth that forces a student to be silent. They see them, rather, as texts like their own — or like their own in that they present methods, terms and examples that a student can use. And even though these are the texts of experts, our students see them in a context in which they have the possibility of speaking back again or of speaking in turn. The goal of the assignments, that is, is to enable these marginal students to participate in an academic project. And it is to demonstrate to them, and to the university, that such participation is possible.

When our university began to plan a program to extend writing across the curriculum, our course was presented as one model for courses in other departments. One of our colleagues in the Psychology Department was quite interested in what we were doing but, as he said, "You know, the problem is that at the end of the course they're likely to get it all wrong. After all, what about Piaget and Erikson? They're not going to get that stuff on their own." He was right, of course. They can only approximate the work of professional academics; they can only try on the role of the psychologist or anthropologist or sociologist. They will not "get" the canonical interpretations preserved by the disciplines, nor will they invent that work on their own. But they will learn something about what it means to study a subject or carry out a project. They will begin to learn what a subject is — how it is constituted, how it is defended, how it finds its examples, ideas and champions, how it changes and preserves itself. And in learning this they will learn something about the work we do that will prepare them to read our texts as they could not were they to remain totally on the outside looking in. There is, then, a way of studying psychology by learning to report on textbook accounts or classroom lectures on the work of the profession. But there is also a way of learning psychology by learning to write like a psychologist — by learning, that is, to assemble materials, study them, and speak of them within the terms and structures of that discipline. In his four years of college education, a student gets plenty of the former but precious little of the latter. He writes many reports but carries out few projects.

It would be wrong, however, to assume that there is no transition when the seminar turns to the published work of academic writers. There is always, in this last section of the term, a feeling of disappointment. Students who have begun to feel their power as readers and writers, working with what they take to be *their* material and *their* ideas, do not take unalloyed pleasure in seeing their work in the context of the professionals. It is not as though our students have come to believe that there was nothing they could learn from the world outside the seminar room. The writing requirements change, and this of course makes the writing more difficult, but it is not responsibilities of learning the techniques of quotation and paraphrase that define the burden they feel. They have been writing essays built upon unexamined assumptions about "freedom" and "independence." They have argued that the changes that matter in a person's life are changes that lead one toward self-possession, and the procedures for reading and writing we have offered have seemed to confirm that readers or writers make meanings of their own. There are strong reasons why freshmen want to believe that education will set them free, and there are strong pedagogical reasons why we want students to believe that they have the power to take command of the texts we bring before them. But the work of reading and writing, as reading and writing stand metaphorically for the competing demands of private vision and public responsibility, is more problematic than this.

The final movement of the course brings forward the presence and pressure of the institution in the work of an individual. These pressures have, in a sense, been withheld earlier in the term, and as they come forward they challenge the versions of self-possession that students have taken for granted. The situation of the reader and writer becomes problematic in ways that students can begin to imagine, and they sense (although we doubt that they know) that they face problems they cannot solve. (They become aware of reading and writing problems, in other words, that are part of the situation of all readers and writers, not just students in a remedial course.) The pleasure of being able to speak back to Gail Sheehy or Margaret Mead is a real one, but its attractions are not nearly so great as the attractions of the belief that a student can be the source of knowledge, an original, someone who has the right to make it all up as he goes along.

The course has argued that students have more to do than speak back the words of their teachers. And yet, at the end of the course, we seem to be saying that they cannot imagine what they say as anything else but a version of the words of their teachers. There is a distinction to be made here, however, one that defines the relation of the student and the institution as a dialectical relationship, that makes reading and writing simultaneously an imitative act and an individual performance. Here is Edward Said talking about the situation of the writer:

> I think that writers have thought and still do think of writing as a type of cosmos precisely because within the discontinuous system of quotation, reference, duplication, parallel, and allusion which makes up writing, authority — or the specific power of a specific act of writing — can be thought of as something whole and as something invented — as something inclusive and made up, if you like, for the occasion. Anterior authority or any rationale based on the prior existence of something else, is thus minimized. It can never be eliminated entirely, for certainly one's childhood, one's present social circumstances, and the historical period in which one lives make their pressures felt regardless.[23]

The paradox of imitative originality or of captive self-possession can be resolved in the image of the reader or writer at work that is present in an artifact, a textual performance. We are offering students, at the end of the term, a way of seeing themselves at work within the institutional structures that make their work possible. What we are offering them is not an affirmation of a person, free and self-created, but an image of a person who is made possible through her work, work that takes place both within and against the languages that surround and define her. Or, as Said argues,

> We need not take this mainly as still another reminder of writing-as-*ascesis* (denial). . . . Rather, it is more positively an assertion of writing-as-action, albeit action of a fundamentally particular sort. To begin to write, therefore, is to work a set of instruments, to invent a field of play for them, to enable performance.[24]

We said earlier that our students begin with a hesitant and tenuous relationship to the materials we put before them, to the terms and imaginative structures that can make those materials available, and to the institutional context within which they are required to speak and to write. The course we've defined above demonstrates our belief that students can learn to transform materials, structures and situations that seem fixed or inevitable, and that in doing so they can move from the margins of the university to establish a place for themselves on the inside. At the end, however, these relationships may remain hesitant and tenuous — partly because our students will remain students, partly because they will continue to make more mistakes than their "mainstream" counterparts (although not so dramatically as before), but also because they have learned (and perhaps in a way that their "mainstream" counterparts cannot) that successful readers and writers actively seek out the margins and aggressively poise themselves in a hesitant and tenuous relationship to the language and methods of the university.

Notes

[1] George Steiner, *After Babel* (New York: Oxford UP, 1975) 473.
[2] In our current semester, there is a larger percentage of white, regular-admission students taking the course than there was when we began, there is a section designed for adults in the evening college, and the course has had its effect on the general development of the college curriculum. It has influenced courses that combine reading and writing at various levels in the English Department, and it has served as a model for the development of courses in departments other than our own — those, for example, designed to serve the university's concern to extend writing across the curriculum.
[3] Bartholomae has more to say about students on the "inside" and "outside" of academic discourse in two essays: "Inventing the University," *When A Writer Can't Write: Studies in Writer's Block and Other Composing Process Problems*, ed. Mike Rose (New York: Guilford, 1985) 134–175; and "Wanderings: Misreadings, Miswritings and Misunderstandings," *Only Connect: Uniting Reading and Writing*, ed. Thomas Newkirk (Upper Montclair, NJ: Boynton/Cook, in press).
[4] Jonathan Culler, *On Deconstruction: Theory and Criticism after Structuralism* (Ithaca, NY: Cornell UP, 1982) 176.
[5] Culler, 176–179.
[6] Culler, 67.

[7] We could offer ourselves, here, in our reading of Steiner as an exemplary case. We have pushed against Steiner, to be sure, in order to make his words useful to us. But in writing this chapter, as in designing the course, we have been bound to the terms and metaphors that gave us our beginning.

[8] I. A. Richards, *The Philosophy of Rhetoric* (New York: Oxford UP, 1936) 115.

[9] Thomas Farrell, "Reading in the Community College," *College English* 37 (September 1975): 40–46.

[10] For a discussion of the English profession's concern with what happens if you turn the meaning of texts over to student readers, see Stanley Fish, *Is There a Text in This Class: The Authority of Interpretive Communities* (Cambridge, MA: Harvard UP, 1980) 303–371.

[11] I. A. Richards, *How To Read A Page* (New York: Norton, 1942) 13.

[12] Cited in Ann E. Berthoff, "I. A. Richards," *Traditions of Inquiry*, ed. John Brereton (New York: Oxford UP, 1985) 80.

[13] We take the phrase, "stories of reading," from Culler, 64–85.

[14] See Hans-Georg Gadamer, *Philosophical Hermenuetics*, ed. and trans. David E. Linge. (Berkeley: U of California P, 1977). We have appropriated the phrase "a past that allows us to say, 'I have understood,'" from his chapter "On the Problem of Self-Understanding." For Gadamer, this past is not only a reader's invention, it is also the past as a history of interpretive acts that has allowed a reader to "understand."

[15] Frank Kermode, *The Genesis of Secrecy: On the Interpretation of Narrative* (Cambridge, MA: Harvard UP, 1979) 45.

[16] The essay students write is based on a short passage they read. We recently abandoned the reading test because it seemed redundant. It didn't tell us anything we didn't already know after reading the essays.

[17] David Bartholomae, *Basic Reading and Writing: A Report for the Dean of the College of Arts and Sciences, The University of Pittsburgh* (Pittsburgh: U of Pittsburgh, 1977).

[18] We chose these readings for their applicability to the theme of the course — "Growth and Change in Adolescence" — but also for the quality of the writing. The chapters move back and forth between narrative account and general discussion. There is no single "main idea," however, announced at the beginning or end of each chapter or at various points along the way. They are texts, in other words, that let a reader read.

[19] David R. Olson and Nancy Torrance, "Writing and Criticizing Texts," *Explorations in the Development of Writing*, ed. Barry M. Kroll and Gordon Wells (New York: Wiley, 1983) 32.

[20] The full text of these assignments is printed in Chapter 2.

[21] Paulo Freire, *Pedagogy of the Oppressed* (New York: Seabury, 1968).

[22] To provide readable texts, we have to define "academic" somewhat loosely. They are, more accurately, academic studies written for a general audience.

[23] Edward Said, *Beginnings: Intention and Method* (Baltimore: Johns Hopkins UP, 1975) 23-24.

[24] Said, 24.

II.

Teaching Reading and Writing

2.

Basic Reading and Writing

Course Materials

DAVID BARTHOLOMAE
ANTHONY R. PETROSKY
with Karen Hjelmervik; Susan Merriman; Mariolina Salvatori; and Marilyn B. DeMario,

Introduction

The following presents the course exactly as it is given to our students. These documents, that is, are the documents we hand out in class, week by week, to mark our progress through the term. This is not to say that everyone regularly teaches from these materials. As a staff, we revise the assignments from year to year, as often as we change the reading list. And it is also the case that individuals will revise assignments during the semester, usually to pick up terms, phrases and examples from class discussion. (This is one way of demonstrating to students that the course is a dialogue and that the work of the seminar relies, in an immediate way, on the contribution of its participants.)

The assignments change from semester to semester, but the basic structure remains essentially the same. What is presented here is a composite version of the course. Where it seemed appropriate, we have listed alternate readings and provided assignments tailored to those texts.

Course Description: To Our Students

The Seminar

Basic Reading and Writing (BRW) is a course for beginning college students that is modeled after a course for advanced graduate students. That is, it is a course where students are expected to develop their own ideas and theories on a subject (our subject

47

is "Growth and Change in Adolescence") and to report what they learned to others. There will be no lectures, no textbooks. For the most part, our discussions will be focused on what you have written. Most of your writing will draw on the work you do together as a group. We will provide the key texts; it will be your responsibility, however, to develop a way of talking about them.

This kind of course is usually called a *seminar*. When offered to graduate students, it allows them to set out on their own to see what they can find to say once they've mastered the basic information and methods of study in their particular academic discipline (economics, anthropology or psychology, for example). In this class, the seminar format is intended to allow you to develop your command of the activities basic to undergraduate study: reading, writing, interpretation, report, discussion. You won't be working within a set academic discipline; you will, in a sense, be inventing one. You might say that the seminar will become the *Center for the Study of Growth and Change in Adolescence*, a new research center at the University of Pittsburgh. We're interested, then, in what you can find to say over 15 weeks' constant study of a single subject; we're more interested in that than in your ability to study and remember the ideas of some accepted, "official" group of scholars. We don't expect you to become experts on adolescent development — at least not as the university defines such expertise. We do, however, expect you to become expert enough to begin to understand and respect the work (not the genius or inspiration) of those the university does acknowledge as expert.

Our seminar, then, is a general introduction to the language and methods of the university. The instructors (most sections have two) will provide a set of reading and writing assignments to organize and direct your work. The members of the seminar (including the instructors) will provide a sounding board, an audience to hear what you have to say and to suggest what you might do next. It is up to you, however, to develop the routine necessary to keep up with the work and to be an active member of the group.

Rules and Regulations

Here are the ground rules for the seminar:

- You have a responsibility to the group to be at all the class meetings and on time. If you know ahead of time that

you'll have to miss a class or be late (and this should happen only under exceptional circumstances), you must let
one of the instructors know. Call the English Department
or call one of us at home, but be sure to get in touch *before*
you miss a class.

- You are responsible for completing all of the work for the
  course on time. Assignments are always due at the beginning of a class. You will have one or two assignments due
  each week, and the work is cumulative — that is, the work
  on one assignment builds from the work on previous assignments. It's difficult to catch up once you fall behind in
  this course; therefore, if you get too far behind, we won't
  hesitate to drop you from the roster.

- You are responsible for participating in class discussion.
  You must be prepared to speak, which means that you
  must be prepared on Wednesday to take the next step in
  a discussion begun on Monday. The work you do between
  classes should always be built on what you did before and
  pointed toward what you expect (or hope) will be coming
  up. So that you will have a record of the work done in the
  seminar, we expect you to take notes in each class — and
  we expect you to take notes no matter who is talking. This
  means that you will be taking notes on what each other
  has to say.

Requirements

Each week you will have two kinds of reading assignments.
There are six required books that everyone will be reading. In
addition, you will be choosing at least four books to read on
your own. You will write a response to everything you read;
this writing will be contained in a journal.

For your journal, please buy a notebook that has pockets
and that will hold (or that already contains) lined paper. This
journal will be divided into three parts. One part will be for
your responses to the required books, and another equal part
will be for the entries you write on the books you select to
read. There should also be a third, smaller part. This will serve
for records you'll keep on your work as an editor. (We'll have
more to say about this last part later in the term.)

You will also have one or two writing assignments each
week. In some cases you will be asked to write about the books
you have read, in some cases you will be asked to write about

your own experience, and in some cases you will be asked to write about both, together. The essays will be different from your journal entries. They call for a different kind of writing and we will evaluate them differently. Please buy a separate folder with pockets for these essays. You must keep all the essays you write, all the papers we hand out in class, and all the assignment sheets in this folder. We will collect it at the end of the term.

We plan to regularly duplicate your essays for discussion in the seminar. The duplication process will go much better if you use only black pen when you write (unless you type) and if you use only regular-sized notebook paper (8½ by 11) with regular-sized lines (no tiny spaces). Please write on only one side of the paper.

We do not put a grade on your journal entries, nor do we duplicate these for the class to read. The writing assignments are not graded either, except for the occasional in-class essay exams. Your grades for the seminar are determined by your performance in the course and are based on our evaluation at the end of the course of all the work you have done through-out the term. You can see how important it is, then, that you keep everything in order in your folder and in your journal.

This course is a six-credit course. It is the equivalent of two courses in the undergraduate curriculum and you will re-ceive two grades: one will represent our evaluation of your formal written work over the term; the other will represent our evaluation of your participation in class and your work in your journal. You may ask us at any time during the term how you stand and we'll tell you what your grade would be, but you will generally know how you are doing from our comments on your papers and our weekly conferences. We will let you know immediately if we're worried about your progress.

Assigned Readings

The following books are required for the course: *I Know Why the Caged Bird Sings*, *The Catcher in the Rye*, *Hunger of Memory*, *Passages*, *The Vanishing Adolescent*, and *Coming of Age in Samoa*. All of these books are available at the bookstore. Please have them all by the end of the second week.

When we assign a book we'll expect you to read it from cover to cover by the date due. We will not work through books chapter by chapter. You will see that there is a pattern to the assignments so that reading and writing assignments are not due on the same day.

In-Class Reading

You will be given an hour a week (usually on Friday) to read in class. This time is given for you to work on the books you have chosen on your own. (You may, of course, read these books outside of class as well.) You can choose anything you want to read. In fact, you should think of this as an opportunity to read those books you've always wanted to read but never got around to. We will give you a list of books recommended by former BRW students, and this includes novels, science fiction, romances, biographies, books on sports, "self-help" books and books on careers. The only restrictions are these: you cannot read magazines, textbooks, books from other courses or "how-to-do-it" books.

Autobiography

There is actually a seventh assigned book for the course. This is the collection of autobiographies that will be written and read by the students in the seminar. Midway through the semester, you will write what we'll call a "section" of your autobiography, one which will deal primarily with the last two or three years of your life. You'll be drawing on the writing you've done for the first half of the course when you write this. The autobiographies from the class will be duplicated and bound into a collection that will become a required reading for the seminar. We will be charging each of you about $3.50 to cover costs.

Writing Assignment 1: In-Class Diagnostic Exam

We are giving you a chapter from Margaret Mead's autobiography, *Blackberry Winter*, and a question asking you to write about what you have read. The question will ask you to write about what you see to be the main ideas in the reading. You will complete this assignment in class. *Be sure* to hand in your paper before you leave.

You will have two hours to read the chapter and write your paper, so there will be plenty of time for you to prepare to write, to write and then to proofread. You will probably not have time to prepare a second draft of your paper, but you may feel free to make changes on the copy you hand in.

Questions

1. We'd like you to describe as carefully and completely as you can the important point or points you see Ms. Mead making about her experience at DePauw.

2. Would you then write about whatever in the chapter seems most important or most significant to *you*? And would you be sure to explain why you feel it is important or significant?

Writing Assignment 2

For this writing assignment, we'd like you to recall an experience you've had in the last two years or so that strikes you as particularly significant, one that has changed the way you are or the way you think about things. We want you to describe this experience as completely as you can, providing us with all the details we need to understand what happened. Then, when you've finished telling us what happened, go on to explain how and why this experience was a "significant" one. That is, go on to explain how and why it affected you as it did.

Here's how we want you to write this paper. This is a rough draft, not a finished paper, which means that you can go back and change things later. In the assignments that follow, in fact, you will be given the opportunity to go back and work on them again. Don't worry about organization, structure, correctness and the like because we aren't concerned with those issues yet. Do whatever you have to do to get yourself ready, and then just start writing. Give yourself enough time to write a full description of what happened and an explanation of what you think its significance might be. Writing time should be a total of one hour, but you will need more time to think.

Questions

When you come to class, would you also be prepared to talk, in detail, about how you wrote this paper? In fact, would you come with some notes written on the following:

1. What did you do first? What second? What came last?

2. What was easiest for you and what was hardest?

3. What gave you the most pleasure or the most grief?

4. Where did you get stuck or bogged down? Why, do you think? And what did you do to get going again?

Thinking about questions like these makes it impossible to say, "I can't write." As you look back over what you actually did while writing this paper, see what kinds of conclusions you can draw about the type of writer you are and about the things you can and can't do when you sit down to write.

Reading Assignment A

We'd like you to read the whole book, *I Know Why the Caged Bird Sings,* by next Friday. This gives you a full week. Plan to sit and read for periods of time that are longer and longer, rather than for many short sittings. When you bring the book to class on Friday, we'll want to know how you went about reading it. Be prepared, that is, to point to passages or sections of the book (if there are any) where you got bogged down or lost. Would you also keep track of the time you spend reading? Inside the back cover, or on a $3'' \times 5''$ card (ask us for one), record the date and times you begin and end each sitting. We'll want you to do this for all the assigned readings this term.

As you read, keep a pencil or pen in your hand or nearby; do not underline or take notes, but if you come across something that seems significant or puzzling or something that you'd like to bring up in class discussion, put a mark in the margin or through the page number so that you can find it later. Monday, when we spend class time talking about *Caged Bird,* you'll need to refer to specific parts of it. If you don't have these marks, or some system you invent, you'll find that you'll have no way of getting back into the book. There will be a book in your hand with a lot of pages, but no record of what you found to be worth a second look.

After you finish reading the book, you'll write in the part of your journal in which you record responses to the assigned reading. Here's how we want you to write. As soon as you can after you have read the book, sit down for one hour and write your response. We want you to write the first things that come to your mind when you think back on what you have read. We're not interested in summary, because we have read the book, too. Tell us, instead, what stands out for you. Then, tell us what things in your own life you can associate with what has stood out for you. These associations may be ideas of yours, feelings, experiences, memories of other books, of other courses, or things people have said to you. You want to move from recording what stands out for you as significant to a way of accounting for *why* these passages or sections are significant. It's very important that you write this two-fold response and that you write for an hour, an hour of straight, uninterrupted writing.

Don't be worried about how your words fall on the paper. Error, structure, organization and the like are not things that we are concerned with in the journal at this time. The journal is an idea book, a place to try things out. We want to read your thoughts as they come to you with a minimum of distractions, even if the words appear funny to you or are not connected or are not nearly how you want them to be.

Read the book; write for an hour. This will be due at the beginning of Friday's class. You will hand in the journal folder as Assignment A.

Worksheet: *I Know Why the Caged Bird Sings*

In groups of three students each, use your books and depend on each other for the following information:

1. Name as many characters in the book as you can.

2. List, in some kind of order, the events in the book as they occurred.

3. When you are done with 2, go back and star (*) those events, or the circumstances around those events, which you think are the most significant because of their effect on Maya's life. Use this space to briefly state the reasons why you have starred what you have.

4. After you work with your group, we'll be meeting as a class to discuss how Maya changed and why. In particular, we will be trying to come up with terms or labels to define the *types* of change that occurred for her. List some possible terms here, with a sentence that explains them.

Outside Reading Journal Entries

Today will be our first hour of sustained silent reading. Once a week you will have an hour of class time set aside to read one of the books that you have chosen for outside reading. (You can, of course, read these outside class as well.) Today, when the hour is up, we will ask you to make an entry in your journal. We'd like you to write a 10-minute summary of what you have read. Think of this as a book that the rest of us have not read, that we can only learn about from you.

The format of the journal itself is important. As we told you last week, the journal will be divided into two large parts and a third smaller part. One of the larger parts is for the required reading assignments. This is where you will write Assignment A (*I Know Why the Caged Bird Sings*) which is due Friday. The other large part of the journal is for outside reading assignments, and this is where today's entry will go.

In addition to the 10-minute summary, there is one other thing we want to do today concerning the outside reading. Get the materials that we handed out earlier that are in your folders. Find the chart where you filled out your three outside reading selections and, next to the title of the book you read today, enter how far you read (i.e., put the page number). Then go to the right-hand side of the chart labeled *date due*. Considering how much you read today in an hour, and considering how many pages are in your book, estimate realistically when you can complete the book. Keep in mind that you'll have an hour a week of class time to read. We generally allow students about two weeks to read their outside reading selections. So pencil in a date within the next two weeks or so as a tentative date as to when you will finish your first book. Next week we will be meeting with each of you individually and we will be checking on these commitments. From now on, after today's entry, you'll not make an entry in this part of your journal until you have completely finished a book.

When you are finished with this book, we want you to write in the journal for an uninterrupted hour. You may certainly write longer than an hour, but you must not write less. This part of the journal will not be read by anyone but us, and it will never have to be rewritten because it is incorrect. We would like you to feel that this is your chance to spout off or applaud or complain or get as personal as you'd like. We may have you rewrite on occasion if the entry isn't long enough or if we don't feel that you've been serious about your work.

The journal entries are different from the reading or writing assignments that we'll hand out in class. You will have to provide enough information about the book in order that we understand the sort of book you are reading and what you paid attention to when you read. But we are not interested in reading simply a summary of events as you are able to list them. We are interested in knowing why this book is worth reading and remembering. Perhaps the book was confusing or disappointing to you, perhaps it came alive or died in unexpected places. We'd like to know what you found to be interesting or perplexing, what you objected to or what you liked. For us to understand this, you'll have to be quite specific in writing your response and to use examples and illustrations so that we can see what you see.

We will also use the journal as a way of having a conversation with you about what you've read. We'll ask questions, ask you to comment on what we've said, push at you to make connections or to clarify or to come forward with opinions or objections or assent. And we'll expect you to write back to us on the next page.

Your second journal entry for this first book will be due on the day you have committed to be finished.

Writing Assignment 3

You've had a chance to spend some time with the following problem:

> We'd like you to recall an experience you've had in the last two years or so that strikes you as particularly significant, one that has changed the way you are or the way you think about things. We want you to describe this

experience as completely as you can, providing us with all the details we need to understand what happened. Then, when you've finished telling us what happened, go on to explain why and how this experience was a *significant* one. That is, go on to explain how and why it affected you as it did.

You've spent a good bit of time working on this experience you've had and what it might mean. You've located a moment in your life and called it "significant" or "meaningful." You've thought about it to a degree and with the attention that writing demands. And you've been forced to find words for some vague feelings or impressions you had about the way things change in your life. Whatever went on in your paper, because you've been writing, you've had the chance to learn something. You've gotten smarter. You know more about yourself and about change (and about writing) than you did before you picked up the assignment.

Now we'd like you to rewrite that paper, and the purpose of the rewriting is to make your paper a more precise and insightful representation of what you know. In part, that means working with what you've already written in order to make it a more complete or complex record of what you can say about your subject. Since you know more now than you did when you began, it also means, however, that you are in a position to go on to say even more, to arrive at a new perspective on your subject and find new things to say.

Carefully reread your paper and note our comments. These comments are our responses as readers to you as a writer. In particular, look at the questions in the margins. Be sure you're giving us a full story.

The goal of rewriting, then, is not only to make your first draft more correct or more elegant. We want you to revise (meaning re-see), not just copy over more neatly.

Questions

The second part of Assignment 3 asked for an explanation as to why this particular event is significant for you. To make your explanation fuller, you may want to ask yourself:

1. Am I telling what made this experience significant?

2. How is this event separate from and more significant than other events I might have written about?

3. Did I learn something? What?

4. What if I had not had this experience? Would I think of myself differently?

Reading Assignment B

When you revise an essay you've got more to work with than memories or wit. When you began working on Assignment 3 you had a written record in front of you of one attempt (yours) to find something to say about yourself and change.

We've attached two sets of drafts and revisions from Assignments 2 and 3. We'd like you to read and study them, making notes and checks in the margins where you see fit. We want you to be prepared to talk about change as it is represented in these papers.

Questions

1. What changed? What changed significantly?

2. What didn't change? Anything significant here?

3. What conclusions can you draw from this about revisions? About the changes a person can make?

Reading Assignment C

For Monday, you are to read *The Catcher in the Rye*. For Assignment A, we talked about how many sittings it took you to read *I Know Why the Caged Bird Sings*. Everyone had different numbers of times that they read and varying lengths of time for their reading periods. For this book we'd like you to read in fewer sittings and for longer lengths of time. Again, do not take notes or underline; if you find something you want to remember or something you don't understand, make a mark in the margin so you can go back to that page after you have finished reading the book.

Once you finish *The Catcher in the Rye*, we'd like you to sit down and write a response to the book in your journal. It's best to write your response as soon as you can after you've finished the book. Plan to write for an hour. In this entry, we'd like you to tell us what you found in the book that seems most interesting or useful, given the discussions we've had about growth and change so far in class. Keep in mind that there are no "right" answers that we are looking for; we have, however, identified issues and questions that most interest us as a group.

We'd like to see more *illustration* of the things you choose to talk about in this entry. We'd like you to cite examples (to include examples) from the text and, if appropriate, from your own prior thinking and experience. Your explanations, that is, should take more than a single sentence and they should be more than a bald statement ("Maya liked her brother Bailey."). Again, however, give us as little summary as possible. We've all read the book. We know what happened to Holden. We want you to help us better understand him.

Worksheet: *The Catcher in the Rye*

In groups, use your books and depend on each other for the following information:

1. Name as many characters in the book as you can.

2. List, in some kind of order, the events in the book as they occurred.

3. When you are done with 2, go back and star (*) those events, or the circumstances around those events, which you think are the most significant because of their effect on Holden's life. Put a check by those that you think are least significant. We are particularly interested in the distinctions you make between the significant and insignificant events. Use this space to briefly state the reasons why you have starred what you have.

4. We'll meet as a class to discuss how Holden changes or does not change, and why.

Reading Assignment C (Alternate)

For Monday, please read *Ordinary People*. This time we would like you to read in fewer sittings and for longer lengths of time.

We ask you to do this essentially so you can train yourself to concentrate on what you read for longer periods of time. You will find out that this book is written in a different style from *I Know Why the Caged Bird Sings*. Can you define the difference? Can you explain why there is a difference?

(If, as you read, you find something you want to remember or something you don't understand, make a mark in the margin so that you can go back to that page after you have finished reading the book.)

Once you finish *Ordinary People*, we'd like you to write a response to the book in the journal. Write your response as soon as you can after you have finished the book. Plan to write for an hour.

In this entry, similar to entry A, we'd like you to tell us what was meaningful to you in the book, and why. Then go on to write what comes to your mind from your own personal experience when you read this book. Although Conrad's life might at first seem remarkably different from yours, you might — if you push yourself to think beyond the most obvious differences — find points of contact with your own personal experience.

The journal entry is due at the beginning of class, on Monday.

Worksheet: *Ordinary People*

In class, use your books and depend on each other for the following information.

1. Name as many characters in the book as you can.

2. List as many events in the book as you can and number them according to the order they occur in the narrative.

3. Go back to 2 and now group those events in a way that is meaningful to you. Try to devise and name at least three or four categories.

Writing Assignment 4

We've spent a lot of time talking about events and how they mark, or cause, change in young people's lives. And we've begun to come up with our own system for identifying what we've called "significant" events and for explaining and labeling the way young people grow and change.

For this assignment, we want you to take a somewhat different approach to the question of change. Begin with a time when you thought, hoped or were led to believe that an event would be significant, but when, in fact, it wasn't. You expected a "turning point," but things just went on as usual. You didn't change. Nothing much changed around you.

Tell us what happened. By now you should be aware that we're not just asking you to tell us a good story (although we're asking for that, too, in a way). We're asking you to provide information for the work of the seminar. And by now you should know what we mean when we say, "Be sure to illustrate and explain." We want you to write at length and in detail. Or, as someone said in class, we need to know what you're talking about if we're going to know what you're talking about.

When you finish reporting what happened, go on in your paper to comment on the difference between a significant event and an event of no significance. You're going to have to give this more than one or two sentences.

You'll have a chance to rework this paper later, so put your energy into what you can find to say. You must, however, hand in something we can read and reproduce for the rest of the class.

Writing Assignment 5

We want you to rewrite Assignment 4, paying attention to the comments we've made on your paper and taking into consideration what we said in class. (You should, by the way, feel free to quote or paraphrase comments made by other members of the seminar.)

In particular, however, we'd like you to work in two areas when you revise your paper.

1. We're still not concerned about correctness (whether the words are spelled correctly or whether the sentences are "good" sentences). We would, however, like you to begin to be more conscious of the way you control the "shape" of your essay. Perhaps the most obvious shape in an essay is the shape indicated by the paragraph indentations on the left-hand margin. Be prepared to explain why you begin and end paragraphs where you do in this revision. Our discussion of papers in class will begin here.

2. The second half of the last assignment stumped most of you. You told a story but that was it. When it came time for you to provide commentary, to tell us what we might learn now that we have all the relevant facts before us, you settled for a one-liner ("I guess graduation is just no big thing") or your paper just ended. It is easier to tell a story about an ugly duckling than it is to draw conclusions, particularly when you need to say more than "Beauty is only skin deep." But this is the problem most of these assignments will pose for you. You've got to devote more time — and that means more sentences and paragraphs — to the role you play as student (not just storyteller) or expert commentator (and not just on-the-spot reporter).

Writing Assignment 6

It's not uncommon to hear people say that change is a necessary part of growth and development. Nobody expects (at least not really) to grow up and have everything remain the same. Change is normal, proper. The real problem is when people refuse to change, when, as it is often put, people "refuse to grow up."

Most of you have written about how unique or extraordinary experiences have made an impression on you. For this paper, we'd like you to write about yourself as a representative case, as a person not at all unlike most people your age and sex. Think of a process of change in your life in the past few years which you believe is probably common to nearly all adolescents. (We're thinking, here, of the list we once made on the board of the sorts of things anyone up to age 18 might be expected to experience as significant.) For example, we said that Maya's first real job was significant, as was her friendship with Louise, and that these two things — the first job and the first deep friendship — might be said to represent the sorts of things that shape and alter any teenager's sense of who he or she is or what the world is like.

Choose an experience of your own that seems to best illustrate a common pattern in and a common process of adolescent development. Tell us about it but, more importantly, tell us what it illustrates. Clearly you're going to have to say more than that getting a job illustrates the process of getting a job. You've got to find another way of talking about getting a job (if that's what you choose to write about) that breaks with the language of storytelling. Think of your paper as your first attempt to develop part of a larger "Theory of Adolescent Development."

This is a first draft. You'll be working on this paper again. You'll be working on your "theory" for several weeks.

Reading Assignment D

For Monday, you are to read *Hunger of Memory*. Plan to sit for periods of time that are longer and longer rather than many short sittings. When you come to class on Monday, bring the book for class discussion. You will need to refer to specific parts of the book.

When you read *Hunger of Memory* do not underline. If you come across something that stands out as important, or as somehow worth discussion, put a mark in the margin or circle the page number so that you can go back and find it easily. You may want to write notes to yourself or to Rodriguez in the margin as well. We're getting to the point now in class where we expect you to be able to use your books to cite examples or illustrations to support what you say in discussion.

Once you have finished the book, we'd like you to write for an hour in your journal. *Hunger of Memory* tells the story of a young man's education. It also tells the story of how the writer, by writing and thinking, comes to understand his education as a process, one that changed him and his relation to his family. Although the book presents many strong and vivid stories, you must have also noticed the sections where he comments on his experience, where he talks as a writer, looking back at the past. For this journal entry, find at least three such passages in the book. Choose the ones that seem the richest or most puzzling — or the ones that seem truest to your own experience. The passages you should look for are the ones in which Rodriguez pauses, after telling you about things that he did, in order to analyze their meaning or to explore their implications for his own development as a person. We'd like you to write down the page numbers for these sections, and summarize what he says in each. Then, when you're done, we'd like you to comment on the words or ideas you've found that seem particularly powerful to you, and to speculate on whether anything similar could be said about your own experience.

Worksheet: *Hunger of Memory*

1. List the experiences that Richard Rodriguez has had that seem to be different from your own. Put a star next to the ones that seemed to have the greatest effect on his development.

2. List the experiences of Rodriguez that seem to be similar to your own. Place a star next to the ones that seemed to have the greatest effect on his development.

3. Using items *from each list*, explain how Rodriguez's experience is representative, how it throws light on the way everyone in our society grows up and becomes an adult. (Use the space below to write notes you can refer to when asked to make a group report in class.)

4. Using items *from each list*, explain how Rodriguez's experience is unique, how it shows the development of a particular individual and not of any group (including Mexican-Americans). (Use the space below to write notes you can refer to when asked to make a group report in class.)

Reading Assignment D (Alternate)

For Monday, you are to read *A Separate Peace*. Plan to sit for periods of time that are longer and longer rather than many short sittings. When you come to class on Monday, bring the book for class discussion. You will need to refer to specific parts of the book.

When you read *A Separate Peace*, do not underline. If you come across something that puzzles you, or if you come across something that seems important to you, put a mark in the margin or circle the page number so that you can go back and find it easily. You may want to write notes to yourself in the margin as well. We're getting to the point now in class where we expect you to be able to use your books to cite examples or illustrations to support what you say in our discussions.

Once you have finished the book, we'd like you to write for an hour in your journal. For this assignment, we want you to tell us what you think is the most important section of *A Separate Peace*. This section could be as short as three or four sentences or as long as a chapter. It may be that this section is the sort of thing that most people would see immediately as "important," or it may be that this section is the sort of thing that only you (or a reader like you) would notice. When you tell us about it, be sure to say where it occurs in the story *and* why you think it is the most important section of the book. We're interested in what you notice, but we're even more interested in what you have to say about what you notice.

Worksheet: *A Separate Peace*

In groups, use your books and depend on each other for the following information:

1. Name as many characters in the book as you can.

2. List, in some kind of order, the events in the book as they occurred.

3. Go back to 2 and put a star next to those events which you think are the most significant. Use this space to briefly state *why* you have starred what you have.

4. For class discussion, be prepared to talk about the way the *narrator* (Gene, the person telling the story; not Gene, the character immediately involved in actions of the past) understands and interprets those events. Use the space below to list page numbers and prepare notes for your presentation on the narrator and his way of interpreting events from the past.

Writing Assignment 7

We'd like you to revise Assignment 6. We're convinced that you can tell good stories about yourself now; these are things you can write with a good bit of conscious ability. So we want you to turn your attention to the part of the paper that develops and explains your "theory."

1. We want to offer all the old words of advice — be precise, provide enough detail, illustrate, explain. We're aware, however, that a "precise," "detailed" explanation of an idea is somewhat different from a precise, detailed account of an event. Still, these are the only words we know how to use. We'll want to see what they might mean in this new context when we talk about drafts and revisions in class. See what you can do to help.

2. Most of you talked about change as something that happens to a situation rather than as something that happens to a person. Most of the papers ended up saying something like, "Before I had my driver's license I had to walk: now I can ride." What can we say in response to this except, "So what?" The "I" in your paper — the person caught up in a moment of possible change, a person defined in relation to everything outside — that "I" is the subject of your paper. You, the writer, by taking the role of a sensitive, intelligent observer and commentator, are trying to learn something about that "I," that person in your paper.

3. We're still interested in the control you can exert over the shape of your essay. If your paper can be said to be made up of "pieces," and if the pieces can be said to fit together into a coherent discussion, we'll be interested in seeing what the pieces are in your essay and how they fit together. Would you, then, hand in an outline or a diagram of your final draft that represents the "shape" of your essay.

Read back over your paper and listen to the writer, the person who is commenting on you and your experience. What does he/she sound like? Do you get a sense that your life is as complicated or interesting as in fact it is? Are we going to end up saying "so what" — or are there more interesting questions we can ask?

Writing Assignment 8: In-Class Assignment

Review *Hunger of Memory*, Rodriguez's "intellectual autobiography," and select a section from each chapter that in some way represents the "heart" of that chapter. Use the sections you've chosen to explain what you see to be Rodriguez's view of his development from childhood to adulthood.

When you have done this, reread what you have written, and go on to explain the key ways in which Rodriguez did and did not have what you have come to think of as a "typical" adolescence.

Writing Assignment 9

We want to introduce a new term: "editing." This may be where we start to become the English teachers you thought we'd be. Now that you've completed your final draft of Assignment 6, we want you to set aside time (begin by setting aside a full hour) to read through your paper once more to see that there are no mistakes. This last act of reading over your work we'll call editing. Sometimes it's called proofreading; sometimes it's called correcting. It requires a very different sort of reading than you are used to doing. You must learn to read each word, and to see that word as black marks on a white page. Usually when you read you don't read each word. You hear a voice or see meaning unfolding, but you don't normally see each word as a set of marks on the page. It's only when you learn to see the word as marks that you can begin to see whether the right marks are there or not.

If you have trouble editing your papers, most of the difficulty will be in *seeing* the errors, not in figuring out how to correct them. You'll get caught up in the sound of your own voice and not notice what's actually on the page. Because of this problem, some professional editors read slowly out loud while they move their pencil (or a ruler) across the page. We'd like you to begin by doing the same. Editing is close, detailed (and sometimes boring) work. It must be done, though. When you are rich and famous you can hire a copy editor. For the purpose of this course, however, we do not want you to get any professional help. You'll be working together in class, but that's the only assistance we want you to have.

We'd also like you to buy a red pen or a red marker. Always bring it with you to class, since you'll be editing each other's papers as well as your own. Before you hand in each assignment from now on (or unless we tell you otherwise), you are to go over your draft, setting aside a period of time well after you've finished writing it. During this rereading you are to make corrections using your red pen. We will not be circling your mistakes for you. The job of editing your papers is yours, not ours. You need to learn to be good at spotting your characteristic brand of mistake. After you've been doing this for a while, we'll begin keeping a record of the errors you *miss*, and we will be helping you to learn to correct those.

Remember — you must be able to write a reasonably correct paper by the end of the term in order to pass the course. Our method for teaching you to produce correct papers is to teach you to edit after you have finished writing and revising.

Reading Assignment E

You have read three books in three weeks: *I Know Why the Caged Bird Sings, The Catcher in the Rye,* and *Hunger of Memory.* Now we would like you to have time to reread and to reflect on these books and what they have in common and how they fit in with the general concerns of the seminar.

We would like you, in fact, to prepare a journal entry that uses these books to make some general point or points about the way young people change and develop a sense of self. Your basic purpose is to say what you can about identity and change on the basis of your reading of these books.

One word of advice: You *must* base your discussion on specific incidents and passages in the text, and you *must* explain the connections between the point or points you are trying to make and the incidents you are using to make them. If you quote a passage and tell us what happened in one of the books, you *must* follow with commentary of your own. (This came out more as an order than a word of advice.)

Be prepared to talk in class about how you went back and worked with the books to prepare for this journal entry. We will spend half of the time of the class on Monday talking about what you are saying in your journals and the other half working in groups to prepare some guidelines to be used for rereading.

Writing Assignment 10: In-Class Essay Exam

You'll have one hour to write an essay based on two of the books you have read, *I Know Why the Caged Bird Sings* and *The Catcher in the Rye.* We're interested in the way you present your ideas and the use you make of the books, so we don't want you to spend any of the time recopying your paper.

We want you to understand that this is not the usual writing assignment or journal entry. It is an essay test, which means we will be looking at the ways you present your recollection of what you have read and at your ability to work with a test question. You need to show that you know what you are talking about and that you can work with the ideas set by the examiner. An essay test does not allow you to write in the personal, write-what-comes-to-your-mind prose that you have been writing so far. At the same time, your examiners (in this case, the two of us) do not want to be bored or told a lot of BS.

Here is your exam: Maya and Holden are very different people. Yet they both experienced adolescence, which means that they had to have experienced some things in common. Write an essay that compares and contrasts Maya and Holden and their particular responses to the problems of adolescence. Use specific examples.

Note: We will spend another class period going over sample copies of your exams after we have graded them. We want to give you a sense of how essay tests are graded, what teachers look for, and how you might best meet these expectations.

Writing Assignment 11

All of us, at one time or another, have said, "This is it. I've got to make some changes in my life." Think about a time when you set out to deliberately change a habit or pattern you knew it would not be easy to change. (Notice that we do not insist that you were successful.)

1. What made you decide that something had to be done?

2. What did you do? Be precise. And be honest. How did you set about producing this change? Please, no stories of miracle cures. No papers that read like this: "I used to be mean to my girl-friend. I realized that it's not nice to be mean. Now I'm really nice."

3. What happened?

We'd like you to write a paper that tells us what happened. It should also be a paper, however, that offers your careful, intelligent observations as an expert on "Change and Adolescence."

This is a draft, part of the work you are doing in preparation for your autobiography.

Writing Assignment 12

So far you've written several papers about your own experience. If you reread these papers carefully, you may notice that you have created a definite image of yourself as a certain kind of adolescent going through certain kinds of experiences. We are now going to invite you to focus your attention upon that character you have created through your writing.

Keep in mind that as a writer you are different from the main character in your autobiography. The *you* who sits down today to write about the past is different from the younger self you are writing about. You're older, wiser; you can see past actions in the context of things that went before and things that came after. And the *you* who is a writer is different from the you in the stories you tell. The writer comments, shapes, connects, embellishes, imposes patterns, even makes things up when memory fails.

Begin this assignment by giving us a full description of the character who appears on the pages you've written.

1. Would you say that the incidents you have chosen to write about so far offer an accurate, thorough, and complete picture of your character?

2. Have you presented a character with many sides or have you presented a stick figure, a character out of a cartoon or a TV drama?

3. What more would you like a reader to know in order to fill out the picture?

4. What do you see or understand now, as a writer, that your character couldn't see or understand? Then, go on to comment on the ways in which your character could be said to be both typical of and different from most adolescents. Use the characters from the books you've been reading and the papers you've read in class as points for comparison.

Writing Assignment 13

During the next two weeks or so, we will be working on our midterm project, a longer paper that might be called a "section" of your autobiography. The first draft is due Monday. After that, we'll work on both revising and editing that draft. A final handwritten draft is to be completed by Friday (11 days after the first draft) and the final *typed* copy is due Wednesday (16 days after the first draft). Be sure to arrange for a typist to type your final copy. Your papers will be reproduced and bound, and this "book" will be our next assigned reading for the course (for which you will pay approximately $3.50).

This autobiography will both describe and discuss some of the major changes you've gone through during that period we call "adolescence." You will want to include events that show how you changed in significant ways during your high school years and the people and situations that had an impact on you. But you will also want to make connections among the events that you describe in order to help your readers understand something about growing up during this period in life. In what way are you the same kind of person that you were at the beginning of adolescence, and how do you account for this sense of consistent identity? On the other hand, in what ways are you *now* a different person than you were a few years ago, and what has made the difference? And on the basis of the experiences you describe, what can you say in general about growth and change in adolescence?

You won't of course be able to write about everything that's happened to you in the last few years, so you'll have to consider and choose carefully those experiences which you feel best represent how you have grown and changed from a child into an adult. You may decide to write about several different events, about a chain or series of related events, even a whole phase in your life. These events may have seemed significant at the time, or insignificant. They may be events you have described in previous papers. All these choices are up to you, the writer. What we ask of you is that you make your readers understand why those experiences have influenced your individual process of growth and change. In writing about them, you will be providing *your* version of adolescence.

There are some restrictions on your choice of events to write about. Don't go back before age 14 or so, except for background material to a story. Be sure that you include enough detail. Try to write about at least three distinct events. You may emphasize certain ones more than others, and you may certainly write about more than three events; three is the minimum. Finally, we want to caution you about writing about the big events everyone thinks are supposed to be significant: that first big date, getting a driver's license, high school graduation, going away to college. These are hard to talk about without sounding like a clone of everyone else: "learning to drive is a way of becoming independent," "graduation is the start of a whole new life," etc. If you choose to talk about these standard events, make sure that you do not use a "ready-made language"; find a way of talking about yourself that allows you to create your own story on paper.

For this assignment, then, write a first draft of your autobiography. Concentrate on generating as much as you can (in the past, the autobiographies have run between 10 and 20 handwritten pages). You may draw on your earlier papers but remember that you are starting a new project. Keep in mind that this is a first draft; you can change your mind if you decide later that some other stories might work better. Do ask yourself, however, if the events you've chosen to write about have enough meaning and interest for you to spend two weeks writing about them. Also keep in mind that the rest of the class will eventually read what you're writing. You may choose to use pseudonyms for other people and places, but your history should have your name in it.

Here is a schedule of the next four assignments:

Assignment 13: A first draft. Due _____.

Assignment 14: A revision. Due _____.

Assignment 15: Another revision. We'll spend time in class editing that copy. Due _____.

Assignment 16: On _____, you must have a final *typed* copy ready for us.

Be sure that you arrange for a typist well in advance. This is the only paper that we'll insist be typed. We want everyone to go through the process of having at least one paper typed and we want you to see what your writing looks like when it's packaged like a professional's. We also want the papers typed so that we can efficiently reproduce them. A collection of auto-biographies will provide the material for the next few reading assignments.

Here are the guidelines for the typed copy:

- The typed copy must be clean and free of typographical errors.
- The type must be dark and easy to read.
- Papers should be single-spaced with two spaces between paragraphs.
- Leave a one-inch margin on the top, bottom and sides.

Writing Assignment 14

These are the revision instructions for your autobiography. It is due at the beginning of our next class. Carefully reread what you wrote and while you read look at our comments. We've read as readers, asking for information or clarification, telling you where we were interested, puzzled or bored. Keep in mind that it is a writer's job to see that the stories all fit together into one package.

Some of you need to add more to the stories. Some of you need to make cuts. Some of you need to shape and rearrange. Some of you need to provide more commentary and explanation.

To save time, you may choose to write numbered or lettered inserts on separate sheets of paper, just as you do in your journal additions. You might also cut and paste — that is, literally cut parts from your paper with scissors (parts to save, parts to add, parts to move around, parts to throw away), take these pieces and arrange them according to how you want to revise, fill in the gaps, and then tape the pieces neatly in order from start to finish with clean sheets of paper as backing.

Your revision is due by our next meeting. We'll work on editing the final draft later.

Some reminders:

- Do you have a typist?
- Have you thought of a title for the class book, the collected autobiographies?
- Have you set money aside to buy the book?

Writing Assignment 15

This is the third step in the midterm project, your autobiography. Each essay will provide a chapter in a class book, a collective autobiography representing the experience of young adults. Each will supply specific examples or case studies. You will be asked in a later assignment to write about all the autobiographies and about what they say, generally, about growth and change during the adolescent years.

You should keep this larger project in mind as you work to put your own autobiography into final form. You can arrange your stories so that they point toward some conclusions. You can use your role as the writer to suggest how you would most like them to be read — what you hope others would see as the connecting threads, the important themes or the key moments in your experience. And you can, of course, come forward and comment yourself on your own experience.

In Assignments 12 and 13, you've been developing your narrative. As we've been saying, in telling these stories you're headed in a particular direction for definite reasons. Use this last revision to see what you can do to further bring the pieces of your autobiography together. If you were working earlier as a storyteller, this is the occasion for you to come forward as a writer. You should begin by rereading your entire autobiography from beginning to end, making notes that you can draw on when you begin to revise.

Questions

Here are some of the questions you might want to ask while you are reading:

1. Step back and look at these stories as though they were about a character you are meeting for the first time. What do they represent? What are the themes or patterns that tie them together? How could you bring them forward so that other readers could see them as you do?

2. What makes these events unique, special, different from one another?

3. What common denominator connects them or is present in each?

4. What movement (progress) do you see between or during these events?

5. What has changed in this character and what has remained the same?

6. You should think also of these stories as chapters in *your* story. Why did these events come to your mind when you sat down to write about your experience? What made you think of *these* stories? And in *this* order? What do they say about you as an adolescent?

7. How might these stories be seen as an earlier phase of where you are now? Of where you are headed?

8. What do you see now in your adolescence that you didn't see before?

9. What have you kept to yourself? What have you decided not to bring forward on paper? Is there any reason to acknowledge that there are things you won't write about, or can't write about, or don't understand well enough to bring forward in an essay?

Writing Assignment 16

This is it. This is the final step for your autobiography. By the next class period, your paper should be finished — at least the handwritten copy. Now is the time to edit and to prepare the copy for your typist.

We'll be spending the next class editing for errors and making sure that your inserts are clear and in order. You may choose at this time to delete anything that seems too personal or too revealing, such as names of people, places, etc. The typed paper (this assignment) is due on Monday. If your paper isn't here, it will not be part of the book, and we will not be able to evaluate you for your midterm grade.

To the typist:

- Put name and title at the top of the first page.
- Use regular paper (no onion skin).
- Single space within paragraphs.
- Double space between paragraphs.
- Number each page in the upper right-hand corner.

Writing Assignment 17

Please reread Chapter 4, "Playing It To the Bust," in *Passages* (pages 62–79). This is the chapter about Dennis, the 22-year-old, black Hotchkiss graduate.

For this assignment we would like you to assume the role of the psychologist. We would like you to identify each crisis that Dennis went through, label it (by using Gail Sheehy's terms and/or your own), and explain the nature and consequence of the crisis. (Why, for example, do you think Sheehy chose to entitle Chapter 4, "Playing It To the Bust"? Can you think of a more appropriate title now that you have worked so closely with Dennis's case?) Be sure to follow this sequence: identify the key moments in Dennis's life, label them, explain the nature and consequence of the crisis.

Then, on the basis of what you've said, go on to tell us what this close analysis of the text has enabled you to see about Dennis that you didn't see before. And go on to tell us what your analysis enabled you to see that Sheehy didn't see (or wouldn't have seen).

Reading Assignment F

This assignment is due Monday. Please read the collected autobiographies. As you read, treat this as you would any assigned book for this course. By this, we mean you are to read this in as few sittings as possible and be prepared to make a one-hour journal entry when you are finished. As you read, make a note next to the things you will want to write about and discuss in class.

In this journal assignment, we want you to write about a pattern (or patterns) that you see emerging in the autobiographies.

What are people saying? Notice what sorts of things most people have chosen to write about. What do you see as the main themes, recurring ideas, and similar experiences in this collection? Use examples and refer to specific papers when you talk about the themes or patterns you have found.

Worksheet 1: *Passages*

Before you begin reading *Passages* by Gail Sheehy, we'd like you to become familiar with the book and how it is set up. We want you to flip through the book and notice the following things: there is a table of contents and an index. Be prepared to demonstrate how one might use them. The book is divided into chapters and larger parts. What do you know about the book from the table of contents? Why do you think Gail Sheehy has titled the book *Passages*?

We are assigning the first three parts of *Passages* (to page 198 or through the "Trying Twenties") to be read by Wednesday. The remaining twelve chapters will be assigned to individuals or pairs of students in the class to read. We want you to be ready to discuss these, also, by next Wednesday.

As you read *Passages*, do not underline or take notes. What you should do is mark a page, paragraph, sentence or word that you'd like to remember for class discussion. You can easily do this by putting a small mark or by writing a word or two in the margin.

We'd like you to plan an uninterrupted period when you can sit and begin *Passages*; designate at least an hour for your first reading. After your first session reading the book, we'd like you to answer the following. Bring this sheet to class.

1. How long did you read? How many pages did you read?

2. What does the title, *Passages*, mean?

3. Have you noticed the different type styles in the book? What are the italics for?

4. What are the subtitles (the short titles within the chapters) for?

5. Have you noticed the little numbers above some sentences?
(See page 18, end of first paragraph.) What are these for?

Worksheet 2: *Passages*

1. In Gail Sheehy's book, as you read the first 198 pages, what
unusual or special terms of the author's did you notice? Write
them below and be ready to explain, in your own words, what
they mean.

2. How is *Passages* similar in style and format to the other three
books we've read? What ways might you connect them? How
is it different? How might you label these two kinds of reading?

Reading Assignment G

This journal entry is due on Friday.

After reading the first 198 pages of *Passages* by Gail Sheehy,
please write an entry in which you *explain* what you believe
Sheehy is saying about the "passages" of one's life, from the
beginning of adolescence to the "Trying Twenties."

Then go on to show us how you can make use of Sheehy's theory *to refine or to refute* the theory of adolescence that you have been formulating throughout this term in your assignments, in your journal entries, in class discussions, as well as in your own private thinking.

In order to do the second part of this assignment satisfactorily, it will be necessary for you to review all that you have written for us during this term.

Writing Assignment 18: In-Class Assignment

We have asked you to review Chapter 6 in *Passages* (pages 92–105). Look back again at the last page of this chapter. As you read through the last two paragraphs, please underline the terms or phrases that seem to be particularly important and significant for your understanding of Sheehy's argument (about finding a "true self"). Use the first part of your essay to present and explain these terms.

After that we'd like you to select a specific case study that appears in the sections you were assigned to read and use those terms to show us what you can say about the form and nature of that individual's search for self-knowledge. We want you to put those terms to work, in other words.

Reserve about 10 minutes at the end of class to edit your paper. We suggest that when you are finished writing, you read your paper backwards, sentence by sentence, aloud to yourself. This way you should be better able to see and hear any errors.

Writing Assignment 19

Your research on adolescent development will be extended, now, to the "case studies" present in the collected autobiographies (or, "The Book," as it has come to be known). We'd like you to use these case studies to draw some general conclusions about the ways change occurs and the types of changes that occur for the adolescents represented in your sample population.

Sheehy says that after she spent hours reviewing the cases she collected, suddenly patterns, similarities, regularities began to emerge. These patterns allowed her to speculate about people in general. She could do more, that is, than talk about Bob and Alice or Ted and Susan. Where she does talk about individuals, she does so because their experience is representative of a common experience. On the basis of what she finds to be generally true, she proposes a theory about, for example, the conflict between young adults and their parents, a theory she explains by inventing such terms as *merger self*, *seeker self*, and *inner custodian*.

We'd like to talk in general about change and adolescence on the basis of the autobiographies, and we'd like you to propose a theory (or theories) that can help the rest of us focus on the work we've done this term.

Your tasks, then, are to:

1. Study the "cases" before you.

2. Identify patterns that seem significant — look for common themes, problems or experiences; and look for themes, problems or experiences that break the mold, that stand out as unique.

3. Report on what you find and begin to explain what these patterns could be said to represent. On the basis of what you find, that is, what can you say about adolescent development?

You may certainly draw on Sheehy's work as you write your paper. There are things we expect you to be able to do on your own, in other words, and there will be places where you will want to draw on what she has done. The two of you are working on similar problems. When you draw on Sheehy, you want to officially recognize that you are using her work. You don't need to use footnotes for this paper. If you use her words *exactly* as they appeared in her book, put them in quotation marks and tell us, in your sentence, that this is something Sheehy said. If you summarize or paraphrase her words, you don't need to use quotation marks, but you still need to announce that this is something she said. If you quote more than a few words (if you quote a phrase, a single sentence, or several sentences), put the page number from *Passages* in parentheses like this: (*Passages*, p. 64) or (*Passages*, pp. 64-65).

We will not guide you through drafts of this paper. You've had enough experience working through drafts to begin to do this on your own. From now on we're primarily interested in your final draft and the work you do as an editor. Set aside time so that you can spend at least an hour editing the final draft. Remember, when you edit you are making corrections; you are not revising and trying out new sentences. Do all your editing in red ink so that we can see the evidence on the page.

Reading Assignment H

The next book to read for class is *Vanishing Adolescent* by Edgar Friedenberg. The book is to be read by Wednesday.

You will notice this book, like *Passages*, has a table of contents and an index. We'd like you to turn to the table of contents and read the chapter titles. As you read the titles, what do you suppose will be the contents of each chapter? What do you suppose the title of the book means?

In flipping through the book, you'll notice the type is similar to *Passages*; there are both the standard roman type and italics. When you read, think about why the author has used italics.

We will be assigning this book to be read in a manner different from the other books we've read. We want you to begin with Chapter 5. This is a discussion of five high school students. These are case studies. Once you are done with the fifth chapter, we'd like you to read the rest of the book. As you read the other chapters, we want you to be looking for specific *sections* or *terms* which will apply to the five case studies. We're looking for connections you can make between each student in the case studies and what Friedenberg talks about in the rest of the book. You will also find parts that may apply to yourself, the autobiographies, the other books we've read in class, and things we've discussed in the seminar. Do not underline or take formal notes; put a mark or a quick note in the margin when you come across something you'd like to remember in *Vanishing Adolescent*.

Once you've completed *Vanishing Adolescent*, we'd like you to write for an hour in your journal. This journal entry will be collected on Wednesday. We are interested in your reaction to and opinion of this book, and we're particularly interested in any comparison you can make to the other books we've read. You may want to begin or end your entry with these comments. When you're done, make a separate list of the terms or ideas you have learned from this book that strike you as useful — things you can apply to adolescents and the theories we've formed in class.

Writing Assignment 20: In-Class Essay Exam

Friedenberg, like Sheehy, seems to think that adolescence is a time of conflict. This is one of the things he says about this period of growth:

Some of the experiences of adolescence which turn out to be the most beneficial to growth are, it is true, painful at the time. Looking for your first job among strangers; learning that your first love is the girl she is but not the girl you need; getting soundly beaten in your first state-wide track meet when you are used to being the fastest runner in town — none of this is fun. But such experiences are not sickening, heartbreaking, or terrifying because, even at the time, they can be felt as bringing you in closer touch with reality. The pain they produce is somehow accepted as benign, like soreness following unaccustomed physical exercise or the pain of normal childbirth. Growth is more satisfying, and far more reassuring, than comfort; though normal growth is comfortable most of the time. (p. 34)

Take the position of either agreeing with or disagreeing with him about his point of view on growth. Explain yourself and your reasoning as precisely as you can, and for evidence draw on the boys he talks about in the chapter that contains the case studies (select, don't use them all).

Plan to be concise; we're interested in how well you come to your point and how well you explain it. Editing is now critical, and you may find that you need almost as much time to do that as to actually write the paper.

Writing Assignment 21

Here is what Friedenberg says about the importance of conflict between "a growing human being" and "his society":

Some youngsters suffer; but those are worse off who never form a clear conception of themselves and what they stand for. These take no stands and fight no battles; in any orchestra they play it cool.

Like Sheehy, he seems to think that the most important thing for adolescents to do is to struggle to define themselves. Sheehy calls this the struggle for "self-actualization," part of the general drama of the "seeker self" and the "merger self." According to Sheehy's account of "pulling up roots," the most crucial struggle for a young adult is the struggle against parents.

Friedenberg, on the other hand, seems to feel that the key struggle takes place in the schools. The schools, he argues, do not allow students to question values or experiment with roles. The schools fear conflict and, as a consequence, they demand "a different sort of behavior than that which exemplifies a well-defined and well-established self." (*Vanishing Adolescent*, p. 203.)

Write a paper in which you use your own analysis of the autobiographies to comment on Friedenberg's account of the role of conflict in adolescent development.

Questions

1. What is his argument? What are its key terms? Tell us what he says.

2. What do you find in your case studies? What can you conclude about the role of the schools in the experience of the individuals you've studied?

3. What, then, do you have to say about Friedenberg's account of the role of conflict?

Hand in a final draft, edited in red ink. Hand in any rough drafts as well.

Reading Assignment J

This book, along with a journal entry, is due Wednesday.

Before you begin reading *Coming of Age in Samoa*, we'd like you to become familiar with the book and how it's set up. This book has a table of contents, but in the back there is an appendix before the index and glossary. Look at the appendix — what is its purpose in this book? Why does the index include a glossary and what is its purpose?

Flip through the book and notice the italics. Which words are in italics? Also notice the footnotes on the bottom of some of the pages. These are designated by an asterisk (*) instead of a superscript (which you've seen before in *Passages* and *Vanishing Adolescent*).

The assignment for Wednesday is to read *Coming of Age in Samoa* in its entirety. Once again, as you read put marks or short notes in the margin if you come across something that catches your interest — something you'd like to mention in class or in your journal. We also recommend that you read this book in as few sittings as possible.

When you are finished with the book, we'd like you to write for an hour in your journal. The response to the book, as usual, may include your opinion of the book, but we'd like you to focus your attention on the following. In *Passages*, Sheehy says:

> The crisis model of young people caught in the turbulent passage between their late teens and early twenties has come to be equated with the normal process of growing up. . . . In short, it's like having flu of the personality. . . . Can't a person get through life without suffering one of these mental blitzes? (p. 80)

In *Vanishing Adolescent*, almost 20 years earlier, Friedenberg said:

> Must there be a conflict between adolescent and society? The point is that adolescence *is* conflict — protracted conflict — between the individual and society. . . . And there are other cultures in which there is no conflict because conflict is thoroughly repressed. (pp. 32–33)

Sheehy's answer to her question is "No." Crisis, like the common cold, is inevitable. For Friedenberg, adolescence is by definition a time of conflict, conflict between the individual and society. If there is no conflict, it has only been repressed.

What did Mead find in her study of the Samoans? Find a passage that, in your opinion, best represents Mead's understanding of the role of conflict in the lives of Samoan adolescents. Record the passage in your journal, using the proper page reference. Then, center your journal entry on the passage you select. Talk about Mead's understanding of conflict for young Samoans and for adolescents in general.

Writing Assignment 22: In-Class Essay Exam

For this essay exam, we want you to describe and explain the key factors in adolescent development that Mead identifies in her study of Samoans. Be sure to cite specific examples to support generalizations you make. Remember: this is an essay exam, not a personal essay.

Writing Assignment 23

Friedenberg's book was primarily about boys in American culture; Mead's book is primarily about girls in Samoan culture. Friedenberg spent a good portion of the book discussing conflict in America; Mead discusses the lack of conflict in Samoa.

Yet Mead also discusses girls who are not part of the "norm." In Chapter XI, she talks specifically about girls who don't get along. She gives the example of Siva and Meta to illustrate how conflicts develop in Samoa and how they are treated.

Friedenberg and Sheehy would say that Samoan girls are not going to end up "rich in personality" because they have not experienced conflict. If conflict is all that is required, then Siva and Meta ought to be the girls who truly mature and grow.

Explain what you see to be the nature of Samoan "conflict" among girls in adolescence; in other words, how does it develop? Describe it; write what sorts of things are done in response to conflict, and *give evidence* from the book. Then, go on to write about the difference between "coming of age" in Samoa (as you can understand it from your reading of Mead) and "coming of age" in America (as you can understand it from your work this term). You may certainly write about how your understanding of the American experience is different from Sheehy's or Friedenberg's.

Writing Assignment 24

This is the last assignment that deals directly with our subject. The last assignment you'll write will be next Monday, and that will be the final exam for this course. You'll be given a passage about college life to read, and then you'll have to write a paper about it.

This assignment will be due on Wednesday, and we want to see, again, at least two drafts of this assignment, one that is clearly a working draft and shows your effort to revise and change things, and the other, a final copy, which shows that your editing efforts have produced a clear, understandable and relatively error-free paper.

Margaret Mead says, in the introduction to *Coming of Age in Samoa*, that:

> if we would appreciate our own civilization, this elaborate pattern of life which we have made for ourselves as people and which we are at such pains to pass on to our children, we must set our own civilization over against other very different ones.

You've spent 15 weeks studying the process of "coming of age in America." Now that you've read about the rites and rituals of the Samoans, and on the basis of what you've learned from your study of the autobiographies, what have you come to understand about the way *our culture* determines the process by which one becomes a "full-fledged adult member of his or her society."

Refer specifically to the autobiographies wherever possible. You are to hand in a final draft. The editing should be done in red ink.

Final Exam: Basic Reading and Writing

You will write this assignment in class. *Be sure* to hand in your paper before you leave.

You will be given a moderately long essay to read and a question asking you to write about what you have read. The essay is a chapter from Margaret Mead's autobiography, *Black-berry Winter.* We will ask you to write about what you see to be the main ideas in the reading.

You will have three hours to read the essay and write your paper, so there will be plenty of time for you to prepare, write, rewrite and edit. Hand in all the papers you use and be sure to identify the final draft by writing *Final Draft* on the top of the first page.

Be sure to put your name and phone number at the top of *this* paper. The purpose of the phone number is to allow us to get in touch with you in the next week.

Question: We'd like you to describe as carefully and completely as you can the important point or points you see Ms. Mead making about her experience at Barnard. Would you go on, after that, to talk about what *you* find to be most significant in all that she's said in this chapter? And would you be sure to explain why you have chosen what you do find significant?

3.

Teaching the Course

MARILYN B. DEMARIO

The procedures used in Basic Reading and Writing address the individual reading and writing needs of the students while discovering and making use of the literate strengths of the group as a whole. This means that while some aspects of the course change very little from term to term, others are reinvented or newly discovered each term. Some of the inventions and discoveries have to do with that mysterious process which makes different classes respond differently to the same materials, while other changes can be attributed to the interests, strengths, and personal styles of the teachers as well as the students in a given term. As I explain what occurs in BRW on a day-to-day level, I hope to provide some sense of the complex movement between the carefully developed structure of the course and those procedures which can reflect the specific needs and interests of the group.

A Team of Teachers

Limited from its inception to an enrollment of no more than 15 students, the course is usually taught by a team of two teachers. Originally one teacher was assumed to be an expert in the teaching of reading and the other of writing (a concession to the charge that the "English faculty doesn't contain any reading specialists"). Since the course emphasizes the interrelationship of reading and writing, however, this division of responsibilities has proved to be unreasonable as well as unworkable. The advantages of having a team of teachers, though, both of whom teach writing and reading, remain clear. In an atmosphere that values a student's oral as well as written expression, and can frequently become as intense as it does intimate, the team teaching arrangement helps to ensure that each student's contributions are heard, and are met with patient encouragement as well as disciplined criticism.

The way in which the team teachers divide their responsibilities is for the most part best left to them. It is important that both teachers become familiar with the work of each student, and that both assume responsibility for writing and revising assignments[1]; but beyond that, their own styles as well as the needs of the students can determine the division of labor. Sometimes both teachers will read all the work of every student, sometimes each will read the work of half the students alternately, sometimes each will work continuously with the same student for some given period of time. In the classroom, one teacher may assume primary responsibility for conducting a given discussion while the other observes, listens, and takes notes on specific points to be pursued at a later time (perhaps in a subsequent discussion or perhaps in a writing assignment). At other times, they may both conduct the discussion, responding to each other as well as to the students. Later, they may assume the roles of observers or participants in student-led discussions.

However these responsibilities are divided, both teachers keep brief but careful notes on every piece of student writing they read. A kind of written communication with each other, these records not only help teachers to pinpoint and clarify those areas where students need to work, they provide a well-documented log of each student's achievement at the end of the term. To this end, many of us keep a folder with four color-coded pages for each student — one for comments on the formal papers or numbered assignments, one for comments about journal entries, one to keep track of outside reading journal entries, and one on which absence and tardiness are recorded. Even though team teachers may spend several hours in conference with each other each week, these communications help to ensure that no important aspect of a student's work is forgotten or overlooked, and that the teachers are in some general agreement as to which writing problems should be worked on first. While not comprehensive, these comments and notes help to point out patterns of difficulty quickly and easily.

Experts and Expertise

Although the real subject of the course is reading and writing, texts and assignments typically revolve on some central theme. Through reading, reflecting, remembering personal experiences, writing, discussing, asking questions, accepting criticism, and revising what they write, students gain the experience of becoming and feeling like "experts" on a particular subject. So, for example, they become experts on "Growth and Change in Adolescence"[2] by reading autobiographies, fictional accounts of adolescent experience, books on the psychology and sociology of adolescence. They see films and listen to tapes on the subject; they write and write again about their own adolescent experiences; they respond in a journal to much of what they read, hear, and see on the subject; they write and publish a collection of their own autobiographies; they discuss, they disagree, and they learn to respect their own opinions in a way that is new to most of them.

In the course on "Growth and Change in Adolescence," eleven books are read throughout the term; seven are assigned texts which the whole class reads, and four represent the students' personal choices. The seven assigned texts, which include the anthology of student autobiographies, are chosen to provide students with a broad range of possible ways to think and talk about adolescence. Typically there are three works of fiction and four works of nonfiction chosen; titles from a recent course on adolescence, for example, included Maya Angelou's *I Know Why the Caged Bird Sings*, Judith Guest's *Ordinary People*, Anne Tyler's *A Slipping-Down Life*, Lee Gutkind's *God's Helicopter*, Richard Rodriguez's *Hunger of Memory*, *Normal Adolescence* by the Committee on Adolescence, Group for the Advancement of Psychiatry, and the student autobiography, *One Life to Live*.

Since the purpose of having students read four additional books is to encourage them to develop their reading skills with books they have a particular and personal interest in, every effort is made to be as liberal as possible about their choice of outside reading. At first we discouraged some genres such as romances or how-to books. To preserve the spirit of this assignment, however, almost any book that isn't a comic book or that has too many photographs or drawings is usually acceptable. More often we find that students choose books which they believe will impress or satisfy their teachers, something that looks appropriate for school but not something they expect to enjoy reading. That books can be read for pleasure is not a familiar idea to many of our students, and when we make this assignment, we need always to remind ourselves that it is not self-explanatory, and that choosing such books requires more of our attention and guidance than we might expect. We encourage them to spend at least one half hour in the bookstore exploring the shelves under three or four different categories before they make their choices, and we talk to them about our own experiences of browsing through bookstores. Some recent outside reading titles have been *The Amityville Horror, Wifey, The Autobiography of Malcolm X, The Old Man and the Sea, Bigfoot, Tarzan, The Sportsman's World,* and *Men Are Just Desserts.*

Prediscussion Exercises

On the first day of each assigned book discussion period, students are expected to have read the entire book and to hand in their journal entries. During the first hour, they work in groups of three or four on the prediscussion or mapping exercises which have been prepared for each book. Early in the term, these exercises simply ask them to list as many of the characters and events from the book as they can and then to star those they consider most important or significant. When the whole class reconvenes, we construct a master list on the blackboard and as students argue, debate, and puzzle over which items should be starred, we begin to work out our own definitions of significance. Throughout the discussion that follows, both teachers attempt to demonstrate, through their responses to the students' comments and the kinds of questions they ask, that speakers bear responsibility for what they say and that questions which do not admit simple or immediate answers are those which are most valued.

As the term goes on, the prediscussion exercises direct students toward more and more complex considerations of character, narrative structure, argument, and personal perception. At the same time, the responsibility for conducting several hours of discussion moves from the teachers to the students.

Writing Situations

Because different writing situations call upon different strengths and abilities on the part of the writer, we try to discover those strengths in student writers by presenting them with at least three different kinds of writing situations. There are typically 15 formal writing assignments in the course, formal in the sense that the goal is to produce writing that is or can become what we usually think of as academic discourse — that is, thoughtful, reasoned, coherent prose that reflects a questioning and disciplined mind. Students are given two days to write a first draft of such a paper. It is read by at least one teacher and returned to the student with comments in the margins. There is a class discussion of a representative student paper, and then students are given another two days to write a second draft.

In another writing situation, students write a full journal entry for every book they read for the course, the outside reading books as well as the required texts. Students may use any portion of the nine days they have to read the book to write in their journals. The goal in composing these entries is not so much to produce correct and coherent prose but rather to experiment with ideas, to risk writing about the connections they see between one book and another or between something in a book and something that was said in class or occurred outside of class.

A third type of writing in which students engage, particularly at the end of the term, is exam writing, that is, writing that must be completed within a brief period of time. Such writing, unlike formal papers and the journal entries, requires that they demonstrate reading comprehension and generate a critical response quickly with few if any mechanical errors.

As we move from one writing situation to another, students are encouraged to learn something about their own writing processes, to discover the conditions that are conducive to their own strengths as writers and to use those strengths more frequently.

Journal Entries

Students keep all the work they do for the course, all their assignments and other classroom handouts in two separate folders. One folder contains their personal journal which includes a kind of dialogue with their teachers. In this folder they keep their journal entries for each book and their written responses to the teachers' questions and marginal comments. (To help ease some logistical confusion, journal entry assignments are usually designated by letters; numbers are used for the more formal writing assignments.) Journal entry assignments begin with general instructions to "sit down for one hour and write your response . . . the first things that come to mind when you think about the experience of reading this book," and later ask for more specific and increasingly complex additions to their entries. An assignment on *A Slipping-Down Life*, for example, asks students to read the first page of the novel several times before they actually begin to read the book and then to write down, along with their specific evidence, some of the initial impressions and expectations they have formed about the book on the basis of this close reading of page one. Later, when they have finished the book, they are asked to include in their entry a discussion of how their expectations were or were not met. As is this one, other journal assignments are designed to help students become more aware of and therefore reflexive about the many decisions and judgments they make as they read and write.

The journals, unlike the papers and exams, are not read with issues such as correctness or formal coherence in mind. Instead, we look for the generation of new ideas, the ability to make connections between one book and another or between something in a book and the writer's personal experience. Our marginal comments are intended to encourage a student to push his or her ideas as far as he can and then farther still. We ask questions; we offer arguments; we request further explanation. Since the purpose of this written dialogue is to provide a forum for students, we keep negative comments and corrections to a minimum. Occasionally excerpts from journal entries may be duplicated as a subject for a general classroom discussion, but the authors are always anonymous, and the excerpts are chosen as subjects for their strengths rather than deficiencies. For the most part, journals are intended to be a place for private experiment, where the writer is in charge of what he or she wants to say and accomplish.

Writing Assignments

In their responses to the more formal writing assignments, on the other hand, students are expected to become familiar with and use the conventions of standard, edited American English. From the beginning, these papers are talked about as though they are being readied for publication. In the first part of the term, students are given assignments which require at least a two-page response of carefully considered, coherent prose. These early assignments invite them to write about significant experiences in their lives and then to go on to think about, and write about, in increasingly complex ways, what makes an experience significant. At the same time that they are being asked to consider and talk about significant parts of the books they are reading, they are also being encouraged to think about their own experiences as something amenable to carefully constructed narrative and therefore subject to similar kinds of consideration and discussion. Just as journal entries are not marked for mechanical or syntactical errors, so too these early papers are not read for errors; instead, the emphasis is on generating coherent and meaningful prose.

Every time formal papers are handed in, one or two are chosen to be reproduced, distributed, and discussed at the next class meeting. It is almost always possible to choose papers which contain representative problems that occur in many if not all of the other student papers. These are problems in a general sense — problems of writing that are also representative of problems in approaching and understanding a subject. It is not unusual, for example, to find that in these early experiments with writing, many students have difficulty keeping a sense of audience in mind; they may tell their readers too little or too much. The purpose of the classroom discussion is to find ways of talking about improving the paper that the writer can use. Even though he or she is anonymous, the writer of the paper has the opportunity of hearing how an actual audience responds to the work.

In addition, all the students become vital participants, as both readers and writers, in a discussion which has as its focus reading-and-writing-in-progress. By continuously noting how meaning and intention change as reading and writing change, students are able to address the question of what reading and writing are good for. For many students, functioning in this way, as serious readers and writers, allows them to see a new relationship between writing and experience. As the course progresses, it is not unusual for students to make comments which reveal a new and growing empathy for the authors of the books being read for class.

Alternate writing assignments require students to write revisions of their previous drafts. With a teacher's comments on their individual papers, and the experience of having participated in a discussion of a representative paper, students are expected to write a substantially new version of their previous draft. This could involve, for example, filling out and ordering information in their narrative in light of their new sensitivity to the expectations of an audience. In addition, they continue to talk about the meaning of the term "significance," and to formulate answers to the question of why some things appear to be significant and others not. In order to help them think about these questions, the assignments remind them to recall class discussions about the books read. Again, for many students this opportunity to revise a paper provides a new kind of writing experience. The process of reflection and change, key themes in the study of adolescence in general, takes on specific and concrete meaning when applied to their own writing.

In-Class Writing

There is yet a third kind of writing required of students in BRW and that is the timed, in-class writing assignments which are given at the conclusion of every book discussion period. Here, they must write "on the spot" with little time for contemplation, reflection, or revision. In addition to the fact that these assignments call for the spontaneous writing skills that students will need throughout their college careers and indeed, in their adult lives, these assignments also work to help students appropriate, and take responsibility for, the writing abilities they have been performing more slowly through the term.

After there has been an average of four hours of class discussion on a given book, students are given the next full two-hour class period to write a paper addressed to a question they have not seen before. The assignments usually ask them to review a specific chapter or section of the book and then, using evidence from what they have just read, to write about an issue that pertains to that chapter or section. Frequently the issue is something that has grown out of their own classroom discussions. As more books are read, students are expected to write about increasingly complex ideas in their responses. Even though they have not seen the question before they must write a response, students are very well prepared for these assignments; they have written journal entries on the book, worked on pre-discussion exercises, participated in, and sometimes led class discussions.

As always, one or two sample student papers are chosen and duplicated for discussion at the following class meeting. After they have read all the papers, the teachers try to choose papers for discussion that demonstrate common writing problems that the assignment may have either introduced or brought to light. In the beginning of the term, representative papers are likely to be those that demonstrate general problems of understanding the assignment and then responding in appropriate ways. Later on, issues related to quoting from a text, or generating and organizing ideas within a brief time period, for example, might be brought up. Since the assignments themselves are revised each term to incorporate elements from class discussions, it is only possible to plan a discussion of writing problems after the student papers have been read. And even then, the issue for discussion may change drastically once it is taken up in the classroom.

These assignments also begin to prepare students for the End-of-Term Review, a college-wide exit exam for Basic Writers that they will have to pass in order to pass this course. The importance of reading the assignment carefully, the need to spend time reflecting before one begins to write, and the ability to concentrate on a single writing task for two consecutive hours are often vitally needed lessons.

Course Structure

This seems to be a good place to pause for a moment and talk briefly about what the course looks like, on paper, from the teachers' points of view. From the first week of the term, many apparently different, though interrelated, activities are going on simultaneously, thus the need for a carefully structured time plan. Perhaps the clearest way to show how teachers can make the best use of their six contact hours each week is to show what a two-week excerpt from the term schedule looks like. (See page 96.)

It would not be possible to overemphasize the importance of working out a revisable schedule for the whole term on the model shown. It is the only way, we have found, to ensure that important features of the course are not neglected or missed. In devising a schedule, we've tried to follow these guidelines:

1. Students are given nine days to read a book and two days to write a paper.

2. Students' written work is always returned at the next class meeting.

3. At least one sample student paper is discussed every time papers are returned.

Week of September 17

Monday 17	Wednesday 19	Friday 21
Collect A Assign B prediscussion exercises discuss Caged Bird	Return A Collect #4 discuss Caged Bird	Return #4 discuss Caged Bird Assign #6 1 Hr. sustained silent reading

Week of September 24

Monday 24	Wednesday 26	Friday 28
Assign #5 (in class) Collect #6 Assign #7	Return #5 Return #6 Collect B Assign C	discuss Ordinary People Collect #7 1 Hr. sustained silent reading

4. Only one assignment should be given during one class period.

5. One hour a week of class time should be reserved for in-class reading.

6. Four hours of book discussion are planned for each book (this includes time for the prediscussion exercise).

7. A two-hour, in-class writing assignment is scheduled at the conclusion of each book discussion.

As might be evident from this sample, no two weeks from this fourteen-week course follow quite the same pattern.

Correcting Mechanical Errors

It may seem to some that as teachers of students who have demonstrated serious writing problems, we are markedly inattentive to errors in student papers in the first part of the term. Indeed we are. Although we can confess to some doubt at times and, in fact, can claim nothing close to complete success, we become convinced again each term that most students cannot learn to care about the correctness of the sentences they write until they care about what they say and how they say it. As with every other aspect of the course, our intention as teachers is to make it clear that students are responsible for the work they do. The habit of writing to please a teacher becomes less and less appropriate as the sense of what writing is good for becomes clear. Punctuation, syntax, capitalization, spelling, paragraphing — the usual subjects of a writing class — are talked about as an integral part of the writer's effort to articulate his ideas in writing in a way that makes sense to him and to others. Near the end of the term, when students have begun to edit their many mechanical errors, we speak more directly about rules and conventions of academic discourse.

It is not, then, until Assignment 9 or 10, the sixth or seventh week of the term, that we even begin to call students' attention to sentence-level errors. At this time, in addition to our marginal comments, papers are returned to students with small check marks at the end of those lines that contain mechanical errors. With no more instruction than this, students are required to turn in corrected pages by the next class period. They may, of course, seek help from their teachers, peers, or people outside the classroom, but the initiative and the responsibility for discovering the errors and making the appropriate corrections rests with them.

Since the mechanical writing errors that adults make tend to be idiosyncratic, it is not always useful to spend many classroom hours in a general discussion of mechanical errors. But again, the needs of the group must dictate the most profitable use of time. Exercises with sentence combining, uses of metaphor, and unpunctuated paragraphs have sometimes been helpful and interesting to many students, but usually a workshop format, where the teachers circulate as students work in pairs, reading each other's papers for errors, works best.

The Autobiography

The focal point of the course, the collective autobiography which students write, edit, and publish over a period of three weeks, brings together many if not most of the reading and writing activities that give the course its purpose and direction. With a suggested length of 10 handwritten pages, each student's contribution often represents the longest and most intensive piece of writing he has done. When the final copies are printed, bound, and sold to students as the fifth textbook for the course, students' interest and sense of pride are almost palpable.

The several assignments for the autobiography take students through three handwritten drafts, peer editing, cutting and pasting, reading both their own and another writer's paper for errors, arranging for a typist (to help them gain a sense of distance from their work, they may not type their final drafts), a slow and careful proofreading session, and a meeting to agree upon a title for the entire collection. Although there may be some group discussion about sections of autobiographies, most of the classroom time during this two-week period is used as a workshop. Each student has a conference regularly with one or both teachers and, depending upon his own preferences, may then work independently or closely with a peer editor. During this period, students often move between a sense of distance from their own writing and a new personal intensity. They may, for example, be outraged by a misplaced comma, no matter who misplaced it, when they work with the typist's copy and some White-Out. Similarly, when they see their own ideas, observations, and discussions in print, as part of a published anthology, they are often surprised, sometimes pleasantly but sometimes not, by how different those ideas and observations look.

As with all the other texts for the course, there is a lettered, or journal entry assignment associated with the collective autobiography. Students are asked to write about some common themes that they see appearing in many of the autobiographical accounts. From this, they are asked to begin to develop their own theory of adolescence, using evidence and data from both the autobiographies and the other books they have read for the course as well.

At the point in the term when the autobiographies have been read and the journal entries written, most students have learned to participate in classroom discussions in productive ways. The prediscussion exercises, which were previously used to help students remember characters and events from books, can now be used to encourage students to raise their own questions and generate discussions. The prediscussion exercise for the autobiography might, for example, ask students to make a list of possible contradictions they see between ideas in one autobiography and another, or between the autobiographies and the other books. When they have had 15 or 20 minutes to work on this in groups of two or three, the entire class reconvenes and each group's observations are discussed, and frequently debated. Some of the most valuable discussions have occurred at this point in the term as students assume the role of discussion leaders, aware of their responsibilities and of the differences between a chat and a seminar discussion.

Critical Reflections

During the last few weeks of the course, students are reading the nonfictional, theoretical books about adolescence. These books, which may have seemed threatening, and therefore "boring," earlier in the term, now provide a background against which students can further develop their critical perspectives. Their own experience with publication has taught them, among other things, that behind the formal appearance of printed words on the pages of a book are one or more human beings attempting to understand and interpret their world. No longer quite so intimidated by authorship, publication, or abstract theoretical discourse, students are now more likely to approach these works with a new sense of respect for themselves as readers, a self-respect which allows them to read the same text several times, argue with it, ask questions of it, and possibly be changed by it.

When students read *Hunger of Memory* (used often as the penultimate text for the course), for example, the journal assignment asks them to "select a quotation for each chapter that in some way appears to get at the heart of that chapter," and then "explain why each quotation you have chosen could be said to capture one of the main points Rodriguez wishes to make." Their written responses form the basis for the classroom discussion and thus eliminate the need for a prediscussion exercise. In many cases students spontaneously assume and share the role of discussion leader as they examine some differences in the choice of quotations and consider the differences in meaning and interpretation those choices could be said to represent. No longer concerned with being "good students" whose job it is to discover what their teachers think a book is about, students can now defend positions which are clearly the result of independent and considered reflection.

This independent critical reflection becomes apparent in the handwritten work we see as well. Papers and journal entries tend to look considerably messier than they did earlier in the term as students cross out, insert, and erase words, phrases, and paragraphs. They complain that writing has become more difficult as they struggle on their own to find the better word and the better ordering of their thoughts. Where they had once been surprised and disoriented by our questions and comments in the margins of their papers, they are now more likely to anticipate our questions and to raise several of their own.

End-of-Term Review

It is with some degree of reluctance and misgiving, then, that we focus most of the group's attention, during the last few weeks, on preparing to take the End-of-Term Review. Along with all students in basic writing classes, Basic Reading and Writing students must take and pass a two-hour exam in which they are first given a five-hundred-word passage to read and then asked to compose a written response to a specific question about that passage. The exams are read holistically by two members of the composition staff and judged as either a passing or failing response. Although students who fail this exam have further recourse and will not necessarily fail the course, passing it represents a significant accomplishment for BRW students. The knowledge that college instructors whom they have never seen consider their writing to be reasonably clear, coherent, and error free affords them a vital sense of confidence concerning their future college work.

In some ways, the kind of writing an examination calls for is inimical to what we have been saying about writing throughout most of the term. In an exam, for example, there is usually time for one draft only. Highly complicated ideas, which frequently call for highly complex and therefore easily mistaken syntax, are perhaps too risky for this situation. A writer's thoughtfulness might be valued as much, but probably not more than his ability to control error.

On the other hand, the ability to compose a reasonably thoughtful and clear response to a passage under the constraints of an examination requires students to consolidate much of what they have learned in the course and to use their knowledge efficiently. They need to trust their own ability to comprehend and interpret a text; they need to understand and make use of their own best writing processes; and they need to know how long it will take them to edit and proofread. Although the in-class writing assignments for each book have familiarized students with this kind of writing situation, in this case students must write in response to a passage they have never seen before, and they must do this alone, without the advantage of a previous group discussion.

Before the actual exam, we administer at least two practice exams. These exams are read and given a pass/fail grade by another teacher in the department. When they are returned, we follow our usual procedure of distributing copies of anonymous sample exams and discussing them in class. Although we expect the discussion to center upon what constitutes a passing or a failing exam, students are often very sure about this (sometimes they judge a sample paper far more harshly than the grader does). Instead, students are more likely to want to discuss the complications and ramifications of the student writer's interpretation of the exam text, to compare different interpretations, and to ascribe merit to some over others. When this happens, we know that our goals for Basic Reading and Writing have been reached.

Writing Vertically and Horizontally

If we were to base the success of this course on the percentage of students who write passing examination papers, the results might not justify the enthusiasm for the course that most of us who teach it feel.[3] For some students, two hours is not enough time to read, reflect, write, and edit; for other students, fourteen weeks is not enough time to achieve fluency in writing. And although, like many teachers who teach literature to reluctant readers, we should probably confess to harboring fantasies that this course will turn our students into bibliophiles, this too would be a disappointing criterion for the success of this course. What we can say is that every student who completes Basic Reading and Writing has had a prolonged and intense experience with language, or languages — his own, his peers', that of selected authors, and representatives of the academy. He has studied writing vertically, from drafts through revisions to final copies, and horizontally, from handwritten to typed pages, to published text, to interpretation and criticism of those texts. He has seen the subtle interaction between language and experience. He has seen at least some of the possibilities that a careful and deliberate use of language can create for him.

Notes

[1] The assignment sequence represented in this volume is a model sequence. While the format remains the same, teachers revise the course (and the reading list) each time they teach it.

[2] There is also a course in the evening school whose subject is "work."

[3] Cumulative results from four recent End-of-Term Reviews show that only 40 percent of Basic Reading and Writing students receive a passing grade on their final exam. When the folders containing their work for the entire term are reviewed by members of the staff, however, almost 80 percent pass the course. These figures are only slightly lower than those for Basic Writing students.

III.

Discerning Principles

4.
Writing, Reading and Authority

A Case Study

SUSAN V. WALL

> It's this lesson that we want to teach students: that reading and writing begin in confusion, anxiety and uncertainty; that they are driven by chance and intuition as much as they are by deliberate strategy or conscious intent; and that certainty and authority are postures, features of performance that are achieved *through* an act of speaking or writing; they are not qualities of vision that precede such performance.
>
> David Bartholomae and Anthony Petrosky,
> *Facts, Artifacts and Counterfacts*

If, as Bartholomae and Petrosky suggest in the essay which introduces this volume, we are to imagine authority as a "posture," a "feature of performance," then we have to define the ability to compose an academic essay not (as one often hears it) as some form of cognitive "maturity" but as a particular form of cultural sophistication. Or, to put it the other way around, what is "basic" about basic writers and readers is not simply their lack of control over the conventional rules of written discourse; it is a kind of naiveté born of their inexperience with what it means to try to sound educated.

For this reason we often hear of the basic student's need to practice the processes of academic reading and writing. As Mina Shaughnessy argued, we can't reasonably expect "miracles" or shortcuts in this business; the teacher of basic students must be ready "to cultivate patience for the slow pace of progress in this most complex of crafts."[1] But the idea of "practice" can be misleading if we take it to mean that by repeatedly engaging in assigned activities of decoding and encoding texts the way a piano student, say, practices certain skills, the basic student will gradually accumulate enough experience to become a "mature" composer. Authority in academic discourse comes from having something individual to say *as well as* from expressing it in ways that do not do intolerable violence to the demands of convention. Invention and social acceptability, in other words, must be demonstrated in combination, not in isolation. Any successful academic text, or any genuine interpretation of one, is a new creation out of conventional forms and meanings. It is, therefore, never wholly predictable or repeatable or capable of being rehearsed.

Posture of Authority

If instead of "practice," however, we speak of a composer's ability in terms of a "posture" of authority, that metaphor of stance is, I think, far more helpful in defining just what we want our basic students to accomplish. Just as one assumes a stance, any stance, only through a constant interplay between effort and gravity, movement and terrain, so, too, academic composing requires us to recognize mutually opposing forces of individual expression and social convention, a negotiation that Bartholomae and Petrosky call "the dialectic that emerges when one moves between private response and public responsibilities." Neither alone will do: the formally correct discourse which has little of substance to say nor (as is more often the case with our Basic Reading and Writing students) the idiosyncratic response which seems to ignore audience expectations. When we label an example of academic discourse as "mature" and "authoritative," what we are admiring is the act of keeping one's balance.

It's easy for experienced readers and writers to forget how hard a stance of authority is to achieve — in fact, we might look at the prevalence of drill-centered basic reading and writing curricula as evidence of a kind of collective amnesia about learning. A key reason, therefore, to compose case studies such as the one which follows here is to dramatize what a long and difficult struggle the achievement of academic authority can be. John, the subject of this semester-long study, is a fairly representative example of our Basic Reading and Writing students. His history illustrates what Donald Graves means when he says that "losing balance, regaining it, and going on, is the substance of learning."[2]

In the early part of the term when John was being introduced to discovery drafting and narrative readings, composing seemed to him to be full of exciting possibilities. It was a chance (as he saw it) to rid himself of a self-image imposed upon him by other adults and to achieve through writing a sense of maturity and autonomy. Later, however, his transition to more planned writing and theoretical readings became a passage fraught with difficulty and confusion. John's sense of empowerment as a writer and reader was very nearly overwhelmed by what he perceived as the need to conform to the languages of other, more powerful adults, in this case his teachers and the authors of the books they assigned. At the end of his first term, John was still ambivalent about his own sense of academic authority. It was only when I interviewed him again two and a half years later that I was able to feel that (to use his own metaphors) John had finally balanced the internal demands of his own needs for expression with the external pressures of the academic community and had achieved a sense of equilibrium as a reader and a writer.

"I Was Uguly, Clumsey . . ."

When John first volunteered to be one of my case study subjects, I was struck immediately by the combination of risk and caution in everything he said.[3] Just as he claimed that he liked to read books that were both "true" and "really amazing," so, too, he'd volunteered for my study "because of the experience I thought I'd get from it. I thought it'd be something different to get interviewed." And yet when he was interviewed, John would typically stop and think carefully before answering my questions, and his responses were often brief and almost inaudible.

I began to understand the caution he felt towards adults when I read John's early papers. Each returned to the same theme, the image he had had of himself before coming to college. His parents, particularly his mother, had pressured him to play competitive sports even though he had never been able to match the abilities of his brother and sister. It was clear from what he wrote that the effect had been devastating:

> I thought that I was uguly, clumsey and had no self confidence in myself. . . . She kept telling me how embarasing it was to go to the swim meets. Which just made me inferior complex grow. In school when I was around someone popular or athetic I felt awkward like I wasn't good enough to talk to them. I always felt like everybody was making fun of me even knowing they weren't.

What John's mother told him he came to tell himself, and what he told himself had become in turn a way of defining how others saw him: "I wasn't good enough to *talk* to them." Such images of the self created out of language had the power to override even more realistic observations: "I always felt like everybody was making fun of me *even knowing they weren't.*"

His high school classes had not helped John define a different, more confident self. He took at least one English course per semester, but there was little reading and writing involved beyond grammar drill, outlining, and composing easy skits, commercials, and formulaic *haiku*. John said that he had often felt he was being treated like a child, not only because such work was trivializing but because there was no real dialogue between teachers and students. His mass media class was a typical example: "The teacher yells and you just sit there." A class in research techniques gave him his one chance to write a substantial paper, a 30-page report on "running," but the teacher left him mostly on his own to compose it. And when he finally got it back, John said, "That's what I think made me really mad. There wasn't any comments on it at all. Not one. I thought it would say something, you know? She might not have even read it for all I know. I got an 'A' but . . . it didn't *say* anything."

Far from feeling sorry for himself, however, John had tried on his own to create a fantasy of a far more assertive and articulate self. "Before I started high school," he wrote in paper five, "I told myself that I was going to change. I wasn't going to feel inferiority anymore." He would dance at parties, compete in gym, and "In my classes I would become involved in group discussion and not feel that my opion was stupid. In general I wasn't gone to worry what my peers thought of me. I was going to have a good time and let my feelings out. Instead of keeping them in because I was worry what people thought of me."

Not surprisingly, this early, drastic attempt at redefinition failed. But eventually there were experiences that afforded John more careful and controlled opportunities for risk and change: running, a sport in which he was able to work up to competitive level with the help of a supportive coach; an initiation into sexual relationships with an older girl; and the steady development of a new circle of friends. John enrolled in a "hard but good" speech class and quit asking his mother for help with his English assignments, efforts supported by his older sister, a physician and teacher, who "always told me I could do it on my own."

Sense of Self

When he came to the University of Pittsburgh, however, his Basic Reading and Writing class gave him an opportunity to define in a new way what "doing it on his own" might mean. The section in which he was enrolled had as its subject the general theme of "Identity and Change in Adolescence." This meant that John would be offered a chance to continue the project he'd already begun: redefining his sense of "self." But the "self" which would be defined through reading and writing was not quite the same in its origins and definition as the identities he had imagined for himself in high school. This self would be a literary one, not one created out of gossip or parental pressure or adolescent fantasy, and so, like any literary construct, it could be deliberately shaped and revised. Instruction in the composing process was crucial here: John's teachers explicitly rejected the intentionalist model of composing in which he would have to know what he would say and how he would sound before he sat down to write. Instead, they actively encouraged him to write an exploratory draft of a paper first, as much as he could get down on paper, and then to reread and decide whether or not he liked the way he had represented himself on paper. Unlike, then, the earlier process of self-definition John had described as his high school experience, this one would be both gradual and inseparable from the processes of drafting, rereading, and revising.

The first cluster of assignments for the course asked John to compose and then revise by elaboration a series of narratives about significant and insignificant experiences during his adolescence. The culmination of this first cluster in the sequence was Assignment 6:

> For this assignment, we want you to be writing about what you think change is in adolescence — what's normal, what's good, what's bad, what happens when things don't change. In order to give your paper some evidence, we want you to write three personal experiences from your own adolescence (discounting anything before age 14). These may be experiences which are significant or insignificant, and they may be experiences which you think are general for most adolescents or particular to you. In other words, everything we've considered in the last books and in your papers should help you begin addressing this task.

While these stories were intended to serve eventually as illustrations for a coherent theory John would be asked to develop about identity and change during adolescence, that purpose had not yet been made fully explicit. At this point in the course, his teachers mostly urged John to explore the fullness of his adolescent experiences in order to make only low-level generalizations about why each was "significant." But I think John very quickly saw further than this. He understood that what was important was the way he "sounded" on paper, what we would call his literary *persona*, and that sounding authoritative as a writer and mature as an adult "self" came down to much the same thing.

A key step in that early realization was John's composing of a story about a time when he sought advice from an older, wiser adult — a typical kind of narrative we get from writers his age. The first version of the story appeared as part of his first draft for Assignment 6:

[Pastor T. narrative, version one]

I cut grass for Mr. and Mrs. T — during my high school career. And I really became close to them. They were like my second parents. After I had finished cutting grass I would go in an talk to them for hours. One day after I finished cutting grass I was really feeling depressed because I thought that I wasn't as good as anybody else. I thought I was ugely, clumsy, and had no self condifence. When I went in to talk to Pastor T. who was minister of a church in my community, He sensed that I was depressed and he asked me what was wrong. I felt he really cared and I need help so I told him that I thought I was uguly clumsy and no wroth anything. . . .

[The paper goes on here to include narrative material from earlier papers: how John had felt shy about making friends, participating in sports, and so on.]

After I finished he said that I shouldn't feel that way at all. Also said instead of saying your not any good say that you are. He said that I was not only intelligent but a good athelic. And he told me that I should say I was better than most people instead of telling myself that I wasn't any good. That was the start of feeling better about myself instead of alway cutting myself down.

The process of self-definition this last paragraph describes can be seen as a kind of revision, a resaying of what John's pastor told him in order to replace what he had learned to say about himself in the past. But remembered conversation is, at best, a free translation: John acknowledged that he could not remember exactly what Pastor T. had told him to say. Writing, on the other hand, permits a more precise, even exact, resaying. In this passage, John borrows and condenses narrative materials from his response to Assignment 5, and he twice reuses terms from that previous text: "ugly, clumsy, not worth anything, no self-confidence." This self-quotation was made possible by rereading what he had written before, that is by that act of literal revision which sets the process of revising apart not only from the memory-dependent processes of spoken discourse but from the initial process of generating written text as well.

Rereading his work, then, provided the essential first step in John's efforts to break out of the very dependence on the words of others that he describes in this draft. Instead of attempting to approximate what he thought he remembered others having said about him, John was freed to create a more consistent self out of terms readily available on paper. Moreover, he could now engage in a dialogue with the self represented by that earlier work, a dialogue in which a new *persona* could be defined. Here, for example, is how he revised his initial draft of the story about Pastor T. as soon as he read over what he'd written:

[Pastor T. narrative, version one]

One day after I finished cutting grass I was really depressed because I thought that I wasn't as good as anybody else. I thought I was ugely, clumsy, and had no self condifence. When I went in to talk to Pastor T. who was a minister of a church in my community, he sensed that I was depressed and he asked me what was wrong. I felt that he really cared and I need help so I told him that I thought I was uguly clumsy and no wroth anything.

[Pastor T. narrative, revision]

One day after I finished cutting grass I was really feeling depressed. When I went in to talk to Pastor T., who was a minister of a parish in my community, He sensed that I was depressed and he asked me what was wrong. I knew that he really cared and I need help. So for the first time in my life I talk about something that I could never talk to anybody else. I told him how I didn't think I was as good as anybody else.

In this revision, brief as it is, there is already a different "John" being described. Instead of someone who is ugly, clumsy, not worth anything or able to feel any self-confidence — instead, that is, of a person set apart from others by sets of absolute categories — there is now a "John" who suffers by comparison with others but still shares their qualities: "I didn't think I was *as good as* anybody else." And by claiming in his revision that he "knew" rather than just "felt" his pastor's concern and by defining the risk being taken ("So for the first time in my life I talk about something I could never talk to . . ."), John now gives himself a share of the credit for initiating a solution to his problems.

Competence and Initiative

This sense of competence and initiative becomes even more apparent when we look at the process by which John completed his first draft of paper six and then revised it. Encouraged by his teachers to write as much as he could (but working on his own at home), John had begun by spending a two-hour writing session composing the narrative of his conversation with Pastor T. (including the part quoted) and two other stories, one in which he'd discovered that sex did not mean he had to make a "fool" of himself, the other in which he'd felt "really proud" at his high school graduation. Two days later he went back to his draft and spent three more hours creating initial generalizations by connecting his experiences to the assigned books he'd been reading, *The Catcher in the Rye* and *I Know Why the Caged Bird Sings.* Beginning by stating that his conversation with Pastor T. was significant "because I started to look at myself in a new way," John went on to say that although Maya Angelou and Holden Caulfield had both been given advice by wiser and sympathetic adults, only Maya had succeeded in feeling "respected." Then he finally attempted some larger generalizations:

[Pastor T. conclusions, version one]

I think everybody need somebody to help them in difficult times. It makes it so much easier if you can talk about what bothers you. After you talk to somebody you feel so much better. The problem might not go away *but know you can ask someone else what to do. And it is a lot easier for somebody to tell you what to do looking from the inside out. They can see things you can't.* Aleast it is not all pent up inside you. *And you can get their advice on what to do.* [Emphasis mine.]

When he first wrote this, John said, he wasn't sure if he would like it or not. He made up his mind only after he read back over what he had written: "I probably thought about it and it just came to me, and I wrote it down, and I looked back and just didn't like it at all. . . . When I read it over again . . . it just didn't sound good." The problem seemed to lie in the sentences I've emphasized. While the general theme of getting advice from helpful adults does connect John's experiences with those of Maya Angelou and Holden Caulfield, the offending sentences didn't "sound good" to John, I think, because they represented a self who was *too* dependent and passive, a John who was still letting powerful others "tell you what to do."

John did not revise these offending statements immediately, however. He did that only after going on to put together a new sentence out of parts from the ones he was rereading: "The problem might not go away . . . but at least it's not all pent up inside you." At this point, John said, he had the insight that "in that sentence right there is what I think I was trying to say, but I had just used a lot of sentences to say it." Having thus "used" these previous statements to get to one which did allow him to sound "a lot more intelligent — on a higher level," John at this point redefined the offending statements: they said "something totally different" from the idea of emotional release (now declared to be "what I was trying to say"), and so they could be cut from the paper entirely.

Once he had scratched out the sentences I've emphasized previously, John felt he had arrived at a general sense of a thesis for this section and did not need to finish the revision right away: "You already have basically what you want to say written down." Instead, he went on to compose six more pages of generalizations about growth and change in adolescence, continuing to explore the themes of gaining respect and self-esteem that he had established through revising his story about Pastor T. In the process, the more assertive and competent *persona* that John had created by revising the Pastor T. section now began to influence his rereading and revisions of the rest of the paper, so that the kind of simple intuitive reaction that governed his reshaping of the first narrative and conclusions ("It just didn't sound good.") was now beginning to be replaced by some sense of thematic purpose.

Sense of Thematic Purpose

Here, for example, is the original conclusion John wrote to the last story in the paper, a narrative of his high school graduation that represented an event that he had expected to be significant:

[Graduation conclusions, version one]

Graduation ceremony is another thing which is built up more than it should be. Everybody thinks wow a graduation starting a whole new life. But the ceremony itself means very little. Because your life would change even if there weren't a graduation ceremony. Either you would go to college or get a job. All the ceremony is a pat on the back.

There's little sense of self in these perfunctory generalizations about what "everybody thinks." The "John" who speaks here is defined by his life, and his life is defined by the expectations of others: "Either you would go to college or get a job." The revision of this paragraph, however, creates a very different *persona*, one who can make choices:

[Graduation conclusions, revision]

That is an example of where you think a change is going to take place but doesn't. When you think that something going to change but doesn't it is a real let down if you think the change would have been good for you. It makes you wondered why you thought things were going to change and why they didn't. The usual reason why you don't change is because of you. If you want things to change you can make them. For example, after graduation I could of told myself that I was never going to worry about what someone thought of me. Then I would of change. If you don't change it mean that your not ready for a change.

Having thus elaborated and reinforced the image of himself as someone who could control situations ("If you want things to change you can make them."), John went back to the first part of his paper, the story about Pastor T., and revised his conclusion to that narrative a second time. The first revision had been little more than deleting several sentences and deciding he'd keep the rest. Now, however, he was ready to look more carefully at what he'd only sensed was important in his first rereading, so that "problem," a term hardly paused over earlier, became the focus of a new and important generalization about achieving a sense of purpose during "difficult times":

[Pastor T. conclusion, first revision]

I think everybody need somebody to help them in difficult times. It makes it so much easier if you can talk about what bothers you. After you talk to somebody you feel so much better. The problem might not go away *but*

know you can ask someone else what to do. And it is alot
easier for somebody to tell you what to do looking from
the inside out. They can see things you can't. Aleast it is
not all pent up inside you. *And you can get their advice*
on what to do.

[Pastor T. conclusions, second revision]

I think everyone need somebody to help them in difficult times. It makes it so much easier if you can talk to
somebody. You feel so much better. The problem might
not go away but at least it is not all pent up inside. And
that is the first step in solving your problems.

Success with Discovery Drafting

I've presented John's composing process for paper six in
some detail because it shows that while basic writing students
suffer in some ways from their lack of writing experience, their
naiveté can also work to their advantage in their efforts to acquire a sense of authority in their writing. Never having been
told that he had to feel certain about his ideas before writing
or that the sequence of composing needed to match the final
sequence of ideas in the finished paper, John felt comfortable
taking his teachers' advice and following wherever his train of
thought led him. Working with chunks of material, not just
single sentences, he moved back and forth among narratives,
generalizations, and revisions of his generalizations, all the while
making notes to himself in the margin indicating the final arrangement he wanted — a method he claimed he'd worked out
on his own about the second week of the term. And he continued to revise as he wrote the second draft of his paper, including, as I've shown, a reformulation of his conclusions about
Pastor T.

In short, John worked through at least nineteen pages to
achieve his main ideas, and he did so by engaging in a kind of
dialogue with the language that was already there on the page.
By the time he began his second draft he clearly had a much
better sense of both *persona* and theme, but he didn't have to
act as if he knew how he wanted to present these right from
the start. Instead, his success with discovery drafting enabled
him to work out a sense of control and certainty gradually, testing out what he "heard" as he generalized and revised on the
basis of rereading what he'd written.

At this stage of John's development as a writer, this dialectic of composing and revising primarily entailed a renaming of terms to define the "self," in particular, the transformation of an internal "inferiority complex" into a more externalized "problem-solving." With this limited goal John was remarkably successful. By careful revising, he was able to write about his past failures without having to feel that his text would itself be a continuation and confirmation of those failures, that is, that the *persona* who spoke in his papers of an immature earlier self would not also sound, as he put it, "stupid" and "like a second-grader." And because of this achievement he was beginning to see writing in a new way, as what Kenneth Burke calls a "symbolic action" that could affect his whole relationship with the adult world:

S: What do you think is the best thing in the paper? What do you feel good about when you look back at it?

J: Well, before I couldn't, I had a hard time even talking about [my inferiority complex], but now that I can write about it, it's not a problem any more.

S: Do you want to explain what you mean by that?

J: Like I think, before I couldn't even, I wouldn't talk to anybody, but then I found somebody to talk to about it. And I think writing it is a final step. If you can write down how you felt, you know, and not worry about what other people think, I think that's a step in the right direction.

While it's true, however, that discovery drafting and revision helped John to work out the main themes of his paper and to define a more confident *persona*, I think it's also true that the ideas and values he decided to develop were not necessarily those which an academic audience would consider intellectually inventive. His first generalization for the Pastor T. narrative, that other people can offer different perspectives to help in understanding a situation, seems more original — or at least more full of potential for original thinking — than the revised commonplace about releasing "pent-up" feelings; but the first point was immediately rejected as making John sound too "second grade." That judgment was more a reaction than a critical response. John knew he wanted to "sound more educated" and "intelligent," but he had little definite sense of what that would sound like beyond the level of vocabulary choice. His terms were named, but rarely explored, explained, connected, moved to a level, as Shaughnessy would say, beyond the sentence.

Evidence vs Explanation

His teachers recognized this as a common problem for the class that had to be addressed in the revision assignment, paper eight (paper seven had been an in-class essay):

> Again, we want you to rewrite the first draft, paying attention to the kind and amount of detail but especially to the quality of your generalizations. This means we want you to be able to distinguish, in your own paper, the difference between writing that is evidence (here we are referring to the stories you wrote about yourselves) and writing that is explanation (here we are referring to *why* you chose the stories you did and what points you want to illustrate with them. . . .). Mostly, it means that you'll have to ask yourself questions like: "Why?" and, "Is this typical?" and, "What is the point I'm trying to make?"

John understood the need for this kind of revision. He could see, he said, "that my experiences didn't blend in the way I wanted it to blend in. They were sort of out of conjunction with each other. . . . It goes from one subject, then all of a sudden you're in another subject." But he had no idea what to do about this other than to wait for a conference with his teacher, hoping she'd tell him what transitions to add to make the paper work.

But his teacher didn't talk about additions or even about form. Instead, she attended to the language that John had already created for paper six. There he had written:

> *If you want things to change you have to make them change.* For example after graduation if I would of told myself that I was never going to worry about what someone thought of me. Then I would change. *If you don't change it mean your not ready for a change.*

The teacher drew lines to the two sentences I've emphasized and wrote in the margin: "These two things seem to contradict — is change internal, external, some of both? and when?" She then discussed these terms briefly with John in their conference, suggesting that he make more use of them and writing them at the top of the page in the form of contrasting opposites: "internal/external." As far as John was concerned, it was helpful advice. While it's hard to see from the passage the teacher noted just where the contradiction lies, her comments seemed to make sense to John. And they also, he said, seemed to him to be genuine suggestions, not orders: "She didn't," John told me, "really say explain what 'internal' and 'external' was," but then, he added, "I had to explain what 'internal' and 'external' was."

It's this sense of "having to" explain that's striking in his comments, as if for John there were something about this set of terms that compelled elaboration. We might account for this in phenomenological terms by saying that his teacher's questions raised for him a significant item of unfinished business in his effort to redefine himself, the tension he had been feeling between his internal awareness of what he thought and felt and told himself and what he perceived as the demands and values of the parents, peers, pastors, and lovers who formed what he calls here his "external environment." But while there's much in his texts and interviews to support this interpretation, this was not the teacher's approach. Instead, she focused on the language John had already created in order to suggest what else it might become. She did this first by placing "internal" and "external" into opposition, enabling John to reread them as what Kenneth Burke calls dialectical terms, that is, terms which "require an opposite to define them."[4] These are, in other words, not static classifications but metaphors of relationship involving both contrast and interaction. Our sense that each "requires" its opposite "is what gives such dialectical terms their power to generate further meanings."

"Ready for a Change"

John's teacher did more, however, than suggest these contrasting terms. She was also able to show him how he was moving towards a metaphor that might unify his paper, making it coherent beyond the level of comparison and contrast. The key word was "ready." It appeared in his statement that "if you don't change it mean your not ready for a change." But an even more important instance came earlier in the paper where John had tried to generalize about his conversations with Pastor T.:

> I think most people have somebody who helps them through a rough time in their life. For example, Maya had Mrs. Flowers. After she was raped and came back to Stamps. She hardly talk to anybody. Until she talk to Mrs. Flowers who gave her encouragement to talk to other people. She really help Maya. Because for the first time Maya was respected not as Mrs. Henderson grandchild or Baily sister but just for being Marguarite Johnson. And this made Maya feel better.

Also Holden had somebody who really cared about him and that was Mr. Spencer. After Holden was kicked out of school, Mr. Spencer had him come over. He talk to him about fluncking out of school and tried to straighten him out. *But Holden wasn't ready to listen.*

I think that everybody need somebody to help them in difficult times. It makes it so much easier if you can talk to somebody. The problem might not go away but aleast its not all pent up inside. And that is the first step in solving your problems.

In the margin next to the sentence she'd emphasized, John's teacher wrote: "I agree. So the 'being ready' seems to be more important than even the individual who helps the kid." Here, again, the teacher invited John to work with the generative power of controlling terms, this time by inviting comparison as well as contrast of "internal" and "external" issues by means of a thematic metaphor: "being ready." It was a move that, I think, enabled John to make sense — and text — out of the third part of her previous question: "Is change internal, external, *some of both?*"

Here, for example, is how John revised the remainder of this section about getting adult advice (the opening paragraphs were left the same):

[Paper six]

. . . But Holden wasn't ready to listen.

I think that everybody need somebody to help them in difficult times. It makes it so much easier if you can talk to somebody. The problem might not go away but aleast its not all pent up inside. And that is the first step in solving your problems.

[Paper eight, revision of six]

. . . But Holden wasn't ready to listen.

Often times when an adult tries to help somebody who is not ready for change it has little effect. Not only must an adult be willing to help the adolescent. But the adolescent must be ready for change internally.

I think every adolescent need and other adult other than their parent to guide them. And to help them through a difficult situation. There are many adults willing to help adolescent. Teachers, parents, adult friends, enpolyer, sister and broter are but a few of examples of people who

could help and adloscent. It makes it so much easier if the
adloscent can talk to somebody. The problem might not
go away but aleast its not all pent up inside. And that is
the first step in solving your problems.

In the process of following his teacher's request that he qualify
his generalizations, John classifies adolescents (some ready for
change, some not) in such a way as to create now a middle level
of generalization upon which his more theoretical statements
and his specific examples can pivot. Thus this first revised paragraph provides a transition from the two examples about Maya
and Holden to the very broad statement that all adolescents
need adults other than their parents to guide them. It also makes
sense retrospectively of the preceding examples; the reader can
now understand, for instance, that Maya was ready for help
even though the term itself doesn't appear in that paragraph.
And it prepares the way for us to understand as we read the
next paragraph why it might be important to name a list of
adults "willing to help the adolescent," a context which, in
turn, sets up the paper for John's later theoretical statements
about how the "environment" must be "ready" if adolescents
are to be able to change.

Defining Terms

Attention to defining terms enabled John, in short, to
make revisions which are true reformulations; they affect the
whole text, not just one particular section as was the case in
his earlier papers. Part of this new unity is thematic similarity.
Having used "internal," "external," and "ready" as terms to re-
see the narratives about graduation and about Pastor T., John
was able then to use them in a way that finally made something
out of his story about sexual initiation:

[Paper six]

Almost everybody experience sex for the first time.
And I think most people are disappointed. It is built up
to be something so great. Not that it isn't but its not as
great as you have pictured in your mind.

[Paper eight]

All adolescent experience sex for the first time. And
most adolescent are disappointed. If the only reason why
the adolescent is doing it is because of peer pressure, he

wants to get practiced or for any other reason than love. Because he wasn't ready for the change internal. Even though he is ready for the change external. What I mean by externally is that the person of the opposite sex is aviable. Internal is that the adolescent must want to do it out of love to truly enjoy it.

Initially, as I've shown, John's revisions evolved from his teacher's request to define the relationship between "external" and "internal" change. But their conversation had very quickly led John to see how "being ready" could be a metaphor for talking about them both. And now that language was beginning to generate a further metaphor that enabled John to carry the discussion to an even more theoretical level. As he revised, particularly as he paused to generalize about each narrative section of the paper, he gradually evolved the idea that under ideal conditions, the "internal" and "external" realms of experience would come to mutually reflect or "balance" one another.

The idea surfaces first during his narrative of Pastor T., which he revises so that their conversations no longer represent the adult telling John what to do but a reciprocal sharing of problems and advice: "Not only did we talk about my problem. He talk about his problems and ask for my advice. For the first time in my life I felt important. Someone actual wanted to know what I thought." A similar reciprocity appears in the revised conclusions about adolescent sex, where "love" is defined as the only viable bond that can unite external "availability" and internal desire. Finally, the metaphor of "balance" culminates in the final section of the paper, where John re-sees his notion of "feeling better about yourself" in the context of what is becoming a much more dynamic and dialectical theory of identity and change:

[Paper six, conclusion]

... The usual reason why you don't change is because of you. If you want things to change you have to make them change. For example after graduation if I would of told myself that I was never going to worry about what someone thought of me. Then I would of change. If you don't change it mean your not ready for a change.

Change is something that happens to everybody. For the good or bad. It is something that make you think and act different than the way you were. People change for various reason. It may because somebody helping you, peer pressure, and because something that happen to you.

I think change is good for somebody who can look back and say I'm happier, I'm feeling better about myself. No matter how you change. Other people might think you change for the worst. But, that isn't important. You are the one who has to live with yourself. And that is what is important.

But on the other hand if you look back and say your not happy. You don't feel good about yourself. Then the change was bad. Even if everybody else say your so much better know that you change. For example maybe you didn't drink and then you start drinking. And you look back and say you were happy before, then you shouldn't drink. Even if you will be like more for drinking. Because you are the one who has to live with yourself. Not your friends or parents. It is extremely important to remember that.

Change can make such a big difference. If you feel good about yourself it can make life so much more enjoyable than when you don't. For example when I felt bad about myself I hated to get up every morning. Each day was a drudgery. I didn't want to see anybody or make new freinds. After Pastor help me which I told you about in the begin I felt better about myself and suddenly I wanted to get up an face a new day. I wanted to make new freinds.

In conclusion I would like to say that changes happen to everybody. And the thing to remember when changing is to make sure you feel better about the change. If not go back to the way you were before. It's not disgraceful to go back to the way were. As long as you are realistic about it.

[Paper eight, revision of six]

The reason why I didn't change was because internal I wasn't ready for change. Even though external I was. I was going to start a new life. I wouldn't being going back to school. But instead I was afaird, I would have to go away from home. I would have to make all new freind and internal I just wasn't ready.

The usual reason why the adoslent doesn't change when he think he is because the adoslent is not ready. He might be ready internal but not external or external but not internally. The enviroenment must be right and the adoslecent must be metally ready for the change. Without both change will not take place.

For example my graduation I was ready external. The envirment was right I wouldn't ever being going back to high school. But I wasn't ready internally. If I wasn't worry about going to college and making new friends. Then I would have been ready for change.

Change is something that happens to everybody. For the good or bad. It is something that make you think and act different than the way you were. People change for various reason. It may because somebody helping you, peer pressure, and because something that happen to you.

I think change is good for somebody who can look back and say I'm happier, I'm feeling better about myself. No matter how you change. Other people might think you change for the worst. But, that isn't important. You are the one who has to live with yourself. And that is what is important.

But on the other hand if you look back and say your not happy, you don't feel good about yourself. Then the change was bad. Even if everybody else say your so much better know that you change. For example maybe you didn't drink and then you start drinking. And you look back and say you were happy before. Then you shouldn't drink. Even if you will be like more for drinking. Because you are the one who has to live with yourself. Not your friends or parents. It is extremely important to remember that.

Change can make such a big difference. If you feel good about yourself it can make life so much more enjoyable than when you don't. For example when I felt bad about myself I hated to get up every morning. Each day was such a drudgery. I didn't want to see anybody or make new freinds. After Pastor helped me which I told you about in the begin I felt better about myself and suddenly I wanted to get up an face a new day.

The American adolsnt has more freedom and desision to make than any other countries. The American adlosent must be ready for change internal and external. Where as other countries only have to be ready for the change internal. Because the external change has already been decide for them.

Which system is better for adlosocent? I think that the freedom is better for the adolescent Because if the adolescent isn't ready for the change at a certain time the external changes is ready he doesn't have to change. For example if an adolscent isn't ready to go to college right after graduation then he can work for a year or so. Until he ready for the change internal. But in other countries change is dictated to the adoloscent. He has no choice to try to change even if he not ready. Which can create problems mentally. You can not be force to change without creating problems mentally, the external and internal has to be right.

For example, if someone throw you into a pool and you didn't know how to swim you would drown. That is the way it would be like in dictated external phase. You have to be mental ready for it. Which would be like swimming. If you could swim then the external and internal phases would be in equilibrium. Which means you can suceed.

John acknowledged that he had borrowed "equilibrium" from Gail Sheehy's *Passages*, a book the class had begun to read. But where Sheehy seems to equate "equilibrium" with stability and tranquility, the opposite of personality change, John here defines it in terms of his previous metaphors of internal and external readiness, as a dynamic cooperation of social and inward states of being which enables personal changes to "suceed."

The revision as a whole is still far from being even adequate college-level prose. The moralizing central section has not been fully reworked to fit John's new theory (although it does take on more of a sense of tension from the new "internal/external" contrast); and while the end attempts to stretch beyond the easy moralizing of the original to meet the teacher's request, "Can you say something about American adolescents from this?" the leap from personal examples to speculation is both too sudden and too broad. Nevertheless, I would argue that the reformulation of paper six into paper eight represents one of those striking qualitative shifts which sometimes occur during the learning process when (to borrow John's terms) the internal and external factors are both ready. There was John's still-unsatisfied desire to define for himself what it meant to become an adult, an issue that, by his own account, was urgent and vital even before the course began. And there was a newer understanding expressed in our conversations that he would never make sense of his individual experiences of growth and change until he had some way of making sense of them all together. But as he clearly said in our conversation about solving his "inferiority complex," John was also beginning to realize that this sense would have to be made *during* the process of writing, rereading, and revising. For this reason the sequenced assignments and especially his teachers' comments and guidance were becoming increasingly important. With their "external" help he was learning to define his terms, to re-see his narratives by means of these metaphors, and to reread his whole text in order (as he now put it) to "pull it all together."

The Generative Process

The result in paper eight is that revision serves the purposes of invention in a way that is significantly different from his previous work. Where before John's revisions were prompted mostly by intuitive feelings, a "sense" of discomfort about how he "sounded," and where before he was content to revise only until he had the basic terms to describe each individual experience, now there is a much more intellectual and systematic analysis of the language of his evolving text. He has created a more abstract and metaphorical language which allows him to explore how one situation may be understood in the same terms as another; his experiences are analyzed as examples of contrasting relationships, classifications within a larger field. And these hierarchical orderings then provide a basis for more elaboration, more illustration, and more superordinate terms, one metaphor leading to the next. This generative process is, as Ann Berthoff rightly says, a dialectic of composing and revising: "You discover what you mean by responding critically to what you have said. Learning to use statements to form concepts and concepts to direct the revision and sequence of statements is learning to compose. You compose by the dialectic of seeing and knowing, naming and defining, saying and naming, stating and forming concepts."[5]

John seemed delighted with the sense of discovery he'd experienced in writing paper eight: "Now we know," he told me, "that change is so much more than chain reaction," a reference to an early class discussion. "'Internal,' 'external' — I could probably write whole pages just on change." This new sense of success came from reading his own revisions; but it was fostered by teaching which had its basis in what he could already do. In terms of the original design for Basic Reading and Writing, the course John was taking was "a sequence of instruction drawing on the syllabus built into the learner, corresponding to his particular competence and the stage of his development in the acquisition of the formal written dialect."[6]

Thus, at the beginning of the term, John was required to write narratives based on his already acquired sense of what a "story" is, but was urged by his teachers to include more details than he would have otherwise composed without their direction. Dubious about this at first, he'd soon changed his mind, seeing that by such elaboration "you might learn something." By a similar stepwise process, he'd been encouraged to compare his narratives in order to work with low-level general terms such as "internal" and "external," then to extend the process of generalization to create further superordinate terms and the further elaboration they called for. Each new assignment and conference had pushed John to stretch his abilities by posing new problems for him to address in his writing; but (in contrast, say, to his own attempted change of personality in high school) these problems were always just one step beyond what he could already do. This was particularly evident in the conference that helped John transform paper six into paper eight. John's success because of that help shows how, as Donald Graves says, "The art of teaching is to ask questions *in the midst of the person's competence.*" [7]

John's Autobiography

The next major effort for the course was the composing of John's autobiography, a project that would take up the next six assignments and most of the month of October. Again, he would be invited to extend his abilities, perhaps by adding more narratives as illustrative examples of the general ideas he'd already developed, certainly by refining his generalizations into a more abstract "theory" of identity and change in adolescence. At the same time, however, his teachers decided to revise the general staff assignments in order to finish the reading of *Passages*, the first theoretical book in the syllabus, before the autobiographies were complete. Given the pressures to cover six books within one semester, their decision is understandable; but in John's case, it was also, I think, a miscalculation. It posed challenges for him as a writer that he was not yet ready to handle.

The problems began when John went back for another conference, this time about the first draft of his autobiography:

. . . She didn't like the way I was explaining "external." And she said, then she started saying something about "seek" and "merge," and then reading Sheehy's book, she used "seek" and "merge" as the main. . . . 'Cause I was using "external" as the environment, which really didn't fit it. But "seeking" and "merging," you explore, then you merge. It made more sense to me.

What the teacher actually told John is, of course, unknowable. But it's clear that he felt his own metaphors of internal and external readiness were no longer acceptable and that another writer's terms made more "sense."

But just what that sense was is hard to tell. Here, for example, is the opening of the final draft of his autobiography:

> In this paper I will explain my theory of adolescence. The adolescent's main goal is to find his identity and to begin to break away from his home environment. But, before he is ready to find his identity, the adolescent has to be ready to change. When he is ready, he will search his surroundings, which I refer to as seeking. If the adolescent finds what he wants by seeking, he will make it a part of his life, which I call merging.
>
> An example of something an adolescent will seek and then not make a part of his life is drinking. A lot of adolescents will drink alcoholic beverages to see if it can accomplish their goal. When they find that drinking doesn't accomplish their goal, they will give it up, and seek for something else.

Although at times awkward and heavy handed, this opening is also in some ways quite admirable, particularly for John's effort to sound writerly in an academic way: the formal diction, the announcement of the paper's intentions, the dropping into exemplification in the second paragraph. The transition from storyteller to composer of expository prose is incomplete, but it's happening. But there's a more serious problem here, not one of approximating a style but of categories and connections, the thought the paper expresses. One of John's teachers caught this by the end of the second paragraph, commenting, "I'm confused. What goal would this be?" As the paper goes on it becomes increasingly clear that the problem is not so much a failure to define the goals of "seeking" and "merging" as it is a more general failure to be able to work with the terms at all.

Sometimes the problem takes the form of narratives without reference to theory. John added, for example, a story about how his parents had pressured him to play baseball long after he had wanted to quit, but it was so unrelated to the general themes of his paper that his teacher had to ask, "Was this a time of seeking and merging?" More often, however, the problem takes the opposite form, an inability to get beyond naming the general terms to either define them or apply and elaborate them in the context of a particular narrative illustration. Here, for example, are some of the many revisions John spent hours in composing (italics indicate what he scratched out as he wrote):

> [John's note to himself here: "end or begin"] Change is a two-part occurrance, first the ad. has to want to seek and he must also want to merge. Even the ad. has to want to seek . . . [incomplete]
> In doing so he must be ready and want to change. *When the adloscent* the first step is for ready he will search his envorment which I call seeking
> the adsolcent explore his surrodening which I call seeking [John's note to himself here: "explain seeking"]
> *When* But before he ready to find his identity and [illegible] he has to be ready to change. *In doing* When he is read so he will search search is surroundings which I refer to as seeking. If he like what he seek he will merge with it.

What these stuttering attempts at revision show, I think, is John's inability at this point to move from inductive to deductive composing. Up until this point his generalizations had been made, as the assignments put it, "on the basis of" a preceding specific narrative. However commonplace they may seem to us, they were nevertheless original terms for John. Even "equilibrium," the one term he'd found in Sheehy, was really not so much a borrowing (he ignored her definition) as a continuation of his own metaphors of "readiness" and "balance." But originality in adopting the terms of another writer means "making it new," as Pound put it, by giving those terms a new context from one's own experience and knowledge. Borrowed metaphors work in the context of something like an autobiography not simply because they are given abstract dictionary-style definitions (as John seems to suggest here by his remark, "explain seeking"), but because they are made to seem an organic whole with the narratives of the text.

It's clear that John didn't see this need for illustration and elaboration. In the previous examples, he seems trapped in the kind of dead-level abstraction that, like the narratives without generalizations of his early papers, typifies the basic writer's lack of movement between general and specific statements. And even when he does try to elaborate his terms, the thought becomes circular, unable to break away from mere naming to showing what names mean, so that "seek" and "merge" finally seem to refer only to themselves:

> For the first time I told myself I was as good as anybody else. Even though I still wasn't ready to merge with the feeling that I was as good as anybody I was getting closer to it. I wanted to merge and sooner or later I would merge.

The problem here is more, however, than John's lack of skill in working with other writers' theories. His general lack of experience with writing also meant that he had not yet developed a sense of authority that would allow him to see his own language in terms of a genuine dialogue with that of a published writer. Completing the autobiography might have helped him achieve this stance; in the design of the course, that midterm project is designed to be a pivotal point in the basic writer's transition to more theoretical academic writing:[8]

> The point of the sequence is to allow students to reconsider the positions they have achieved in their own study of adolescence by defining new positions in relation to the more formal representations of psychologists and anthropologists. But their own attempts to categorize and label provide the source of their understanding of Sheehy, Friedenberg and Mead. The labels and categories of academic culture are not given prior to the students' attempts to make sense out of the subject in their own terms. As a consequence, the students are allowed not only an aggressive stance in relation to these ideas, but also, and this is the most important point, in relation to the intellectual activity which these ideas represent. Theories, in other words, are seen as things real people make in order to try and make sense out of the world, not as gifts from heaven.

By reversing the sequence of the syllabus, assigning Sheehy prematurely before John could complete his autobiography, his teachers reinforced rather than remedied the already intense ambivalence he felt about the value of his own language in obtaining the respect of powerful adults.

We can see one side of this ambivalence in the way that John readily relinquished his "internal/external" theory rather than defending it in conference with his teacher. And once he saw the disappointing reaction of his teachers to his autobiography, he told me at our next interview that the "next time" he would show that he had learned his lesson: he would be "sure I use definitions everybody else uses." It was a theme I'd heard before in our conversations, a belief that getting an education meant not sounding like a "second grader," and that the way to do this was to depend on books and teachers to provide him with a ready-made language, with "better words, educated words" to use in his papers.

On the other hand, however, John was by midsemester no longer the naive basic student I mentioned at the beginning of this essay. He had experienced too much success with papers six and eight to fully accept a passive theory of education, just as his earlier experiences with sports, girlfriends, and Pastor T. had led him to realize that he was no longer able to accept unquestioningly his parents' definition of him as "ugly, clumsy, and not worth anything." He insisted, when we first talked about his autobiography revisions, that he had freely chosen to use "seek and merge," that his teacher didn't order it. And later as we talked he expressed his developing desire for his own authority over his written language — even as his ambivalence continued to pull him the other way:

> I changed words completely. I never even used "external" or "internal." I'm not at all happy about it. . . . I think it would be best to develop your own set [of terms], but 'cause you're trying to get a good grade you want to give them what they want. They might not want you using their ideas, but it seems like that's what they want. . . . I think you learn more [with your own terms] because you're not using someone else's ideas. You're using your own ideas, so it's all yours. You're doing it by yourself. It's all you. I never sat down and thought about, "Well, they shouldn't push me, I should be on my own," but that's what I thought.

Autonomy and Adulthood

I do not want to suggest, however, that John's problem with his autobiography was entirely due to his teachers' reshaping of the course syllabus. It's possible that had John had a chance to compose his entire autobiography before going on to deal with another writer's theory of identity and change in adolescence, he might have been more confident about the value of his own terms. But even so I doubt seriously whether his ambivalence about his own authority would have disappeared; it was a problem he would have to face sooner or later. Everything he had said or written up to this point suggests that he was continually conducting a dialogue with himself about what it means to be an autonomous adult, a dialogue in which there were several conflicting languages for defining what maturity means. Does becoming adult mean feeling accepted, part of a larger network of relationships? From that point of view, one seeks advice, goes out for competitive sports, begins dating, makes what others do "a part of" one's life — and that includes their language, the "educated words" that are required for admission, function, and status in the academic community. But there is also a language for adulthood that insists on taking risks, becoming independent, and valuing original language because, as John said, "when you use your own ideas — it's all you." The issues here are far more than a problem of basic reading and writing: as Shaughnessy argues, we need "to see the difficulties of so-called remedial students as the difficulties of all writers, writ large. For the problems of getting an idea and beginning to write, of remembering where one is going as sentence generates sentence, of sustaining the tension between being right and readable and being oneself — these are problems few writers escape. The BRW student merely comes to them later than most and must therefore work harder and faster to solve them."[9]

That catching-up process that Shaughnessy mentions can be exhilarating, as we saw in John's delighted response to his final draft of paper eight: "I could write whole pages just on change." But the risks of such sudden growth can also become overwhelming to someone as unaccustomed as John was to seeing the authority of his own language as competitive with that of teachers and books. In his papers, including the more coherent parts of his autobiography, John could acknowledge intellectually the need for some way to mediate the multiple languages he had to work with, to "balance" or "take steps" or "be ready" to handle the ambiguities of conflicting attitudes. But appealing as such mediation can seem in the abstract, the growing it requires can be painful; as Graves observes, "Options produce temporary paralysis and new orthodoxies."[10] Finding the demands of his autobiography more difficult than he expected, John was, I think, seduced by the simplicity of saying that change is entirely in his control. "Seek and merge" as John uses them are not dialectical terms but really a single process, one entirely originating with the self and oblivious to external forces. As a metaphor, "seek and merge" represents a dream of growing up as a controlled and nearly problem-free process, ending (as John says revealingly in one draft) at the point where a person arrives at adulthood and "everything falls into place."

Poor Reading

John's problem was further complicated by that twin problem to the basic writer's difficulty in handling complexity in
writing: poor reading. His attempt to oversimplify his own writing was matched by an equally simplistic approach to the interpretation of academic texts not his own. Not only did he ignore
the meaning of Sheehy's terms when he first borrowed them,
he didn't return to the book when he ran into problems redefining them in his writing. The terms are invoked as if we are to
know their meanings, but these meanings are not given. And in
our conversations, too, it's as if Sheehy's ideas didn't exist:

> I really didn't use anything exactly from Sheehy. . . .
> But I just took those two terms to use and explored them
> in my paper . . . not that I really took her theory. 'Cause
> I read the book and I didn't like it. It was boring. I just
> like to use those terms. I didn't even go back to the book
> once I got started. . . .

John's papers in the last month of the term also reflect this
superficial and perfunctory attitude towards difficult reading,
and even when he has take-home assignments, it shows in his
writing as well. Here, for example, is part of his response to
reading the most theoretically challenging work in the syllabus,
Coming of Age in Samoa. He is discussing Mead's contention
that "a person in Samoa who is ambitious would be better off
in the United States":

> I agree with Mead. An ambitious person would be
> better off in the United States, where as someone who
> was not ambitious would be better off in Samoa. Just look
> at two of the books we read. Maya was ambitious and al-
> ways exploring her environment. Thus, she succeeded. On
> the other hand, Holden was not ambitious and did not
> explore his environment. He was overwhelmed by his
> choices. Holden would have been better off in Samoa. He
> would not only have had less choices, but he would have
> been given as much time as he needed to mature.

While even this brief paragraph demonstrates real gains in coherence, hypothetical deductive reasoning, and academic diction
(all emphasized during this final part of the course), there is
also something formulaic about John's response, even simplistic
where Maya and Holden are concerned, and his own values, feelings, and experiences are nowhere engaged with what Mead has

to say. Gone, too, is the process of extensive exploratory drafting and the generating of new ideas it could produce. John's final papers are textbook examples of composing: an outline, rough copy, and final clean draft. I felt concerned at the time my study ended that much of what John had learned about composing had been abandoned.

Epilogue

Fortunately, this story has an epilogue: I was able to talk with John two and a half years later, at the end of his junior year. In order to fulfill the requirements of his major, he had just completed a reading and writing course for engineering students, "English 87: Literature and Ideas." He'd not only earned a solid "B" for his work, but (he said with considerable satisfaction) his teacher hadn't even known he'd taken a course in basic writing.

Early in the term John had decided on his own to return to the process of exploratory drafting that he'd learned at the beginning of Basic Reading and Writing. He'd felt "more comfortable" writing this way, he said, and "It came out better — more ideas." Judging from the extensive drafts he showed me for his papers — multiple versions with large chunks of writing added, deleted, and cut-and-pasted together — the description of his composing process that he included in his final essay was quite accurate:

> I no longer restrict my thought to one aspect, but rather I write down anything that comes to mind and worry about the order or relativeness later. I then leave the paper for a day, then come back, reread it, and do massive patch-up jobs or rewrite the entire paper in a logical manner. I go through this process as many times as necessary until I feel that what I have written expresses what I am thinking.

Is personal satisfaction, I then asked, the chief criterion for deciding whether the text is expressing "good ideas"? "No," John said, "'good ideas' mainly goes with what the teacher wants." I felt for a moment that we were back where I'd left him two years ago. But this time he moved to qualify what he said in ways that suggested that the relationship between writer and academic community was no longer being seen in simple terms. A good paper, he said, was neither entirely what the writer wanted nor what the teacher wanted, but "some of both." And neither was simple to determine. As a writer, after saying what one wants to say, it's important to take a reader's stance: "I look on it, I try to be like another person, try to be open. . . . What you want is not necessarily a good idea." Nor, he said, does giving the teacher what she wants guarantee that the paper will have any good ideas. And even "what the teacher wants," he added in a further qualification, was something that had to be interpreted from class discussions and assignments.

Similarly, John said, "You can read a book and decipher it in so many ways; no one way is right." At this point he turned to self-criticism: "I learned a lot from reading those books [in English 87]. I never really sat down and tried to figure out what the author was saying until I had that course." What, then, about Basic Reading and Writing? He acknowledged that his teachers had tried to help him to become a more careful reader, but (echoing his metaphor from paper eight) "I don't think I was ready for it back then." He described a younger John who was trying to memorize professors' lectures, who believed a book's meaning could be understood immediately without rereading or thought or discussion, who was reluctant to ask questions when he did not understand the material. As a result, he had not been able to make the books he read during his freshman year into more than just what he'd defined them as: "educated words," not whole systems of thought with which he could become engaged. In fact, in a comment that was symbolically appropriate, he misremembered his autobiography as the last paper he'd written for that earlier course.

The effect, then, of being able to take a second course in reading and writing was that John was finally able to complete the process begun two years before, to make academically mature connections between reading, writing, and his sense of authority. Here, for example, is how his final paper describes his response to reading Ralph Waldo Emerson's essay, "The American Scholar":

> I can remember when I first started reading Emerson I pictured myself in a large auditorium very uncomfortable. I was looking all around not paying attention to what Emerson was saying. I kept looking at my watch hoping to get out of there as soon as possible. I now realized that the reason why I felt this way was because of my poor reading skills. I was not able to interpret what Emerson was saying and to avoid the resulting frustration I did not

pay attention. Through class discussion the reading was interpreted for me and I realized the fullness of the essay. Each time I read another essay I increased my ability to interpret what the author was saying. Eventually I was able to answer questions that were presented in our class discussions. I no longer felt that I was in a big auditorium but rather I now felt that although Emerson was elevated above me he was actually talking to me.

English 87 had done little, John said, to give him specific help with composing; reading and discussion had been its focus. It was John himself who put what he was learning there together with what he had learned in Basic Reading and Writing to see that both are essentially acts of interpretation: "I now realize," he wrote, "that when reading or writing a paper, one has to keep thinking about what the author is saying." It is clear, I think, that the ambiguity of that statement is intended: "the author" refers to both the academic authorities John has been reading and to himself, the writer and reader of his own texts. Others might, as he put it, be "elevated above" him in their ability, but they were all still about the same business; they could "talk" to each other. John summed up these changes in his feelings about authorship and authority in his final paper for English 87, singling out of all he had read this one sentence from Emerson: "Meek young men grow up in libraries, believing it their duty to accept the views which Cicero, which Locke, which Bacon, have given; forgetful that Cicero, Locke, and Bacon were only young men in libraries when they wrote these books."

Notes

[1] Mina Shaughnessy, *Errors and Expectations: A Guide for the Teacher of Basic Writing* (New York: Oxford UP, 1977) 293.

[2] Donald Graves, *Writing: Teachers and Children at Work* (Exeter, New Hampshire: Heinemann, 1983) 231.

[3] For the original study, see: Susan V. Wall, "Revision in a Rhetorical Context: Case Studies of First Year College Writers," diss., U. of Pittsburgh, 1982, 48–118. John and I met for 50-minute interviews ten times during the 14-week term. I saw all his texts — notes, drafts, and final copies — and course materials, interviewed both of his teachers twice, and had access to his high school records and his composition placement exam. John is middle class, white, and grew up in a small town near Pittsburgh. His mother is the only member of his immediate family without any college education.

[4] Kenneth Burke, *The Philosophy of Literary Form: Studies in Symbolic Action*, 3rd ed. (Berkeley: U of California P, 1973) 109n.

[5] Ann E. Berthoff, *Forming/Thinking/Writing: The Composing Imagination* (Rochelle Park, NJ: Hayden, 1978) 111.

[6] David Bartholomae, "Teaching Basic Writing: An Alternative to Basic Skills," *Journal of Basic Writing* 2 (Spring/Summer 1979) 87.

[7] Graves 213.

[8] Bartholomae 95.

[9] Shaughnessy 293.

[10] Graves 244.

5.

The Dialogical Nature of Basic Reading and Writing

MARIOLINA SALVATORI

> The understanding of a text has not begun at all as long as the text remains mute. But a text can begin to speak. (We are not discussing here the conditions that must be given for this actually to occur.) When it does begin to speak, however, it does not simply speak its word, always the same, in lifeless rigidity, but gives ever new answers to the person who questions it and poses ever new questions to him who answers it. To understand a text is to come to understand oneself in a kind of dialogue. This contention is confirmed by the fact that the concrete dealing with a text yields understanding only when what is said in the text begins to find expression in the interpreter's own language. Interpretation belongs to the essential unity of understanding. One must take up into himself what is said to him in such fashion that it speaks and finds an answer in the words of his own language.
>
> *Philosophical Hermeneutics, p. 57*

Most BRW students have never read a book from cover to cover; those who have, clearly have not been educated to think of reading as a "dialogue" that gives a "voice" to an otherwise "mute" text, a dialogue that "interprets" the text and in the process yields "understanding" of that text and of its reader.

Like most students coming from American schools, these students have at most replied to a few identification questions or written answers to questions that almost invariably are little more than a restatement of the questions themselves. Their more successful counterparts have learned to turn the very

137

questions they are asked into props by means of which they construct their own "individual" responses ("I think the theme of this novel is . . . "; "The main idea of . . . is . . . "; "In my opinion, this author uses x-symbol to convey y-idea."), and they have been rewarded for this kind of performance by being defined "mainstream." BRW students, however, have learned to think of themselves as incapable of learning to read, or to write, or to think.

Knowing that as long as they think about themselves in these terms, they will continue to act as if they were incapable of learning to read, to write, and to think, our first pedagogical move is to demonstrate that they know more than they think they know. What they need, however, is to learn to structure that knowledge and converse about it in ways that open up rather than close off understanding (understanding of both their knowledge and themselves as knowers). For this reason we try to find ways of making it possible for them to see what they have said as if their words were a text that they can read, write, revise, and have dialogue with — a text they can speak to and that will speak back to them in turn.

However, since the most salient characteristic of BRW students is their willed obliviousness to both intellectual and social conventions, particularly to the academic convention of group discussion and cooperative learning, as teachers we initially encounter great resistance to the methodological enactment of our theoretical and pedagogical premises. When, from the very first day of class, we invite our students to talk about how and what they think they learned when they read a book, wrote about it, and discussed it in class, when we define ourselves as participants in their learning process, as facilitators of knowledge rather than distributors of information, many of them initially respond with dismay and suspicion. This response is likely to be channeled into two distinct and equally destructive behaviors: a docile acceptance of the demanding course requirements (which they seem to consider either as a necessary punishment for something they refused to do, or a remedy for something they were unable to do), or overt disruptiveness (by which they seem to want to remove the threat of the possibility of any cooperative effort). Good will on our part, encouragement, compassion and patience are necessary but they are certainly not enough to overcome this negative stance.

In BRW, to the surprise of both the docile and the disruptive student, both attitudes are immediately acknowledged and analyzed in terms of their causes and motivations, and questioned in terms of the learning experience they can or cannot make possible. In what can be considered the first move away *from* a monological *toward* a dialectical system of education, we ask our students, perhaps for the first time in their scholastic experience, to assume responsibility for what they say, and to become reflexive about why they say what they say.[1]

The classroom then becomes the center of everything, the place where teachers continuously discover, test, and modify ways of stimulating students' intellectual resources, and where students learn to understand and to assess the roles they have and can come to take in their own education. The *remedial* approach is replaced by one of *mediation* as both teachers and students learn to ask and to answer questions that make texts speak, and speak away silences with "voices" that *mediate* and *remediate* understanding in continuous, enriching dialogues.

What follows is both a description of the design of BRW and an attempt to recall the voices that rescued it from its "lifeless rigidity."

BRW: The Design of the Writing Assignments

BRW students write in response to 24–26 writing assignments.[2] The total number includes the "diagnostic test" administered in class at the beginning of the term, the six in-class assignments on the required readings, and about three assignments, at the very end of the term, whose format is the format of the End-of-Term Review exam which students must pass in order to graduate from Basic Reading and Writing. As the course progresses, the assignments become increasingly difficult as they make reading, writing, and thinking increasingly problematic activities. The basic design of each assignment retains throughout (though less overtly in the first four assignments) a tripartite scheme which guides students through what Gadamer names as the three fundamental phases of the hermeneutic process: (1) *to understand* first of all, (2) *to interpret* that understanding, and finally (3) *to apply* the knowledge gained in the act of reflexivity (i.e., the ways in which one thinks and the reasons for thinking that way) to the subject matter under investigation and to life experiences.[3]

Assignments 2 through 15 provide students with ways to organize and to direct their exploration and revision, their critical formulation of what they know and have so far learned about adolescence. These assignments culminate in the midterm project, the "autobiography," a text students keep rereading, reformulating and revising as they think through the three theoretical texts that are the required readings for the second half of the term.

Significance

The most evident feature of the first assignments (2 through 6) is their redundancy. Instructions are spelled out and repeated to make sure that students do not skip important steps in the development of their essays. Assignments 2 and 4 ask students to describe in detail a "significant experience" in their adolescent life; Assignment 3 is a return to what they write in 2; Assignment 6 introduces them to the concept and function of revision. Term after term students demonstrate that, at this point in their development as readers/writers/thinkers, their understanding of "significance" is not very sophisticated and neither is their ability to reflect on why *they assigned significance* to the particular experience they narrated. (Our definition of "significance" and "significant" rescues the etymological meaning of the word *to signify*: from Latin *significare*: *signum*, sign + *ficare*, to make.)

Initially their selection of material is haphazard. (They usually say: "It's the first thing that came to my mind" or "It's the only thing I could think of.") Their essays reveal a view of both writing and reading (reading of the assignments, of the "text" of their experience, of the teacher's marginal and final comments) as mechanical acts, in which thinking and reflexivity either have no part or are unnecessarily complicating "steps." However, in the class discussion that precedes and follows their writing, students learn to demonstrate that they know how to think, that they know how to reflect on the presuppositions that govern their acts of knowing, and that they can engage as interested and interesting participants in the collective critical inquiry. Our job is to bring forward the students' roles as active participants — to make this their discovery as well as ours. It can, of course, be argued that their thinking, reflexivity and engagement are then neither autonomous nor spontaneous, that they are in fact *forced* responses to their teachers' questions. Although at this point their responses may seem as characterized by a lack of autonomy and spontaneity, it might be more appropriate to define them as *guided* responses to assisted invitations, the ambiguity that the absence of the grammatical agent generates in this phrase functioning, I suggest, as a reminder of the reciprocity of the process in which teacher and students continuously and alternatively guide and invite each other.[4]

To remind students that in writing as well as in discussion one generates meanings by thinking, engaging in dialogue with oneself, questioning and counterquestioning one's assumptions as well as others', Assignment 4 makes an overt link with, and reminds students of, those very activities that in the classroom enabled them to produce sophisticated insights:

> We've spent time talking, writing, and thinking about what makes something significant. We have been discussing the significance of events and people in Maya Angelou's life, and you have made a start in explaining the significance of the experience you wrote about in 2 and 3.
> This assignment calls for a new rough draft. . . .

The assignment is worded in this way for another important reason. We are beginning to tell students that we expect them to view the critical thinking in the classroom discussion as a model for the thinking that should sustain and guide their reading and writing. The seminar, then, is an opportunity to begin doing collectively what they will later do individually, i.e., to use any of the team insights gained in discussion when they are writing, to connect the public and the private work.

Connections

Assignment 5 (their first in-class assignment) functions as a step toward bringing to fruition their newly acquired understanding:

> As we noted several times in class discussion, it often happens that what appear to be insignificant events or characters in this book can seem more significant when we think about what Maya Angelou would like us to understand about her life.
> For this assignment, we want you to read Chapter 17 of *I Know Why the Caged Bird Sings* (pages 93–100) and summarize the chapter in a sentence or two. Then, go on to write about and to explain how the apparently insignificant events of this chapter turn out to be significant for your understanding of Maya Angelou's experience as a whole.

This assignment has a crucial function in the design of the course. It invites students to bring forward the observations they made

in group discussions (for example, that the importance/signifi-
cance of a character isn't a function of the length of his or her
presence in the story but rather a function of both Angelou's
and the reader's perception of his or her influence). It encour-
ages them to make an effort to *interpret* their understanding of
characters' and other people's points of view, and it stresses for
them the fact that events, characters, experiences do not *possess*
significance or insignificance, but that the student's *act of reflexivity* confers those attributes. Assignment 4 is also a prelude to
Assignment 7, in which they are asked *to apply* their understanding and assessment of concept formation, of definition, and of
their power as critical thinkers, in an essay that describes and
explains how they came to the conclusion that something they
"expected to be significant" "turned out to be insignificant."

The assignment legitimizes what was seen as an illicit activity. Students thought that they had *missed* the significant parts
of the text and that the things they noticed were trivial. The
assignment is designed to bring forward their roles as readers,
to show that the process of assigning significance to what you
notice is a way of reading, not a way of bluffing or covering
your tracks.

Autobiographies

At this point in the course students are about to begin to
work on their midterm project, their autobiography, which asks
them to produce a piece that will represent significant moments
in their adolescent lives. They know that the text will be read
and analyzed and discussed by the whole group and, although
they each know that they're free to choose a pseudonym, they
also know that they will be able to recognize each other's writing.
That they can recognize a certain use of language as characteristic of a certain language user is in itself a sign of their maturity
as readers. But this can also be a problem. Some students, in
fact, in a gesture that is indicative of the mutual trust and support that by now has come to characterize the teaching/learning
context, will ignore our suggestion that they do not narrate
events or circumstances that might be too personal, and will
volunteer astonishing glimpses at the complexity of their lives.
But such glimpses — at times moving, at times tragic, at times
unbearably cynical — can jeopardize, in the affective response
they cause, the critical stance that the writer, the teacher and
the other students must adopt in order to discuss the work at
hand. Because we want neither to invalidate their gesture, nor

our function as teachers, we have devised an assignment which in the name of narrative theory and in the name of the theoretical premises of the course asks them *to reflect* on the distance that the act of writing imposes on life.

> So far you have written about two kinds of experiences in your life — one was defined as significant and the other as insignificant. If you reread these papers carefully, you may notice that you have created a definite image of yourself as a certain kind of adolescent going through a certain kind of experience. We are now going to invite you to focus your attention upon that character you have created through your writing.
>
> Keep in mind that, as a writer, you are different from the main character in your autobiography in at least two ways: first, the you who is the writer is different from the you who went through certain experiences, and second, the you who exists today is different from the younger self you are writing about.
>
> Would you begin this assignment by giving us a full description of the character who appears on the pages you have written? Would you say that the incidents you have chosen to write about offer an accurate, thorough, and complete picture of that character? Can you confidently say that you have presented your readers with a picture of a complex character rather than an oversimplified one? What more would you like a reader to know in order to fill out the picture?
>
> Then, would you go on to comment upon the ways in which your character could be said to be typical of or different from most adolescents. Use the characters of Maya, Conrad, or the boys in *God's Helicopter* as points of comparison.[5]

The distance required for the writer and the other readers in the seminar depends on an acknowledgment of the distinction between the "I" who narrates, and the "character" in the narrative (both fictions invented by the writer). This acknowledgment, however, is obviously easier for the teacher to make than for any of the students. But since it is a fundamental prerequisite for the critical analysis of the students' texts, we spend a considerable amount of time exploring what this concept of fictionality means, looking for and discussing places in the students' and in the assigned fictional texts where tense shifts or adverbial markers seem to signal different temporal perspectives and mark the character's "otherness." Students are initially perplexed by the double fiction they have to weave and unweave; but the discussion itself, focusing as it does on the conventions of language use and language users, has a healthy distancing effect for them.

The last paragraph of the assignment invites them once more to make connections with the fictional texts they have read so far, so that they can learn to explore the complexities of *their* "character" with the same kind of critical understanding they were able to achieve in their analysis of the characters in the assigned texts.

The next four assignments guide students through a rough draft and the various revisions of their autobiography. The two most important features of these assignments are the emphasis on re-seeing as an opportunity to enlarge their understanding of personal experience and a movement to place the autobiography within the "project" of the last half of the term. As part of this project, students propose and test a theory of adolescent development.

The collection of all the students' autobiographies becomes another assigned text to read. From a pedagogical point of view, this is a very important move. Although students' papers have already been regularly discussed in class — a practice by which we implicitly and explicitly argue that their writing is worth reading and their reading is worth response — their writing has never appeared to them as "official" as it does now, cleanly typed and bound as a book. This collective text is now juxtaposed and equipoised with the three fictional texts they have read so far, and will be the text they will continually re-read, revise and rewrite in the second half of the term as they move through the assigned theoretical readings on adolescence. From a theoretical point of view, the *reading* of the *text* of their experiences reaffirms the fundamental premise of the interconnectedness of the two activities; in fact, it demonstrates that *to understand* the nature of the activities of reading and writing means *to interpret* and *to apply* that interconnectedness.

A Student's Private Dialogue

Let me now focus on one exemplary text, the autobiography of a student who, because of the questions she learned to raise about the texts we all read, turned the collective inquiry in "Growth and Change in Adolescence" into a text that *she made speak* and *made her speak* a "dialogue" which ultimately yielded an impressive understanding of the very critical questions she posed about parent/child relationships. Let me introduce Robin by using the "character analysis" she constructed in response to Assignment 10:

> The character I just read was a young girl who was extremely shy and withdrawn. All of the events she tried, she did so to try to rid herself of some of her shyness. Trying out for her class play and joining the matriculation were both her way of proving to herself and showing others that she could do, and she could be more than any of them had ever expected. . . .
>
> This young girl's problem with proving herself was not trying to improve herself, but the reasons why she did such things. Her first and utmost reason was for others. The main people being her family and friends. Then her last reason was for herself. There is nothing wrong with doing things for others, but she should learn that she doesn't always have to.
>
> This character thought by trying all of those new things that they could change her life. After all of them she seemed to return back to the shyness she was trying to overcome. This doesn't mean that what she did was wrong, but that it was a very long process. By continuing to do these things, time after time, it made easier for her to begin.

This paper demonstrates the extent to which Robin's improvement as a writer is connected to her improvement as a reader. Seven weeks earlier, when Robin took her diagnostic test, we thought she could have made it in a more advanced course. Unlike most BRW students, who initially can seldom write more than one paragraph, she could at least produce considerably long texts, though laden with errors. When we gave her the choice to try to move up, she chose not to because she knew, she said, that she needed help in reading. She needed this help, she explained, because she did not know "what to do with what she read."

Though Robin could produce long texts, she was unable to control them. She made many surface errors (verb endings, missing words, and unnecessary and erratic doubling of words). Her long, winding sentences were often so loaded with words as to stifle meaning. And when she read them, she was apparently unable to understand what needed clarification and what needed to be corrected and why, even when the problematic parts were pointed out to her. But she was a very conscientious student. She put her papers through three or four revisions, rather than the customary two; and it was through her incessant revisions that she learned a way of reading that within four or five weeks dramatically reduced the syntactic blurriness and the number of errors in her writing. Learning to read as a way of engaging in a dialogue with and questioning a text (and her reading) took her much longer, however.

Robin was painfully shy. She sat quietly during class discussion taking voluminous notes, but she resisted questions about what she had said and why she said what she said, and courted silence. Her "dialogues" took place privately. In her case, we had to modify our pedagogical approach. We learned to carry on these dialogues outside of class — in conferences, or through marginal comments on her papers. We accepted her nonparticipation as we learned to read her silence as something other than a sign of hostility or apathy.

Dialectical Relationship

In the paper I have just introduced, Robin — though still tentatively — is beginning to engage in a dialectical relationship with the text she had earlier constructed. She is asking questions of that text that have less to do with extrinsic features (the abundance of details and the effectiveness of a character's description) than with intrinsic ones (the motives for that character's construction). But although her questions lead to a substantial analysis ("This young girl's problem was . . . "), she questions her questions in such a way that at this point she fails to keep the horizon of her understanding open; one senses, in fact, in the last paragraph of the excerpt an attempt to justify the "character's" persistence in doing "things that could change her life." It is important to notice that the justification, the rationalization which blocks the questioning, comes after the critic's remarkable insight into the reasons for the shy girl's self-imposed gregariousness.

As emotion supercedes critical distance, Robin's reflexivity loses focus; the merging of the two I's causes logical and syntactic blurriness. The paper rambles on for one more page until a new voice emerges. Trying to address herself to the assignment's question, Robin writes: "Maybe if the writer had written about an event that was significant, but which she didn't succeed or win in, we'd be able to tell more about the writer." This sounds like the objection of a book reviewer who questions why the manuscript is not what it could have been. In this case, however, the reviewer is also the reader/critic of her own text, and the question raised can hardly be thought of as arbitrary; the question Robin is raising about her text indicates that she is now engaging in a dialogue with herself about the *choices* she made as a writer and as a thinker. She is on her way toward a significant "revision of knowledge," one that will guide her inquiry through the rest of the term.

Robin's autobiography was a long, well-constructed narrative which included, as she herself put it, three events that "revealed my growth, my ability to understand myself, know my limitations, and know the goals that I was able to achieve." Here is clear evidence of her growing ability to use writing as an opportunity to question and to expand her understanding of those experiences, why they were significant *then* and what their significance is to her *now:*

> The audition was simple. I had to sing a verse of "Oh, What a Beautiful Morning," act out a scene with Mrs. Ban, and act out a given scene doing pantomime. It's funny, now I say it was simple, but when I tried out, I remember saying how difficult the audition was, and so did everyone else. We said it to preserve our egos. Instead of having to blame ourselves for lack of talents, we could blame it on the difficult audition.

Emotions are kept in check; the collective self-deceit is unmasked; the critical question prevails; the understanding brings about bemusement. Remarkable for the clarity of vision it engenders is Robin's moment of reflexivity, located in the present yet not entirely disregarding the past: "It's funny, now I say it was simple. . . . I remember saying how difficult the audition was. . . ." And here is evidence of her ability to connect insights from different moments and different contexts:

> By the time I had tried out for the class play, I had gone through enough experiences to make putting on the class play much easier. I learned to use my nervous energy to make my performances better. I used it, instead of it using me. My shyness was overcome at those critical moments by me not being myself. I wasn't myself, but I was the character Laurie, whom I created for the play. She was a part of me, yet very separate from me. The character was my shield on stage. I couldn't be seen, for I was hiding behind her.

The vocabulary of Assignment 10 seems to have become Robin's, but perhaps, at this point, this very vocabulary (which is not yet fully hers) "shields," "hides" from her the realization that although she may have learned to *use* nervousness to her own advantage, her shyness is still very much with her. This is, in fact, the acknowledgment she makes in the "conclusion" that prefaces her autobiography:

> Being an extremely shy and withdrawn person, I spent much of adolescence trying to prove myself. When I was a young child, I received attention from being shy. While the other children were being loud and mischievious, I, the quiet one, sat quietly in a corner and watched them. According to the adults I was "the perfect little girl." As a matter of fact, I was no longer anything at all. All of a sudden, all the people who were once so fond of me, now had nothing to say to me. I don't think my family realized how heartbreaking their sudden withdrawal of attention was for me. I sometimes wondered if I hadn't been reinforced in my behavior, if I would have grown out of my shyness.

She seems to be viewing her shyness as a sin, a fault that needs to be identified and traced to its origin so that it can be amended. The question she asks at the end of the paragraph is particularly painful in this respect. Perhaps it is a question she had been subconsciously asking of herself for a long time but which, rhetorically framed as it is, closes off, rather than opens up, fruitful inquiry. From now on, however, Robin questions and assesses the validity of her questions, which change in the second half of the term from "whose fault, whose blindness" it was to the extent of parents' responsibility to their children *and* children's responsibilities to themselves and to their parents.

Parents' Vulnerability

Reading Robin's responses to the assignments sequentially, it is even possible to locate the moment when this question was fruitfully reframed. It happened, it appears, when she read *Hunger of Memory*, a text in which, she states, " . . . Richard Rodriguez, the author, tells the reader of the effect these educational changes had on him and his family especially." Although Robin is clearly sensitive to Rodriguez's initial "feelings of inadequacy," she is equally sensitive *to his parents'* feelings of inadequacy. As she tries to assess the function of the Catholic

Church in both Rodriguez's and his parents' lives, she argues that for Rodriguez the Church " . . . was the constant when everything failed. Church was his dependable friend. It reconciled all differences. It was the place where he felt the intimacy of his family once again." For Rodriguez's parents, however, the Church was " . . . the only institution that treated . . . [them] with intellectual respect." She suggests that "Maybe that is one of the reasons his mother and father had so much respect for this Church. The Church respected them." Although Robin does not elaborate on this, she suggests that Rodriguez's suffering (due to a loss of intimacy) is equal in intensity to his parents' suffering (due to a loss of respect). She is, in other words, seeing the possibility of viewing the relationship between a child and her parents equally. Both suffer. The question is not who is at fault but how to understand the suffering. In so doing, she is preparing herself to question the text of her own experience in more complex and critical ways.

Robin's new insight into parents' vulnerability seems to give her a new self-assuredness. Having acknowledged that parents can suffer, she now moves to question how long one must protract one's suffering. The once shy, introverted, and hesitant writer offers this critique of the possible excesses of the Judeo-Christian ethic (in a response to *Normal Adolescence*, the penultimate text we read in the course):

> One of the theoretical issues offered by this book was that of the "Judeo-Christian ethic," which, taken literally, means that everything we do, we should do out of our love for God, and when we do not do something out of the love for God, we should carry and be burdened with the guilt of that sin. This is the "official" ethic of our culture. There is nothing wrong with this ethic, but there is a part that needs to be added, and that is that we need not carry the burden of our sins, but we should ask God for forgiveness of them.

She means, of course, that an uncritical acceptance of this ethic can result in unnecessary self-punishment, and she cites Maya Angelou (*I Know Why the Caged Bird Sings*) and Conrad Jarret (*Ordinary People*) as appropriate examples, although she doesn't mention the "character" she had analyzed in response to Assignment 10. But having established children's responsibility for their own well-being, she goes back to parents' responsibility for their children. Of parents, she asks that they *reflect* on their teachings, because when "an adolescent leaves high school, and goes on to college, or to find work," some things may happen that are "unlike the things he's been learning all of his life. People spend all of their lives learning the importance of 'being your own person,' only to find that they'll have to conform to the wishes of others, or be considered an 'outcast,'" Her final perspective on growth and change in adolescence is a commonplace:

> Adolescence has many psychological effects on a person, and these effects determine the kind of adult that person will make.

But when she argues, reflecting on her own experience, that it is extremely important that parents make sure that

> their children understand the things they [the parents] are saying, so that as they grow they do not become confused, and they are able to function as adults

her observation is compelling in terms of the reflexivity it demands of her readers, particularly when the readers are themselves parents.

To assign that much responsibility to parents may seem, at first, a reversal to Robin's former position — an abdication of the adolescent's responsibility toward her own change and growth. But a more careful reading of her text yields a different understanding of what she is suggesting. For children to understand what their parents are saying and for parents to make sure that their children understand, a certain kind of relationship is obviously necessary — a relationship initiated and sustained through dialogue, a relationship in which questions and counterquestions can ensure that the *application* of what one has learned follows from the appropriate *interpretation* of what has been *understood*.

BRW: The Design of Class Discussions, Reading Assignments, and Prediscussion Exercises

BRW asks a great deal from its students in terms of the amount of work,[6] the intensity of involvement required, and the high performance levels expected. This, however, is done less to test students and confront them with the limits of their knowing, than to make *them* test and confront the possibilities of their knowing.

Our course description defines BRW as a "seminar." And a seminar it is, in the sense that the group does engage in "original research" under the guidance of two teachers who meet regularly with students for reports and discussion; but it is also a "seminary," that is, a "place," an "environment," where the conditions conducive to such discussion are introduced, nurtured and ultimately carried away by the students.

Class Discussions

Reclaiming its etymological meaning, discussion (to discuss = Lat. *dis*, apart; *quatere*, to shake) in the BRW classroom is conducted in such a way as to become, for all its participants, a "shaking apart" of fixed, uncritical ideas and assumptions in order to generate a dynamic rearrangement of concepts into new and more complex ones, into revisions and modifications of opinions.

Of course, this kind of discussion doesn't just happen; on the contrary, it must be carefully prepared, though not predetermined, and effectively guided, though not imposed. For the first week or so, the dialectic of questions, answers, and counterquestions is mainly initiated and sustained by the teachers as they interact with the students both in their responses to students' papers and in the classroom conversation.[7] As the course progresses, however, the responsibility to lead and to keep the class discussion going is eventually delivered to the students.

Since we expect our students to care about and to assume responsibility for their own education, we make a point of showing them that whatever they say, even the tentative and offhand comments they make, can be turned into something that matters and is worth exploring. Comments like "I could not read it because I found it boring" or "I could not relate to it" are not left to pass unnoticed or unchallenged. Urged by the teachers' questions and counterquestions, the student who in defiance or in frustration makes such comments comes to recognize in them a method of reading and begins to understand the consequences that such a method of reading and thinking can have for the learner. When critically examined, they become an opportunity to reflect on the reader/learner's responsibility *to make* things meaningful, *to make* things significant and relevant. The focus on the making of meaning rescues the signifying power of "meaningful," "significant" and "relevant" from that "lifeless rigidity" — to use Gadamer's words — in which common usage has imprisoned them.

The questioning and the counterquestioning are good humored, even relaxed, but intense, relentless. In the beginning of the term, when students don't yet understand or believe that the course will be built around their work, the questions can cause frustration, dismay, even anger. But the risk of arousing and dealing with such emotions is worth taking. Students will say that they are uninterested in Maya Angelou's experience (because, as one of my students put it, "I never had those problems, and can not understand them"), or that the book is useless ("because this happened in the past, it's not like that anymore"). Others will find only momentary and superficial contact with Angelou's suffering ("because it reminds me of my own").

The class will be happy to take these various statements as expressions of "different people's opinions" and to leave them at that. To accept this is to encourage students' *automatism* as thinkers, not their *autonomy*. It makes dialogue impossible and turns the class into a place where each individual speaks his or her piece, in a single statement, and then lapses into silence; it makes students miss the opportunity to discover the extent to which prejudgments may preclude understanding, unexamined foreknowledge can preclude further knowledge.

Almost invariably, in fact, it happens that the student who so warmly and articulately responds to *I Know Why the Caged Bird Sings* is unable to empathize with Conrad's suffering *(Ordinary People)*, whereas the student who left *Caged Bird* "mute" will be able to say something about *Ordinary People*. In other words, most students cannot "relate to" those experiences they find "alien" (and alienating), but they can recognize something they already know. They are willing to offer a single statement but not to continue on — to listen to others or to listen to themselves.

To assume that single sentence responses are enough from Basic Writers is to define them, in Freire's words, as "objects" of a palliative, remedial education rather than as "subjects," that is initiators, of an education based on dialogue, on give and take. It seems that a more appropriate strategy is to acknowledge their responses (to write them on the blackboard, for example), but at the same time for a teacher to remain silent and demand a second sentence, and then a third, and then a response to the material on the board from someone else in the classroom. To do this is to explore the reasons that made such responses possible and to create in the next assignment, in the next class discussion, the opportunity to test that new understanding and to discover the difference that the application of that new understanding makes.

Reading Assignments

The course demands the active and sustained involvement of both the teachers and the students in the process of learning. But it also makes that involvement both feasible and possible.

For example, to prepare students for group discussions, and to ensure their participation, the course is structured in such a way that on the day we begin discussing the assigned text, they hand in their "journal entries" on that book. They come to class, in other words, having already worked out a point of view, something to say. They do not wait to be told what to say about a book but begin with a substantial investment in a reading that will be questioned and validated by others. Because we want them to experiment with their responses to the texts they read, we tell them not to be too concerned with correctness. We do expect, however, that the journal be a continuous sustained investigation of "Growth and Change in Adolescence" (the course's theme). For this reason, we not only require that they revise perfunctory entries, but we also make sure that each successive reading assignment raises questions that loop back to include observations made or issues raised in previous assignments or class discussions. And because we acknowledge that, at least in the beginning, their performance is still affected by their lack of practice in and appreciation of what the reading activity entails, we embed specific directions in the reading assignments themselves.

Thus, for example, in order to make students reexamine and revise the assumption that reading is passive, that in reading it is the text's function to do something to the reader, we ask them to increase their reading time to fewer and longer sittings so that they learn to concentrate and to sustain their concentration in that activity; and we direct them to take notes, as they read, to fold page corners, and to mark the text they are reading so as to pay attention and reflect on what they more readily forget and more easily remember, so as to establish and to locate specific points of connection within and among narratives.

So that students realize that all readers develop strategies to combat forgetfulness, we have found it particularly instructive to reproduce a page from one of the texts we have read and marked in preparation for our class discussion. It is helpful to ask students to reconstruct the system we have devised to reflect on the various parts of the text we have selected as places to return to, and to retrace the network of signs that traces our active participation in the reading process.

Prediscussion Exercises

We carefully prepare our students and ourselves for class discussions. Drawing on our past experiences and on our current observations about the strengths and weaknesses of the group with which we are working, we have devised a series of prediscussion exercises by means of which we both acknowledge the particular reading difficulty that they may encounter with the text we are reading, and show them how, though they might not realize it, they are capable of transcending it. During these discussions we must be prepared to be quiet and they must be prepared to speak.

On the first day we discuss a new text, we divide our students into groups of four according to the particular strengths each student can offer to the others, and we assign them an in-class exercise to direct and focus our subsequent discussion. This exercise comes in the design of the course after they have written their response to the text in the journal entry and before they get involved in the collective inquiry. (Although it might seem that these exercises ask for factual information, it will become clear that what we are interested in discussing is not only *what* they can recall, but also and especially *how* and *why* they recall what they do.)

For example, for *I Know Why the Caged Bird Sings*, we ask students (1) to name as many characters in the book as they can; (2) to list, in some order, the events that shaped Maya Angelou's life; (3) to go back to (2) and to star (*) those events, or the circumstances around those events, which they think are the most significant in their effect on her life, and to state the reasons for their evaluation.

After the students in each group have conferred and made their decisions, one of them dictates the answers to us. One teacher writes that student's answers on the blackboard and, at the same time, incorporates the other groups' additions, deletions and modifications; the other teacher makes sure that every student participates.

When the text of their response is on the blackboard, students must begin to make something of that text. We begin by asking students to reflect on the various ways in which readers *actively* remember, in fact recollect their memories of characters (by names, according to the author's physical descriptions, in clusters, by association, sequentially, by comparison) and how memories of events may or may not activate memories of characters, or how, on the other hand, the two acts of recollecting can have a mutually integrative function.

Students find these discoveries about the intricacies of the reading process "interesting," though clearly much less than we do; but by the time we get to discuss their answers to the last question, they are usually eloquently committed to defending and giving reasons for their interpretations. They drive home a point by showing the page corner they have folded, the paragraph they have marked, and by reading the passage that they have now taken as the center of the text. They take equal pleasure in adopting the language of our marginal comments to serve as critical machinery they can turn on each other.

I remember one time when our discussion of *I Know Why the Caged Bird Sings* was going nowhere. Our students' observations about the structure of the book (observations they had recently learned to make) allowed them to say only that the book was confusing and fragmentary. One student, soon aided by others, began listing various reasons why he didn't think *Caged Bird* was a "good book." There were "interesting parts followed by flat ones"; certain chapters just did not seem "to belong . . . like Brother Taylor's chapter"; he was confused by the "many places where Maya lived"; he had difficulty with the "many names [by which] Maya's Grandmother was called"; he couldn't understand Maya's reticence "to make friends"; and he couldn't make out the connections between Maya's rape (which he suggested should be taken out of the narrative), her search for a job, *and* her pregnancy.

As I was writing this list of complaints on the blackboard, I realized how those comments were an indication both of how much he knew and of how much his lack of reflexivity prevented him from appreciating how much he knew. The crucial pedagogical step, at that point, was to make him (and the other students) understand that his confusion, puzzlement, and difficulty *were* appropriate responses. The sections he could not, at first, put together marked the starting point for his active work as a reader, as a reader who had to compose a coherent account of a fragmentary text. As I was writing the list of complaints on the blackboard, I realized that each comment could serve as the starting point for our collective inquiry; but I had to choose. That day the class discussion concentrated on the role of the rape in Maya's experience. After the discussion, Doug, the student who found the book confused and confusing, revised his journal entry, acknowledging the rape as the source of confusion in Maya's life:

> Maya, when she was younger, was raped by Mr. Freeman. Maya became confused. She did not know what to do.

The rape was also, however, the reason for her precocious maturity:

> Maya was maturing. From a time she couldn't make decisions to an adult who knew what she wanted and went after it. She was now making her own decisions. She was not confused as she was when she was younger. Within weeks Maya realized that her classmates and herself were on different paths. Her schoolmates were concerned and excited over the approaching football games, while Maya had in her immediate past a race down a dark and foreign Mexican mountain. Her classmates were concentrating on who was worthy of being student body president, and when the metal bands would be removed from their teeth, while Maya remembered sleeping for a month in a wrecked automobile and conducting a streetcar in the uneven hours of the morning. . . .
> So I would say, Because of Mr Freeman, racing the car down the Mexican mountain, the recked car she slept in, the job on the streecar and all other events that Maya had gone through, Maya matured faster than any of her schoolmates.

This text represents an extraordinary revision of "opinions." What had seemed at first to this student a disconnected sequence of arbitrary events is now reconstructed as relevant examples of the protagonist's growing maturity. In his revised reading he has now reinterpreted the confusion he experienced as he read Angelou's text — not as a threat to his competence as a reader but as a challenge.

Like the writing assignments and the reading assignments the prediscussion exercises predicate that *to know* means *to understand, to interpret,* but most important *to apply* the knowledge acquired through reflexivity to new ideas, situations, contexts. For this reason, each subsequent exercise assumes that students, like the student I just wrote about, will put whatever knowledge they have acquired into practice. At the same time, each prediscussion exercise acknowledges and focuses on a particular difficulty we foresee our students may encounter as they read that particular text. For example, the nonchronological narrative technique of *Ordinary People* becomes, when students are asked to come to terms with their understanding of Conrad's problems, an opportunity to discuss and to discover how readers make meanings by reordering, restructuring, in a way rewriting, the texts they read.[8] *God's*

Helicopter, on the other hand, offers the possibility to investigate, once more, the fact that events and people do not *bear* significance in and of themselves, but are given significance in different ways by different readers.[9]

As students' oral responses become "written texts," we ask them to analyze those texts, to bring forward their possible presuppositions. (What assumptions about childhood, for example, make one student assert that Maya was responsible for Mr. Freeman's raping her? What assumptions about a child's need for a father's love, on the other hand, make another student sensitive to Maya's innocent obliviousness to Mr. Freeman's perversion? What assumptions about parents' responsibility to their children make some students so harshly judge Beth's rejection of her son's demands for love in *Ordinary People*?) According to the possibilities for understanding that such presuppositions may open up or close off, students learn to understand and revise their own reading strategies. At the same time, by "writing out" their responses — which, at first, often seem disjointed and chaotic — students see the abundance and the complexity of thoughts that the reading process can generate and the role of writing in structuring or in ordering that process.

The exercises and the assignments delineate a method which students are expected to, and eventually do, enact in their reading, writing and discussions, and which later they are expected to consistently demonstrate when they read and write, and when they are in turn given the responsibility to lead class discussions. The student who succeeds in using BRW as an opportunity to reflect about the ways in which the learner makes learning possible is the kind of student who comes closest to enacting Gadamer's view of reading as synonymous with understanding. Clearly, unlike Gadamer's ideal reader, BRW readers are not expert questioners, but the design of BRW is such that it does put students in the position to practice and to reclaim the power to initiate and maintain their own sustained inquiry.

A Student's Public Dialogue

Beginning with the third book we read, the structure of our class discussion undergoes a radical change. We assign our students (two or three each time) the role of discussion leaders, and we assume the role of recorders of what is said in the classroom. Our two sets of notes, integrated with each other so as to record as many voices as possible, and subsequently typed, become the text for the next classroom discussion. The shift of responsibility, far from being casual, has two major pedagogical goals: (1) to give students the opportunity to assess and to reflect on the potential for their questions to further the discussion, and (2) to discover the extent to which the fruitfulness of their questioning is dependent on the other discussants' willingness to be questioned and to question in return.

As an indication of the extent to which BRW students can learn to use class discussion as an incentive to further their knowledge, let me reconstruct a class discussion that took place on the ninth week of a 15-week course.

The voices we were able to record are the voices that spoke loudly enough for us to hear (we sat away from the group), and coherently enough for us to transcribe in complete sentences. The other voices — those barely audible, those unintelligible — consigned themselves to muteness. Although on that day there were two leaders of discussion, Rich and Gerard, I will focus on Gerard's questions more than on Rich's, because of the two, Gerard retained an apathetic, noncommunicative stance for a longer period of time in the course. But before I comment on Gerard's ability to "make a text speak," let me loop back to that time in the term when the consequences of Gerard's silence were evident in more than his classroom behavior.

When Gerard took our diagnostic test, his writing showed poor control of sentence boundaries, of grammar (particularly verb endings and homonyms) and above all a poor understanding of, and response to, the passage he had to read and write about. At that time Gerard, like most BRW students, could not engage in a public conversation, let alone a critical discussion about a text, be that text his own or somebody else's. Although he wrote and spoke about texts, Gerard's texts were "mute" and to a large extent they induced silence in their readers. His inability to engage in a dialogue with a text was evident even when the text he spoke about was the text of his own experience, a text which because of its familiarity, some may argue, should not have been as difficult to understand as another's text. Gerard's inability to question his text and to question himself as producer of that text is symptomatic of his inability to raise and to formulate questions about any other text, and is a clear indication of the ways in which the activities of reading and writing, both in theory and in practice, are mutually supportive and ultimately inseparable.[10]

During the second week, in response to the third *writing* assignment, Gerard had written:

> My experience in camp was great. In camp you do alot of diffrent things so you can abroaden your horizon on the world and yourself. In this paper we will talk about a few of my experiences in camp.
>
> My camp was called Gree Way Academy, in New Jersey, I was 9 years old and first time away from home. Before I wen there I was scare and ready to go back home. When I got their I unpack and after a few days got myself settled.
>
> After the family left things started to happen. Things like meeting new peoples, play games, and being to enjoy myself. Their I went swimming, I played basketball, baseball, soccer and football. We also did things like acts and crafts, talent and dances.
>
> At Green Way Academy I learned how to mix with diffrent cultures and diffrent personalities. There were older kids in which I learned alot from just by watching them. I learned how to relate to all colors, attitudes, and life styles.
>
> The memory of the few months their in camp is significant because it brought me closer to diffrent people it helps me to relate to diffrent people. Them months I'll never forget.

In the text he has written, the 19-year-old Gerard seems to have silenced the nine-year-old Gerard; had he been given a chance, had he been asked the right question, the younger boy might have "spoken," and he might have contributed to his older counterpart's understanding of what it feels like to be left behind.

Of the people at camp, the writer claims that he learned to get close to them and to relate to them "just by watching them." He gives us no idea of how that happened, because, I believe, it did not even occur to him that he should ask such questions. To argue that time and distance may be responsible for the flatness of this text is to imply that to remember is a passive act instead of an active recollection that attributes significance to the past; it is to suggest that texts distant from us in time and place will remain silent.

Had Gerard asked more fruitful questions of the text of his experience, he wouldn't have produced such a blank text about that experience. What I find particularly intriguing and

painful is the list of things done, the list of words crowded on
the page so as to fill it, so as to achieve the minimum length, as
if the *naming* of those activities could stand for the *experience*
of living them. Gerard's language — "I learned . . . just by watching them," "I learned how to . . . " — is emblematic of the learning experience it can be said to be an enactment of: a learning
experience in which the learner is told how to do certain things
and whose questions about what happens in the learning process and how that happens are not envisioned as a possibility; it
is a learning experience, in other words, which is the outcome
of a teaching method that neither questions itself nor asks productive questions of its participants.

In contrast to Gerard's remoteness from the text he had
produced earlier in the course, the text of the class discussion
bespeaks Gerard's involvement in the process of discovery. The
instructions of the prediscussion exercise were very simple and
direct: (1) list the ways in which Richard Rodriguez's experience has been totally different from your own; (2) explain the
ways in which Rodriguez's experiences have been similar to
experiences you have had. Gerard's understanding of the questions led him to give *Hunger of Memory* a voice that interprets
Rodriguez's text in terms of Rodriguez's change and the growth
that change can be said to represent.

For the first five minutes, on the day of the discussion,
Gerard was silent. Arms crossed on his chest, an impenetrable
look on his face, he watched Rich as Rich struggled to initiate
the discussion.

> RICH: How you do feel about the book?
>   (silence)
> RICH: I know it was difficult, but . . . But what did you
>   learn?
> WALTER: He [Rodriguez] did not know who he was.
> RICH: What conflict did he have?
> WALTER: At home, with his parents. He had to learn
>   English. In school he was always considered still a
>   Mexican.

Rich's first question, vague, unfocused, did not get any
response. Uneasy with the silence, he looked at me. I forced
myself to ignore his uneasiness. I wanted to help him, but even
more I wanted him to make it on his own.

With a hesitant, ingratiating smile, Rich tried to enlist the
sympathy of his fellow students: "I know it was difficult, but
. . . But. . . . " The forcefulness with which he spoke that

second "but" reminded me of the restrained impatience with which I usually respond to the comments of students who, having defined a task too difficult, abdicate their responsibility as learners too soon, too quickly.

Rich's question was again met with silence. Then, Walter's reply seemed to suggest to him a new lead: "What conflict did he have?" At the time I thought his new question did not connect at all with Walter's comment, a comment that signaled Walter's interest in Rodriguez's confusion of identities; but as I see it now, that lack of connectedness is more apparent than real; it is a lack of connectedness created by Rich's inability, at the time, to phrase his question in such a way as to make apparent to others the causal link he saw between Rodriguez's not knowing who he was and the conflicts that his ambiguity about his own identity generated in him.

Walter, however, pursuing his inquiry into Rodriguez's confusion, made Rich's question work for him and gave an answer that, as a demonstration of conflict as much as of the confusion of identity that can be the result of that conflict, actually mediates his line of inquiry with Rich's:

"At home, with his parents. He had to learn English. In school he was always considered still a Mexican."

Throughout all this, Gerard still kept silent. Rich looked at him, expecting him to begin to share the responsibility of leading the discussion, but Gerard did not move. With the exception of Walter, nobody else had spoken yet. Then Rich, repeating the pedagogical move by which his teachers had so often transformed oral discussion into written texts, turned to the blackboard, and after rephrasing his interpretation of Walter's contribution — "He was between two cultures, the Spanish and the American" — he asked a question, very deliberately addressing it to the whole class: "Which characteristics did he have of those two cultures?" He wrote in capital letters SPANISH and AMERICAN; he drew a line down the middle of the blackboard; and he turned around, chalk in hand, looking at his classmates, waiting for answers. The answers came. Lots of voices could be heard. He actually had to ask his friends to calm down, so that he could transcribe what they had to say. Pretty soon he had two lists of characteristics:

SPANISH	AMERICAN
dark complexion	education
religion	speech
environment	environment
language	language

But he no longer seemed to know what to do with them, and where to go from there.

At this point, Gerard took over as leader.

GERARD: Were these characteristics with him throughout the book? How did he feel about that change?

LISA: He had lost his intimacy with words. He had to give up the ties with his family.

GERARD: Was he close to his parents?

EARLEEN: Yes. But he later moved away. His parents could not cross over that line he had crossed over. It was difficult for him to do that. He wanted to find a way back by trying to remember what he had known.

GERARD: Has anybody ever been left out because of that change? As he went on with his education, how did that affect him as a person?

WALTER: He was confused. He did not know where to turn to. As a person he was considered a minority; but as far as he was concerned, he was not. But he was left out. I don't know. Other Mexicans spoke Spanish. He could tell who they were, but he could no longer relate to them.

GERARD: And how did that affect him socially?

Gerard's questions both look back at the text Rich has assembled on the blackboard, and move that text forward by suggesting a direction to take, that direction being the *change* and the lasting consequences that that change was to have for Richard Rodriguez.

As he pursued his inquiry — relentlessly, cogently — Gerard's successive questions became more and more clearly "directions," "assisted invitations" to expand the possibilities for discovery of the first question ("How did he feel about that change?"), which he posed again from at least three different, though mutually enriching, perspectives: the perspective of Richard Rodriguez's changed relationship to his parents ("Was he close to his parents?"), to himself ("... how did that [change] affect him as a person?"), and to others ("... how did that affect him socially?"). But his questions perhaps represented too closely his interpretation of Rodriguez's text for them to elicit the responses he was hoping for from the other students. They also did not seem to connect with either Walter's or Rich's line of inquiry.

Visibly uneasy at his colleagues' renewed unresponsiveness, Rich tried to redirect the inquiry into change from a new perspective, the perspective of faith:

> RICH: What about his faith? The change from Latin to
> English Mass — he felt it's not like Church any more.

Rich's suggestion did not produce any result until Gerard re-
phrased it in his own terms:

> GERARD: So, he really did not change completely?

The way in which Gerard both picks up Rich's new thread
("What about his faith?") and weaves it with the thread he is
following ("So, he really did not change . . . ") is a remarkable
demonstration of his absorption in his own dialogue with the
text he is examining, and of his *selective* alertness and receptiv-
ity to whatever material will forward his inquiry. But, it can be
argued, Gerard's commitment to his own inquiry is too univocal;
so much so, in fact, that it makes him impatient toward those,
like Lisa, whose comment, actually a delayed response to Rich's
question, momentarily forestalls the advancement of his exploration.

> LISA: Faith — it provided him with a place where to be
> in touch with his parents.
> GERARD: So, his faith was just a key by which he could
> open a door and be with his parents?
> LISA: Faith remained with him.

Lisa was not going to give up her skeptical reading of
Hunger of Memory. "It was so boring. Nothing really happened,"
she had said the previous day. All her interventions, like her
journal entry on this text, seemed to be meant to prove the use-
lessness of engaging with and discussing *Hunger of Memory.*
Gerard, on the other hand, who had read it as an exemplary
tale of change ("How can you say that?" he countered Lisa's
remark. "Look at how much he has changed by the end of the
book!"), and saw change as a symptom of growth, seemed to
have difficulty reconciling any kind of stability or continuity
with change. Or so I thought. And, fortunately, I was quite
wrong.

In what at the time I considered an escapist move on his
part, Gerard, after a brief silence, turned again to Lisa and asked
her:

> GERARD: How about his complexion? How did he feel
> about it?

It seemed ironic to me, then, that he should choose to discuss Rodriguez's complexion, that complexion that after all is

the indelible sign of continuity between him and his parents. What I did not realize was that, beginning with his question: "So, he really did not change *completely*?" he had begun to discover a way of mediating change and continuity. The question about Rodriguez's complexion followed logically from there. Rodriguez's change, his radical change, invisible — especially to Lisa — was represented by his acceptance (perhaps even exploitation) of his color.

Lisa's answer disoriented him: "He really never was a minority. . . . " It was with intense frustration that he turned her comment back to her: "What is a minority?" And her answer, seemingly sophisticated, actually only glib, "A word," he refused to dignify as an answer. Leaning toward her, his hands grasping the end of the table, he said: "The question still stands. What is a minority?"

But Lisa was already packing her books. And so were a few other students. The class was over.

As I reread this script and recollect that particular experience, I am reminded of Rich's and Gerard's absorption in the discussion. Whether or not they were conscious of what they were doing, they chose two different but mutually supporting roles as discussion leaders; and whenever necessary they shifted roles, just as they had observed their teachers do throughout the term.

It was obvious that to be the leaders of the discussion did matter to them; and it was equally obvious that they were going to make it matter to others. I remember my surprise when Rich used the blackboard, exactly when I would have used it, to focus the discussion and to keep it going. I remember my initial unease when Gerard kept rephrasing his questions, and my fear that he might be mimicking me, and my relief when I realized that, if he was indeed mimicking me, he was doing it so well that he had turned the game into an effective pedagogical strategy. And I also remember my frustration at having decided to become less conspicuous as a teacher, since it prevented me from pressuring them further, from questioning their questions so as to help them make their inquiry even more effective.

As a concluding remark on Gerard's growth, I want to reproduce here the first paragraph of his journal entry on *Hunger of Memory*, a text which he had clearly learned how to read; a difficult text with which he had begun a private dialogue that made possible the public dialogue he later generated in the classroom:

>The first chapter of *Hunger of Memory* is "Aria." I don't know what the title means but if I go by what he says in the chapter, I may be able to guess.
>
>The first chapter gets into the difficulty that he was having with school and his parents. Rodriguez was not doing very well in school because he couldn't understand English. When one of the teachers came to his house and asked his parents to speak English with him, they did this so he could cope with the American society better. After this he started to improve. . . .
>
>From what I can understand from the first chapter, "Aria" might mean a change of culture.

Gerard's reading strategy ("I don't know what the title means but if I go by what he says in the chapter, I may be able to guess) echoes Gadamer's description of the act of understanding:

>The understanding of a text has not begun at all as long as the text remains mute. . . . One must take up into himself what is said to him in such fashion that it speaks and finds an answer in the words of his own language.

I want to point out, however, that in the classroom discussion, the very voice that bespeaks Gerard's understanding of the text, the voice that traces his involvement in the process of discovery, occasionally tends to silence other voices and to prevent them from questioning and counterquestioning that understanding.

Considering Gerard's initial apathetic stance, for a teacher to suggest that his assertiveness might actually preclude further knowledge may seem inopportune, even arbitrary. Not to do so, however, might mean to designate Gadamer's first phase of the hermeneutic process as the end rather than the beginning of this student's inquiry and ultimately to set up arbitrary and condescending limits to how much a BRW student can learn.

Notes

[1] Here, in the metaphor of educational dialogue, as elsewhere in my paper, I am indebted to Paulo Freire's work. See particularly *Pedagogy of the Oppressed* (New York: Seabury, 1974) and *Education: The Practice of Freedom* (London: Writers and Readers Publishing Cooperative, 1976).

[2] The numbers and the text of the assignments I will be referring to come from Marilyn DeMario's and my revision of the assign-

ments the last time we taught BRW. They do not correspond exactly to the number and the text of the assignments in the book.

3 Hans-Georg Gadamer, *Truth and Method: Parts I and II* (New York: Continuum, 1975), and *Philosophical Hermeneutics* (Berkeley: U of California P, 1976) 3–94.

4 The phrase "assisted invitations" comes from I. A. Richards but through Ann E. Berthoff. See Ann E. Berthoff, *Forming/Thinking/Writing* (Upper Montclair, NJ: Boynton/Cook, 1978); *The Making of Meaning* (Upper Montclair, NJ: Boynton/Cook, 1981); and "I. A. Richards," *Traditions of Inquiry*, ed. John Brereton (New York: Oxford UP, 1985) 50–80.

5 This assignment is Marilyn DeMario's contribution to the course.

6 In addition to the 25 essays (which include seven or eight in-class exams), BRW students write six journal entries on the assigned books (*I Know Why the Caged Bird Sings, Ordinary People, God's Helicopter, Hunger of Memory, Normal Adolescence, Passages*) and four on books they choose.

7 Mariolina Salvatori, "The Teaching of Writing as 'Problematization,'" *California Education Quarterly* 10 (1983): 38–57.

8 To encourage students to construct a meaningful and coherent interpretation out of the nonlinear narrative structure of *Ordinary People*, the prediscussion exercise asks them (1) to name as many characters in the book as they can; (2) to list as many events in the book as they can and to number them according to the way they occur in the narrative; (3) to go back to (2) and group those events in a way that is meaningful to them, and then to devise and name at least three categories for those events.

9 This is the prediscussion exercise for *God's Helicopter:*
We all know that the three main characters in *God's Helicopter* are _____, _____, and _____.

1. Under each character's name, list the names of the characters you closely associate with each of them.

2. As you look back at the list you have constructed, you will notice that some characters appear in each of the three lists, yet those characters have not necessarily influenced the three main characters in the same way or to the same extent. Go back to the list and underline or circle the characters that seem most important for each of the three boys.

3. To what extent does the personality of each of the three boys explain why some characters are more important for one than for the other(s)?

10 For a similar discussion of another student reader/writer, see my "Reading and Writing a Text: Correlations Between Reading and Writing Patterns." *College English* 45 (1983): 657–666.

6.

Empowering Revision

NICHOLAS COLES

Basic Writers, notoriously, do not like to revise. Indeed recent research comparing the composing processes of inexperienced and experienced writers suggests that the willingness to write multiple drafts and to make major changes while composing them could be taken as an index of a writer's maturity.[1] Some inexperienced writers apparently see no need for revision; they believe in inspiration: their one-draft wonder has spontaneity and truth-to-feeling, and to change it would be falsification.[2] Others look on their papers as something over and done with, an assignment completed and turned in for a grade — there is another one due next week. Those whose teachers have specifically asked for revision may have come to see the request as evidence that the first draft was a mistake and as confirmation that revision itself is a form of punishment — especially when it has been assigned as extra work.

Such rewriting as they can be persuaded to undertake typically consists of changes at the level of the sentence or smaller and principally in vocabulary, the kinds of changes Lester Faigley and Stephen Witte classify as "meaning-preserving."[3] Believing, as Nancy Sommers suggests, that "the meaning to be communicated is already there . . . and all that is necessary is a better word, 'rightly worded,'" these students are unable to imagine using revision in the way many professional writers do: as part of the ongoing process of invention — that is, as a technique for *producing* meaning.[4] Much of their writing experience, in fact, will have come in forms which inhibit discovery drafting and major rewriting — the carefully outlined five-paragraph theme, the exam-style in-class essay, the book report. What these inexperienced writers may never have experienced, in other words, is any authentic reason for engaging in an activity so painstaking and time consuming as revision. They may never have been provided with a context in which they could use revision as I believe most of us use it, to get further into a subject we care about.

I want to suggest here that a semester-long sequence of assignments on a topic students know something about can provide such a context, and I want to demonstrate how, within that context, teachers and students can together foster the habits and methods of revision.

The Basic Reading and Writing classroom, in which writing is subject to discussion and response by 15 students and (usually) two teachers, offers a rhetorical context in many ways like that in which we ourselves work. For we feel our writing to be addressed to a community, however loosely defined and internally divided, of scholars, teachers and fellow writers, whose own work and whose responses to our work challenge, sharpen and affirm what we do. So too students in BRW are members of a group of people with common life experiences and a shared project of exploring and researching them through writing. They constitute for one another not only an "audience" to be "considered," but in a real sense a community of writers — a community based on commonality of experience and also on respect for one another's work with language.

There is another way in which we can look to our own practice as writers, and our own reasons for revising, to identify what it is we would offer our students as the value of the activity. The growing number of case studies of experienced writers at work suggests that we perform revision not only in a rhetorical context but in what, borrowing from Kenneth Dowst, we might call an "epistemic" context.[5] We use it, that is, as a means for generating knowledge within our field of study. Revisions for us represent stages in the ongoing process of working out what we know and what we can say about the subject that engages us, a subject, moreover, which may engage us for weeks, months or years. Student writers do not usually have the kind of long-term commitment to a project that keeps us going, reformulating our ideas as we recompose them. But a semester-long sequence of assignments on a topic of primary concern to them offers an approximation of the experience of sustained immersion in inquiry which gives our rewriting its meaning and its context.[6]

The subjects about which students in BRW write and read — "adolescence" for the day-school undergraduates and "working" for continuing students — are chosen because they represent matters about which our students already possess a wealth of information in the forms of direct experiences, observations and memories. Throughout the semester, the assignments lead them to explore this information from varying perspectives, transforming it by degrees into what we can recognize as the data and concepts of a discipline.

The direction of the assignment sequence corresponds roughly to James Moffett's hierarchy of abstraction, in that we move through narratives of personal experience to generalization and theory-building.[7] Many earlier assignments begin with stories students can tell about significant events in their adolescence or at work, while later assignments are transactional in that they ask students to respond to the language of other writers, in and out of class, on the issues of the course. But this abstractive formulation is too simple, for the sequence is not a one-way progress through levels of discourse. The assignments are, rather, persistently recursive, looping back to reengage previous reading or discussion, reviewing experience written about earlier in light of fresh theorizing. The cycle of abstraction, in fact, is rehearsed in assignment after assignment, "in a movement of thought" which, in Vygotsky's terms, "constantly alternates between two directions, from the particular to the general, and from the general to the particular."[8] Assignments foster this movement by calling not only for a single task, such as a story about a specific incident, but also for reflection on the meaning for the writer of the story he has written: what could he be said to have learned from it that would contribute to our understanding of our subject?[9] The sequence, then, enacts writing and rewriting as a way of knowing one's own knowledge (in Josephine Miles' phrase), and it is from the vantage point of the achievement of that kind of disciplined self-awareness that I believe revision, as a means of getting there, can be said to be worth the trouble.

There is a sense in which assignments sequenced in this way are all revisions of one another. Students are asked to reconsider papers they have already written, perhaps to compare or combine the conclusions they came to there with what they now have to say. Occasionally, as when they turn to treating their autobiographies as "case studies," they may find themselves quoting and commenting on their own words from earlier papers. But this "sequential revision," as we might call it, while it provides the necessary general context of a continuous review of ideas, is not itself the same activity as textual revision. It doesn't teach the same skills, nor offer the same local opportunities for meaning making, as does the thorough rewriting of an achieved text.

In textual revision the writer confronts problems — of the sense he makes or fails to make, sentence to sentence — which can be avoided when he just moves on to the next assignment. But he confronts them with the reviser's advantage that he no longer has to invent the whole discourse of the paper; he has the relative luxury of being able to look closely at fragments, to focus on one issue at a time, pretending temporarily that other complications don't exist. Yet the rest of the paper will still be there when he is ready for it. And this luxury of knowing that he can make changes later releases some of the anxiety governing the first draft: he doesn't have to imagine that what he is writing now — with all its vagueness, chattiness, evasions, missed connections, *non sequiturs* — is what he will end up with. He learns to trust the revision process to get him eventually to a product he can be satisfied with, for now. To teach this process, the numbered sequence includes assignments which call specifically for revision of the previous paper; that is to say, time and space are allotted for textual revision within the sequence, and students are therefore expected to devote as much time and energy to their revisions as to their initial drafts.

The sequence of assignments, I have been arguing, allows students to work as we do in the sense that it provides an overarching direction and purpose to the writer's activity; it proceeds by stages which complicate and advance students' knowledge of their subject, their changing sense of the shape of it, the important issues within it, and the abstractions they can formulate about it. Those pairs of assignments which specifically call for revision give students the further opportunity of composing, as many of us do, in successive drafts: generating a paper without worrying too much about how it sounds, getting it correct, and seeing what goes with what; and then rereading and re-seeing what they have there in order to develop it.[10] But this re-seeing, which we may take for granted assuming our students can see what we see happening in their papers, is of course a habit that will need to be taught, and we have at least two methods for this: in-class reading and discussion of first drafts, and teacher commentary, either written or offered in personal conferences. I will take these in turn, looking first at a paper revised primarily in response to class discussion and then at one guided by my written comments.

Class Discussions

Discussion of papers in a workshop setting offers the general incentive for revision, described by Susan Wall and Anthony Petrosky, that "a writer writing for a specific context and an immediate audience often has an opportunity to discover first-hand that what he said did not produce the imagined effect on the audience, or that what others observed does not correspond to what he feels he said."[11] The writer can then direct his revision to both intentional and rhetorical matters: Did he say what he meant? How could he say it so that they would understand it as he does? But an audience of peers who are working on the same sequence of assignments also comes to a fellow writer's paper with a special kind of interest — a shared preoccupation with a common set of issues which keys and enriches their reading. They can offer not only "feedback" and judgment, but informed response and support, including other possible interpretations of what the writer has described, other possible conclusions to be drawn from the story he has told. The students are functioning, in fact, as a form of scholarly community, a community which is in part generated out of their discussion of one another's papers.

The following paper was written by a student I will call Eric in a section of BRW designed for continuing adult students. The theme of the course was "working," and this particular assignment was the second of a linked pair of assignments which asked students to describe incidents of, first, paid and then, unpaid (usually volunteer) work, and to use these stories as the basis for some tentative generalizations about the kind of worker they see themselves to be and about their relationship to work. Here is Eric's first draft:

[Assignment 4 (first draft)]

[1] Everybody does unpaid work everyday of one's life. It all depends on what you call work. The work you get paid for, your livelihood depends on it. The work you don't get paid for is that of your own choosing whether you work for yourself or someone else. But to me, I wouldn't call it unpaid work, I call it helping your neighbor. For instance last summer, a neighbor and also a very good friend of mine, his plumbing was bad and had to be replaced. It would be very costly to hire someone to dig up the yard ten feet deep and about sixty feet long especially when you don't have the money. The interesting part about this was he wasn't able to take part in any of

the digging or cementing, its not that he didn't want to help. But he had a very good reason.

[2] The following week he was to be operated on for a hernia he suffered at work. So his uncle and his two sons and his brother-in-law were going to help replaced the bad underground plumbing from his back porch to the city street which was about sixty feet in all. The City wasn't responsible for property which you own but if your plumbing ran into the street which the city owns it would be responsible for that. Once I heard they (his uncle and uncle & two sons) were going to start digging, I went over and ask them if they needed a hand, which they were only more than too gladly to hand me a shovel which I accepted. The hardest part in digging was we had to dig six feet under the porch and house which was on a slant, which made it narrow and difficult, because the shovel wouldn't fit.

[3] We also had to overcome a lot of difficulties. The side of the house had to be replaced also which was just as narrow, cause the two houses were only four feet apart, Which made it difficult to dig cause the dirt wall would fall back down the hole so we had to wheel-barrel it down the yard and dump it. We only had to dig down five feet to meet the decayed pipe which wasn't too deep, it was twenty feet long, though. Then we dug fifteen alongside the porch also about five foot deep. But then came the hard part, Even though his uncle had dug up back yards before, for the same thing. This time it wasn't that easy cause we had to intersect two pipes down at least ten feet, but we dug the wrong path. After we got on the right path we discover other pipes that didn't belong, it was because the previous plumber who work on it thirty years ago put in some mickey mouse pipes that didn't belong.

[4] Then after we got all the pipes all dugged out The weather didn't cooperate with us, it rain for two or three days and transform the yard into a swimming hole. So after we waited for it to dry up a little, we started to dig again only to have it collapse almost on us while we were in the hole ten feet down. This was about two weeks after we started that we finally got the pipes layed in and covered up, for at least another half century. If the digging wasn't bad enough then came the laying of the cement.

[5] It was like quicksand, we were knee deep in it and trying to race against time, before the cement had a chance to dry and set. The truck that delivered the cement

gave us twice as much as we needed. He delivered the cement from the top of the hallway and filled it all the way down til the bottom. Then we had to rake it down to the backyard along the porch and down towards the alley, we didn't want to cement the whole yard just enough for a walkway a half a side walk. We filled two or three small dump truck loads that we didn't need and gave it to another neighbor down the street who could use the cement around his swimming pool, which took away a couple of our helpers because we still had to finish smoothing out the cement, then a couple of neighbors across the street came over to give us a hand, It was starting to get hard so we had to wet it down, which your not suppose to do to cement, but that was our only alternative.

[6] We had gotten the cement at 4.30 in the afternoon and since most of us had other regular jobs, that we didn't get off until 5 o'clock, but his uncle's sons were there to recieve the shipment of cement but couldn't do much until the others got off work. It was close to 10.30 at night before we call it quits. What I didn't know at the time was you aren't suppose to get your hands and body in wet cement too long, but it was already too late cause I've already been kneeling on my hands and knees for two and a half hours trying to smooth the cement out. I found out the next morning my hands and knees were both raw and chap with cement dirt still sticking to my knees and wouldn't come off until a week later.

[7] I would have to say it was a memorable experience that I learn alot from, not only from plumbing, digging, cementing but because it turn out to be a block effort of the neighbors helping together. I think mostly because to put in a regular shift at a job for 8 hours and then come home and work another shift.

[8] But what meant the most to me is that I was apart of it, a group effort for a good cause, in helping out a neighbor. It made me feel good, I only wish it would happen more often.

Revision Activities

I wanted to use this paper to talk with the class about two interrelated revision activities which are basic to the early part of the course: reshaping a narrative so that it provides a substantial basis for generalizations; and, conversely, forming those generalizations within the specific context of a particular story. I chose Eric's paper because in his effort to be as detailed as possible, he had clearly gone overboard and had not yet found any principle of selection for shaping his story. By the same token, however, his attempt to tell us everything showed, I felt, that what happened was important to him and that he cared about our being able to appreciate it. His brief concluding gesture about "helping your neighbor," repeating dutifully the formulation he began with, is also symptomatic of first drafts at this stage of the term, an instance of the Basic Writer's tendency, when confronted with the formidable task of forming a general interpretation of what they have just been saying, to fall back on the ready-made languages of cultural convention. And yet, a formula like "helping your neighbor" could serve to provide some safe ground from which to explore the unanticipated meanings of an experience like Eric's — something he in fact started to do when he wrote, "I think mostly because . . . " But this attempt became a syntactic fragment and was abandoned in favor of the slogan "a group effort for a good cause." If this "conclusion" was evidence that the writer had not gotten far in conceptualizing his experience, the density of detail in the narrative augured well, I thought, for his doing so on revision.

   The class's laughter at the last line ("I only wish it would happen more often") when I read the paper aloud was probably as instructive for Eric as anything that was said in helping him see the disparity of tone and feeling between his narrative, essentially a chapter of accidents, and his upbeat conclusion.[12]

   "What's so funny?" I asked.

   "This ending, how he wants to do it more often. How many times a week does he want to go through this kind of hassle? I mean, I know he says it's for helping your neighbor and all, but . . ."

   " . . . you're not convinced?"

   "Well, if it was me, I'd just be glad it was over."

   "So even though he says it felt good, because it was a group effort, and so on . . . ?"

   "Right, he says it, but he doesn't prove it. You know, he just sticks it in there."

   "I agree with Joe," says Michelle. "It's one of those stuck-on conclusions, where you've got to say *some*thing. . . ."

   "Maybe. Notice he even starts it that way: 'I would have to say it was a memorable experience. . . .' That's like, 'Well, if I'm forced to say something about this . . . '"

"And these paragraphs at the end here are real short compared to the rest of the paper," Michelle adds. "Maybe he just got tired after writing all that about laying the pipe. That's all he had energy for."

"I think you're being too hard on the guy. He says right at the beginning it's about helping your neighbor. That's the whole reason why he did this, and that's what he sticks to at the end."

"Yes he does. And is that what you admire in a conclusion, Walter, when it sticks to what the writer said in the introduction?"

"I don't know. I'm just saying he's . . . the ending's not just stuck on out of nowhere."

"But it doesn't fit with the rest of the story," Michelle insists.

"OK, we need some examples of text to work with here. What part of the story doesn't fit with the conclusion? Michelle?"

"The part about the wet cement, it doesn't relate to how it's a good cause and a group effort and everything. It just deals with *him* and the hassle he went through getting his knees torn up. . . . I just don't see this being about how it feels helping your neighbor — more about laying pipe, or cement."

"What title might you give this paper, then? What would you call it to show what you see it being about?"

"How to — or how not to lay cement."

"How about 'Mud, Sweat and Tears'?" says Shannon.

"Not 'Helping your Neighbor'?"

"Well, it could be, but you'd have to change it around."

"Change what exactly?"

"The story. He should have told more how he felt about it, doing work for a neighbor and not getting paid for it. He could put more feeling into it. I wrote about something like this — I have this neighbor who's blind that I cut her lawn for her — and it's a drag sometimes but it's the feeling you get inside. And I don't feel that here, the way he told the story."

"OK. Before we look more closely at the story itself, I'd like to get clear about the problem we're having with this conclusion. Is it that it's too short, 'stuck on,' a string of clichés about 'group effort' and so on? Or is it that it's not a fitting conclusion to the story the way he told it?"

"It's both. I mean maybe it's short because he didn't know what to say. Because the way his story turned out, it's not about group effort and how good it feels and all that. . . . At least, how I see it."

"What did it turn out to be about, mainly? And I should say that I'm assuming maybe he had to tell the story one time, this way, before he could *know* how he felt about it, or how to say it anyway. So . . . now that he's written it, what has he got, a story about what, as far as you're concerned — leaving aside for the moment what he tells you in the conclusion? Look back over it and see what stands out for you."

"It's like what Shannon said before, 'Mud, Sweat and Tears.' I see mainly how hard the work was he had to do."

"Where are you?"

"At the end of paragraph two and the next paragraph. He says how hard it was three times at least, about the digging and the bad plumbing. And then he goes on, 'If the digging wasn't bad enough . . . ,' and into the cement story. Every thing goes wrong that could go wrong."

"Maybe his point is," says Eric (whose name has been left off the dittoed paper and who has chosen not to identify himself as its author), "they had all these difficulties but they *overcame* them, like it says at the start of that paragraph. It was real hard but they dealt with it by working together."

"Where do you see the working together aspect?"

"Well, it's mainly in the conclusion, which is kind of thin. But he does say the neighbors came over to help with the cement. That's the group effort."

"So you don't see the same problem as Michelle, that the story doesn't quite lead up to . . . "

"Yes, I do think he needs to deal more with the neighbors, his relationship with them. Less about just himself, the things he did, and more about them working together."

"OK, so we're agreed that what this paper needs is not just extending the conclusion or making it fit with the story. You'd want to change the story around too, to rethink what it's a story about really, what the writer wants it to emphasize. And that's his choice, as the writer, and his responsibility. These are the kinds of large decisions you have to make in revising, about what you are going to make the experience mean, what *kind* of experience this story represents. Let's get back to the story as we have it here for a minute. How did you respond to it as a story?"

"How do you mean 'respond. . .'?"

"I mean, what do you notice about it, about the way it's written?"

"It seemed like it rambled a lot, to me. I mean, it kept my interest — you felt like you were there and everything. But, I had trouble with the way he rambles on. He could have said it simpler, get to the point."

"Do you have a section that would show rambling?"

"Like in the third paragraph, 'The side of the house had to be replaced also which was just as narrow, cause the two houses were only four feet apart, which made it difficult to dig cause the dirt wall would fall back down the hole so we had to wheel-barrow it down the yard and dump it.' It's all one big sentence, just stringing it all together, all those details."

"That confused me too," Sue agrees. "I think there was too much emphasized on the location. Because if you don't know what this house looks like, and the porch and everything, you don't really know what he's talking about."

"Where do you get confused exactly?"

"In that same paragraph, the third one, where he's giving all the measurements, 'four feet'... 'twenty feet'... 'five foot deep.'"

"I didn't have any problem with that," says Philip. "I mean, he's showing you what the house looked like, and the dimensions of the yard and everything they had to do. I thought he did a good job on that, so you could see it like he did. I've done this kind of work, on my mother's house. It's a great de-scription, digging the mud out and having it fall back on you, all the stuff you have to put up with. And you need to know how narrow the space is they had to work in. What can I say, I like how it is."

"So the details work for you? Is it that he's trying to re-construct the whole scene, to help us imagine it?"

"But he drags it out too much," says Shannon. "He gets bogged down in all these details. . . . Maybe it's impossible."

"What's impossible?"

"To tell the whole story, with the location and everything that happened."

"He gives it a pretty good shot."

"Yeah," says Philip, "I still don't see your problem with it. The way it is here, that's the way it happened. I mean, what do you want him to do? Because he was there, you know, and we weren't. So he's got to tell it the way he sees it, the way it happened. It wouldn't be true if he started changing it around."

Representation and Interpretation

At this point we were up against a common and inhibiting assumption of basic writers — that telling a story is a matter of

literally reconstructing history and that there is only one faith-
ful way to tell it. Philip's articulation of this assumption gave
me a chance to call it into question and to raise the issues of
representation and interpretation, and their inescapability in
storytelling. I wanted Philip and the class to begin to see that
what Eric had provided was not the experience itself but a representation of it, that "what had actually happened" was now
past and gone and recoverable only through a form of fiction —
of reinventing and remembering the experience. I wanted to
suggest also that the events — the "facts" as we had mercifully
not yet called them — can't help but be represented from a
particular shaping perspective, the point of view not simply of
"the writer himself" but of the writer at different times in his
life and at different stages of composition. The process we call
drawing conclusions or telling what this experience "meant" to
the writer will be in part a process of identifying and clarifying
the perspective which is implicit in the composition of the details of "what happened." My hope obviously was that the idea
of writers choosing how they will represent their experience
and what they will make it mean would be worth more to my
students than the illusion of essential truth-to-experience —
that they would be willing, in Moffett's terms, "to trade a loss
of reality for a gain in control." [13]

"OK, here's a question for you as writers of stories. It's
Shannon's question really: Is it *possible* to tell the 'whole
story'?"

"Everything that happened? You'd go crazy. And anyway
you can't remember it all."

"Well, this writer's remembered quite a lot. Should you
just write down everything you remember, then?"

"Not everything. . . ."

"So, if you can't tell everything, can't tell the whole truth
and nothing but the truth, what can you do?"

"Tell part of it, I guess."

"Which part?"

"You have to decide, the writer."

"How will you decide?"

"What's important . . . what's most significant to you?"

"That sounds right, but how will you recognize it? What
would you see as most significant for the writer in this paper?"

"The way he feels about helping his neighbor. That's the
strongest part for me. Because I know you can put up with anything when it's for a good cause like this."

"How can you tell that's most significant to him?"

"Well, I don't know if it's *most* significant. But it's what I mostly see in the story."

"Where?"

"Well, like where he says, 'I asked if they needed a hand . . . and they were only too glad to accept.' That's the feeling he's getting into, the kind of satisfaction you feel when you volunteer for something, versus the frustration he might have with his paid job . . . if it's anything like mine. I know that's what I want to get into more in my paper."

"OK. And what else seems significant to the writer from the way he tells this story?"

"What we just talked about: how hard it was, his struggles with the mud and cement, the 'mud, sweat and tears.' That's the main feeling I got. That's what he talks most about, for like four whole pages."

"All right. This again is part of your option as a writer, especially in revising your narratives. You're going to be selecting the parts and the details that will help show what was most significant to you. Essentially you're choosing which version of the story to tell, and that'll be the version which will help us understand what this experience meant to you — or means to you, I should say, because of course what it meant to you when it happened may be different from what you saw in it when you wrote your first draft, and that meaning may change more with all the thought you'll be giving it as you revise."

The revision assignment is typical of BRW in that it calls for a reworking of the first draft (Assignment 4) and for reconsideration of the issues raised in that assignment from a new perspective — in this case, a comparison of the values of paid and unpaid work:

[Assignment 5]

For this assignment, we'd like you to revise the paper you wrote in response to Assignment 4, the paper in which you told about a time when you did work for which you were not paid.

Like the revision you did for paper three, this revision is a chance to rework your narrative (the story part) into a form that is as full and informative as it needs to be for a reader to understand what you're trying to say. This may mean adding more information, or perhaps cutting factual material that doesn't seem to contribute much to the paper's point. This may mean providing more explanation of your motives (why you did or thought something), which means you may need to reconsider just what you did think and feel, both during and after this experience. Or this revision may mean doing some rearranging of the order in which you say things in your paper. These are all ways in which writers make more sense out of what they have written, both for themselves and their other readers.

We are also, however, asking you to do something different with the final section of your paper than we've asked in any previous assignment. This time we want you to create a longer conclusion that will compare and contrast what you say about your experiences with paid and unpaid work. First, read back over what you wrote in papers three and four. Then write responses to the following questions:

When you contrast what you can say about paid work with what you can say about unpaid work, what important differences do you see? How, that is, do these two kinds of work have different meanings for you?

When you compare what you can say about paid and unpaid work, in what ways can you draw similar conclusions? How, that is, can you group paid and unpaid work together, judging from your own experience?

Finally, what can you say now about your relationship to work and about what "work" means to you?

Take some time with these conclusions. They are a chance to discover how you think. Give at least a page or more to this concluding part of your revised paper.[14]

Eric's paper on this assignment was also dittoed and handed out to the class. We do this because discussion of drafts and their revisions not only trains the process of rereading and re-seeing which leads to rewriting, it also offers everyone in class a vision of transformation, of the gain in meaning, control and self-awareness which is possible for them also in revision. Here is Eric's revised draft:

[Assignment 5 (revision)]

[1] Everybody does unpaid work everyday of one's life. It all depends on what you call work. The work you get paid for, your livelihood depends on it. The work you choose not to get paid for is your decision, whether your working for yourself or someone else. I wouldn't call my unpaid work, work, I rather call it helping out your neighbor.

[2] For instance last summer a neighbor who's also a very good friend of mine was caught in a jam. His sense of timing was off, everything seem to happen at the wrong time and all at once. His underground plumbing had to be replaced and he was also scheduled to go into the hospital the following week. The only good thing for him was he didn't have to take part in the digging, not that he didn't want to, he said laughing. I heard his uncle and two cousins and a brother-in-law were looking for some help, so I volunteered my services. They were only more than happy to hand me a shovel when I showed up. Before I could even say a word, I was in the shallow hole they've already dug.

[3] In no time it was twice the size and they literally had to pull me out for a breather because I didn't want to stop. I was really pumping away, huffing and puffing, the sweat was pouring down my face. I just got into it, I didn't want to stop. So I took a break and that ice tea really hit the spot after, working up a sweat, I almost forgot what it was like, because I haven't work out that hard in quite awhile, but it sure felt good. It was tiring, especially after putting in eight hours.

[4] This might seem crazy, but I like physical work. I think it's better than sitting down in some office for eight hours, because I would be bored to death. But physical work is demanding, tough, hard work, it consumes you, you have to bust, you have to give it everything you've got. There isn't no time for bullshitting, you got to concentrate on what you're doing. There was no question about it, it wasn't going to be a piece of cake, we had to put up with quite a few setbacks. One thing, the weather didn't cooperate with us. It rained two or three days off and on, filling up the yard and converting it into a swimming hole. That took a couple days before we started again and it still wasn't completely dry.

[5] Because the deeper we dug the muddier it got which was like working in muck. But we took turns alternated two in and two out because the mud was sticking to your shovel and you would be lifting over your head which was tiring, plus doing double work when it fell back down. So the two people above would scrape your shovel and clear it, because we were running out of space to throw the dirt.

[6] It was a group effort and if you were too tired to work one day it was understood, because after all we

all had day jobs too. We also had to put up with a cave in and then the cementing hassle of running out of time before the cement had a chance to set. We didn't panic though, we stuck together and work through it. Most of those nights we work with the aid of a spotlight, so we wouldn't be able to see our finished product until the next day. The only thing unprofessional about our work was we didn't have the companies stamp of approval. But our footprints had a better impression.

[7] During those three weeks of working together I learned a lot about plumbing, digging, laying pipes, cementing, but most of all the other neighbors down the street, his uncle's cousins and neighbors across the street. It's not that I didn't know them or talked to them before. It's more than a Hi and saying hello now, you felt more closer and got to hear them talk about their lives, their day jobs, and compared them to yours. You could hear their voices with concern, that they really meant it and cared. I just wished it could happen more often. . . .

I read just this much to the class, stopping here to look at the textual revisions of the earlier draft, before going on to the extensive reflections on paid and unpaid work which this revision made possible.

The class had no trouble seeing what had changed — the deep cuts in some sections of narrative, the condensation of others — but they were not agreed as to whether these changes improved the paper. Philip, who had dissented from the class consensus on the first draft, maintained his stance. He regretted the loss of details such as the neighbor's hernia operation:

"That was important to know, that he had a hernia and that's why he couldn't dig. I mean, it sounds to me like he cut away too much, a lot of the best stuff too . . . like when they nearly got buried in the hole when the mud caved in. I thought that was interesting, and he doesn't tell you the cement story either. I have to say I thought his first paper was more interesting than this, with better details."

"What does it matter whether he had a hernia or arthritis or what he had?" Sue wanted to know. "The main thing was he couldn't do the job himself, so that's where the neighbors come in."

"Well, those of you who do feel this is an improvement, how would you demonstrate it to Philip? Is it just a matter of leaving things out, condensing details? What else has changed?"

"No, it's the way he tells you, you know, how he related to the work, how he jumped into the hole and they had to pull him out for a breather. That wasn't in it before."

As discussion moved from the more obvious cuts to the many small additions of significant detail — the iced tea, the spotlight, the footprints were all admired — it became clear that these changes were more than mechanical (deletions, additions, condensations), that they represented not only "improvement" in fluency and coherence, but a broad shift of emphasis. In place of an attempt to "cover" the entire event, we were now seeing a rigorous subordination of detail not merely to "feeling," which we had all wanted more of (as if it were an ingredient to be added according to taste), but to a purposeful exploration of "how he related to the work." Connie described the direction of this shift in terms of a change of pronouns: "The first draft he did, he was only talking about all that *he* had done, not relating it in general to what people can do, by working together. Because as far as when he said 'I,' it seemed like he was struggling through the whole thing, but when he changed to 'we' then it came easier, by them working together."

Another element in Eric's recasting his paper was that whereas "group effort," "helping your neighbor" and "feeling good" had served before as conventional labels he had fallen back on to round out his first draft, he had now begun to appropriate them to his own purposes in this act of writing. They were no longer confined to those ghettoes of conventional wisdom, the introduction and conclusion, but were now at large and at work in the paper explaining and organizing the details Eric had selected to represent his experience. We noted, for example, how in paragraphs 5 and 6 his description of their system for dealing with the mud — "we took turns alternated two in and two out" — gave definition to the general label "group effort," which in turn introduced the mutuality of "if you were too tired to work one day it was understood. . . . " One result of this prior generalizing is that when Eric comes to define the outcome of this communal work in paragraph 7, he now has something to say which we can recognize as his own general reflection on his particular experience. We noticed, however, that he ended as before: "I just wish it could happen more often."

"You've heard that before, right? That was his last line in the first draft and we thought it was funny. Why not now? What's different here?"

"Because he set it up. You know why he'd want to do it again, for that good feeling of helping your neighbor."

"I'm thinking it's more than *helping* your neighbors," Sue says. "It's them working together, like Connie said, all the neighbors together. He's gone beyond what he said before. He's talking about the *feeling* of the neighborhood. 'Their voices with concern' and that."

"Yes, it's as if he is almost creating a neighborhood, a real community, byt working with the others on a common project. Notice by the way what he did here as a reviser: he kept a line that he liked, or that seemed true for him even though it was a bit absurd in the context of the last paper. But he didn't just cut it because it didn't come up right last time. He made it make sense, by 'setting it up,' as Walter said, by giving it a context where it could sum up how good it felt. And I like your notion, Sue, that he 'goes beyond' his old idea of 'helping your neighbor,' which is really a bit of a cliché, something anyone could say. He uses revision, then, to go beyond where he got to in the first draft. Is there anywhere else that you see him going beyond formulations from his paper 4? Anything new here that adds to the sense of what it meant to him to do this work? Anything that we could say he's discovered as a result of writing up this experience? Anything that surprised you?"

"Where he talks about how he likes physical work. That was different. He really gets excited about it."

We read over paragraph 4 again. "What's he doing here?"

"It's like he's letting you know why he would do this. I mean what's in it for him, his motivation for himself, that he gets a real workout. I know that feeling, when you're just pumping away. You can really get high on it."

"You mean it's not all for the sake of the neighbors, all this effort, or for the neighborhood? Not only the 'we' Connie was talking about, but an 'I' as well . . . ?"

". . . saying what's in it for him — never mind the others."

As we talked about it, paragraph 4 came to represent for us the way in which a paper undergoing revision can grow a new branch of meaning, in this case taking a turn which was anticipated in the first draft only by its absence, an absence the class pointed up by asking: What felt good exactly? Why go through all this painful labor? One answer, the expected one, lay in the revision's articulation of what it can mean to "help your neighbor"; the other lay in Eric's writing his way through the conceptual blockage of that way of labeling his experience, to the point where he could see himself as a responding subject of the work he did.

There is, then, a curious two-way movement to Eric's revision: on the one hand, in disentangling himself from the dense particularity of the first draft, he distances himself from the immediate experience so as to be able to take up a perspective on it and to recompose it according to his vision of an emerging communal "we"; on the other hand, clearing out that mass of detail also opens the way for him to come much closer to his own relationship to the work so as to define the "I" who performed this work and wrote about it, and in doing so transformed it and gave it meaning.

While we all came to see some version of this transformation, we were never agreed in seeing it as an improvement. And revision, perhaps, especially a first revision, will not always produce what we would recognize as a more coherent and finished piece of writing. It is necessarily messy, this business of rethinking what before came pat. The new material will have the raggedness of a first draft; the cuts may feel like amputations. There are certainly some losses — of specificity, perhaps, and "interest" in Philip's terms — among the gains in feeling and purpose in Eric's revision. Philip and Walter missed the account of mud falling on the diggers, and I felt that an abbreviated version of the cement episode, referred to only tangentially in paragraph 6 as if we already knew about it, might have worked now that it could be set in the newly developed context of what made it all worthwhile. Perhaps Eric took some of the class's responses too much to heart and cut away too much. Class discussion of papers is, after all, inevitably a process of estrangement: the class takes the paper away from the writer so that it is no longer simply his language, his experience; it belongs for a time to the class as a basis for their comments about writing and working. It becomes, that is, a text bearing meaning for others, open to their reading and interpretation. In that process it comes to be seen as something whose meaning can be shaped by a reader's activity. At the moment of revision, however, it is the writer who must become that reader. Estrangement and the distance that allows perspective are followed by reacquaintance as the class gives the paper back to the writer with renewed power to make it his — even if, in the end, it is impossible to separate what is "his" and what "theirs."

Improvement or not, there was no doubt that Eric's elaboration of the meaning of this work for him put him in a position to draw much more interesting and useful comparisons between paid and unpaid work than would have been possible on the basis of paper 4's one-line conclusions:

[8] . . . The difference between being paid and not being paid is like the difference between night and day. Work that you get paid for your doing it for a couple of reasons. One you really love the work and being paid is the bonus, which doesn't happen to very many of us. The other is your only doing it for the bucks. You start out loving getting that paycheck, cause you work hard for that, but the novelty wears off, cause you expect that paycheck and more. The work you do goes unnoticed, you first start the day really working your tail off, but by the end of the day your tail is dragging. Mostly because you only got a half hour for lunch, no breaks. They almost expect you to be superman, never getting tired, or frustrated or sick of doing the same dam thing. Someone's always making or telling you to do something, you always got to check with them, as if you can't make a decision on your own. But you can't make a decision even if you wanted to because they never tell you anything.

[9] They come out of that air condition office, and see you once the whole day and that's the time when you're taking a breather, so they give you a look of intimidation, never saying a word, but you know what they are thinking, "get back to work slave."

[10] With unpaid work, it's not that the work is more easier, but working for yourself is the most satisfying, because you choose to do it, and your the person controlling the situation. Doing this unpaid work you would feel you wouldn't care too much about it, but you actually spent more time in doing it right. You get to see the whole job through from beginning to end, the progress, the setbacks, the mistakes, and time to learn and change them and to do it right this time. But most of all it's the finished prodcut, you say did I do that, you stand back and your proud of yourself and you look back when you started, you thought you were never going to finish. Some days when you felt you didn't do too much, you say tomorrow another day. You take it one step at a time, if you tried to take it all on at once, you would go crazy and sometimes you do, that's when you feel like giving up. So you got to pace yourself, so you don't run out of steam.

[11] The only thing that was the same was when I was working with other people, at my paid job the only

time I really enjoyed working was when we were unloading the trucks, we could take our time, and talk to the truck drivers. So you would talk to them once a week and get to know them. One guy was driving a Pepsi truck for forty years. I ask him how he liked it, he said he had another year to put in before he retired, and told me to stick to school and get an education and be someone.

[12] So work whether it's paid or unpaid and as long as your treated decent, is like riding a bike and you come to a big hill, you don't look at the top because you can't see it, and if you did, you would never attempt it. So you shift gears and take it one pedal at a time, and pace yourself, don't try to check your progress too much, because then you don't feel like your moving, and before you know it, your at the top and can't see the bottom no more, you say to yourself, that was a breeze, because you were patient.

How to account for the emergence of these new ideas, developing, as they do, some of the deepest concerns in Eric's relation to work and his goals for the future? There is little here that can be seen to be directly anticipated in class discussion of paper 4. And while it is true that Eric's revision of 4 made certain of these reflections possible (the emphasis on overcoming obstacles and the satisfactions of physical work are brought forward indirectly), much also is missing (the redefinition of "helping your neighbor," for example). Yet these new ideas had been prepared for; they are in fact new only in the sense suggested by James Moffett, that "a new thought is a further thought about an old one," a new synthesis of old ideas. The sequence of assignments Eric was working on is structured to foster this dialectical process of rethinking: each new act of writing builds on and away from what has been written and thought before. It was, I believe, Eric's previous reading and writing for the course which put him in a position to sustain these new thoughts about control over one's work.

In his journal entry on selections from Studs Terkel's *Working* (our first assigned book), Eric had admired and envied those workers "who loved their jobs": "They are the fortunate ones because they had a freedom of choice to be what they wanted. They stuck with it because of the pride it gave them in working hard at it . . . never sacrificing their quality of work or giving anything less."

The first writing assignment had called for an essay in response to "The Secretarial Proletariat," an article describing the work experiences of a pink-collar worker.[15] Eric empathized strongly with her powerlessness: she was "just a body they have control over for eight hours to command as they wish, and no respect to be given on your part. But they treat you on a different level as if your incapable of making a decision on your own, which would make your work a little more easier and bearable for you to do. . . . I respond to what everything Ann is saying Because I have experience some of the same things she went through."

In Assignments 2 and 3 (3 being a revision of 2), Eric went on to recount some of those experiences. In 2 he told of an incident on his job as a stockboy in a wholesale supermarket: in trying to deal generously with a good customer — alerting her to an upcoming sale — he ran afoul of the manager who "chewed [him] out" in front of the customer for overstepping his duties. Eric concluded that his part in the incident demonstrated his "pride in helping people get the most for their money" as well as his "pleasure in getting to know the regular customers. . . . Because this was my only relief from management when I was talking to a customer and way of getting back at them, through the customer getting their most satisfaction, & to make sure they weren't getting rip-off."

In Assignment 3 Eric added a parallel story in which he went to the aid of a customer whose muffler had been caught by some protruding railroad tracks in the store's parking lot: "He offered me money but his thanks was quite enough I said. It felt good helping out another person in a jam." To do so, though, he had again to defy his boss, exercising freedom of choice when officially he had none: "I knew I was right. Right in meaning to stand up and say this was wrong [leaving the tracks sticking up], even if it was worth losing your job." He was in fact fired a month later, Eric wrote — hence his return to school.

Writing next about volunteer work became an opportunity for Eric to explore his responses to work which is neither bossed nor timed — work, in other words, in which he could exercise "freedom of choice" and "decision making," and in which he could take considerable pride. It was, then, an act of "sequential revision" — putting his volunteer experience, as he had recomposed it in paper 5, against his earlier narratives of paid work — which gave rise to these new possibilities: that it may be, paradoxically, the presence of bosses which prevents one from doing what one considers a good job; that a paycheck is no incentive to working hard; that, whereas pride on the job came mainly through work done in defiance of boss and work rules, pride in voluntary work lay in labor itself and in its "finished product"; that "working with other people" can be a major source of satisfaction in work; and finally, that work, like riding a bicycle up a hill, takes continuous effort and gets you somewhere you want to be. Through these reflections, Eric was in the process of forming the three distinct lines of concern he was to carry forward into the semester, each of them deeply personal and representative also of certain political and psychological conditions of work in general: (1) the role of structures of power in determining one's work experience; (2) the role of work in creating community, and conversely, of community in validating the work one does; and, (3) somewhat in contradiction of this, the sense of work as a solitary confrontation with external obstacles and with the limitations of the self suggested in the closing cycling metaphor.

That final paragraph (12) shows that Eric still has the Basic Writer's tendency to want to end with a moral, to offer his conclusions — what he "learned" from this — in the form of a guide for future conduct. Yet the cycling image as Eric has elaborated it here works, I think, because in drawing on his most committed spare-time occupation as a metaphor for work, "whether it's paid or unpaid," he was imagining possibilities for fulfillment in all work — "as long as your treated decent." Privately, I admired the metaphor also for the rich analogy between Eric's view of work here and his experience as a writer in the BRW classroom.

Teacher Commentary[16]

Few students can have their papers discussed as thoroughly as was Eric's in any given week, and fewer still will make his creative use of that discussion in revising. The most continuous and insistent way we can represent our reading of our students' papers, and thereby model their rereading, is in our written commentary.[17] If there is a distinction to be made between the kinds of concerns addressed in discussion and in commentary — and this will vary from class to class and teacher to teacher — I'd say that discussion typically helps most with matters of intelligibility, proportion and emphasis. Students, in other words, can help a fellow writer shape his narrative and explain his thinking, but they're generally reluctant to read papers dialectically. They're unlikely, that is, to see problems of dissonance, contradiction and other disturbances as promising invitations, even more unlikely to deliberately force a writer back into the chaos of his ideas, to encourage changes of mind or radical reformulations. Fostering this more challenging and uncomfortable dimension of revision is, I believe, primarily the responsibility of the teacher, a responsibility which rests on our authority as both the class's most experienced writer and reader, and, whether we like it or not, as "the teacher."

Written comments, then, are our chance to move beyond the terms onto which discussion continually threatens to fall back — terms of adjustment: more feeling, less detail, a longer conclusion. Our more pointed comments can invite the writer to question and explore the language of his paper in such a way that rewriting becomes a deliberate method of rethinking his subject. We may, for example, direct a writer's attention to shortcuts and simplifications, to places where his effort to elaborate an idea has been abandoned, often at a point of fruitful complexity, and a chunk of conventional wisdom wheeled forward in its place. We notice clichés and repetitions, then, not as errors, but as alternatives to going forward into the thicket of all the other possible sentences. We point out contradictions, gaps, and breaks in logic, not so much as lapses requiring reconciliation or bridging, but as possible openings to a dialectical shift in the train of thought. As in guided class discussion, the intention is always to draw the writer into becoming an active reader of his own paper, so that, on the basis of what he is able to see taking shape there, he may go on in the next draft to produce a fuller, smarter, more satisfying representation of himself and his relation to his subject. While we acquaint him with the emerging shape of his thinking, however, our commentary seeks also to indicate the possibilities of choice and change in how he thinks about his experience and what he will make it mean.

Page 191 shows a first draft of a BRW paper which was later revised with the aid of my comments. The assignment, which occurred about halfway through the sequence on adolescence, asked the student to draw on his experience in order to respond to a passage by Edgar Friedenberg, of which the paper's first paragraph may stand as a simple precis.

The major difficulty with this paper as I read it is that it claims to represent a conflict which is, in fact, foreclosed in favor of one side — the advisability of conformity to "athority" — before the conflict has really been explored. One sign of this capitulation is that the history of the conflict is described only in an abstract and skimpy way, albeit with some feeling; it is

① *Good summary*

In Friedenberg's <u>Vanishing Adolescent</u>, he brings up the idea that a conflict between society and an individual going through adolescents is essential for his growth in his individuality. I agree with his idea because I have had experiances proving him right in my eyes.

One of the experiances that I had that follows this is a personal revolt against athority. When in high school, I would not listen to teachers or any other person in athority in the school system. Because of this I was constantly being punished. Being punished was interfering with how I could go about doing things when not in school. My will wanted to do one thing while the teachers wanted me to do another. After a while of doing this, doing wrong and getting punished for it, I started to <u>comply</u> to what they said. I also started to <u>agree</u> after a little while longer, to what they did and said. It was hard for me when I didn't comply. I was miserable and very frustrated because I couldn't do what I wanted to do. Now that I look back at it, I feel more sure of myself about what I did was right. That is to comply to society or the teachers.

why not?

How punished?

② *Was it a struggle giving in to them?*

② *I like this distinction. Can you say more about the difference between complying and agreeing?*

The conflict was going against what my teachers which is society, said. It does lead to adulthood because this conflict teaches you things that you didn't know before and does lead to their <u>critical</u> participation in society because you finally do <u>conform</u>, such as I did, which is assuming your place in society. The reason though the conflict is even there is because the individual doesn't agree with what society says is right. This causes the conflict, but after a while of trial and error the individual realizes that <u>to function freely you have to conform</u> and in conforming you realize that everyone benefits and not only yourself.

④ *How is conformity critical?*

⑤ *This is an interesting paradox. Can you explain what you mean by it?*

⑥ *Sam, when you revise this, look again at the quotation from Friedenberg. The situation you describe reads to me like conflict as a process of getting beaten into shape. Is that what you mean, or what he means, by conflict being essential to one's growth.*

not enacted in the writing with the kind of specificity that could allow Sam to draw from it a personally informed conclusion about the value (or the damage) of conflict in adolescence. Another sign of his turning away from what was obviously a painful complexity is the suddenness of his conversion to conformity in the middle of the second paragraph; there is no account of the process of change. Some of my comments, then, are addressed to the skeletal nature of his account of the conflict, while others dig at the neatness of his premature resolution of it. My intention is to provoke Sam into reopening the question. As I go through my comments and explain my intentions, I am, of course, retrospectively supplying a rationale for what arises much more spontaneously than this explication implies.

1. "Good summary" because Sam has succeeded in translating the terms of the passage into a proposition he can now go on to test against his experience, as I ask him to do in my final comment (6). Sam clearly understands Friedenberg well enough to be in a position to see what he does not yet see, that the experience he relates does not fit Friedenberg's notion of benign conflict as neatly as he assumes.

2. Here I am appealing for some narrative detail and explanation, hoping that in bringing with it more of Sam's feeling about the conflict, it will provide a more tangible basis for exploring what the conflict was about.

3. In "comply" and "agree" the writer has found useful terms for a distinction which I see as central to his subject, since the distance between complying and agreeing may encompass considerable growth in individuality (or its erosion). But he has not yet said what these terms mean to him, nor how he got from one to the other.

4. As the contradiction in the sentence implies, Sam uses Friedenberg's impressive-sounding phrase "critical participation" as if the adjective "critical" were not there. I am pointing out the word in hopes that he will notice how its contrast with his use of "conformity" goes to the heart of the issue he is engaged in writing about.

5. Whether one agrees with it or not, the aphorism that "to function freely you have to conform" embodies a sophisticated insight and I wanted Sam to explore its implications. But, as it happened, I scared him away from his own wording here by giving it my teacherly label "paradox," which Sam took as a

sign of something wrong, to be eliminated. The idea itself, though, recurred with greater definition in the revision.

6. In my final comment I am asking Sam to reconsider the relation of the situation he has described to the formulation from Friedenberg he began with by telling him what this version of his experience sounds like to me: "a process of getting beaten into shape." As it turned out, I was also giving him a hint of an alternative language he could use to disconfirm the language of "authority," including the published authority of Friedenberg, which was holding him powerless to take a more critical view of his experience.

Revision of Sam's Paper

The next assignment called for a revision of the Friedenberg paper. I have excerpted only the concluding section of Sam's revised draft which offers, I believe, another example of what thorough revision may be said to do for a writer. It begins with his reflections on what had become a more concrete and engaging narrative of the conflict as an ongoing war with authority, escalating from trouble with teachers over homework to more serious altercations with parents and the law:

> ... It got to the point were I would go out of my way to do something wrong because "authority" didn't want it. Well since I live in a society, the things I did were hindering society's flow so they corrected me to conform to the rules they made. Their correcting me was actually punishing me. The punishments ranged from getting a good crack across the head from my parents to being made to help in the old folks home from the local J.P. or the juvenile court. This made me angrier because they were treating me like a dog and giving the respect that I had the intelligence of one also. By a dog I mean that if you don't want a dog to do something you punish it, and sooner or later the dog won't do it in fear that he will get punished. So I kept doing worse things and in return got worse punishments. After about two and a half years of this I started to realize that to do the things wrong just wasn't worth the punishment I would get. Just like the dog that realizes it just isn't worth the beating to go on the rug but easier or less painful to cry at the door. So after a long while I started to accept society's ideas not for the reason that I agreed or understood why but because I was almost actually trained to.

As for right now that I am a little older and have passed through some of my conflict, I do agree with some of society's ideas not because I was so well trained that I really believe them but because I see now that for everyone to do as much as they want to can't be done without hindering someone else. I have been hindered because of disrespect for my being which isn't right. After this I look back and see that I wasn't only being trained but it was an indirect way of teaching one respect. There are though things that I still don't agree with such as doing homework but I have learned I will do it for a better grade so I can do better in later life, which is just respect for myself. Maybe later in my life I will agree with the things I don't agree with and maybe change my mind about the things I agree with now.

It all comes down to you have to have conflict to get your individuality. If you didn't have the conflict and conformed to whatever society said, then you would react the way society predicts you to act and would be a social puppet. If you did have conflict then you know why (for the most part) society has the rules of which it does, and they are based on respect. Those who have had conflict learn respect by first hand experiances. Since they learned it by first hand experiances, they will have their own way of reacting to disrespect and have their own degrees of respect to what they want to respect; which is your individuality. The more of a conflict the more you think on your own therefore the more your individuality will come out.

What seems to me to have happened in and through this revision is that the fleshing out of Sam's story has been the means to his engaging in a much more complex and sustained examination of the issues of freedom and conformity it raises than was the case in his first draft. One mark of this is the emergence of the metaphor of the dog which signals a reformulation of Sam's conception of himself in relation to authority.[18] It is possible that my comments about "giving it to them" and "getting beaten into shape" prompted the new image; but the writer's development of the metaphor, particularly his giving it that poignant twist whereby the reward for learning not to "go" on the rug is not to be let out to sniff around the neighborhood, or even to be taken for a walk, but instead to be left to cry at the door — this is his own. That the avoidance of pain should lead to more pain suggests perhaps that Sam is not as assured as he later sounds that the rewards of conformity are worth the costs.

In any event, the metaphor provides him with a new term for this process of enforced conformity: he was "trained." However — and this is the mark of someone exploring thought in writing — as soon as he has his new label, he begins to question and qualify it: he was "not *so well trained* that he really believes [society's ideas] ''; he "wasn't *only* being trained." And what he now sets against the notion of "training" is his previous term, "agree," an opposition which enables him to refuse the total capitulation training implies and reclaim a space for himself as someone who will make up his own mind about society's demands (including mine as his teacher) and who can, when necessary, negotiate a pragmatic compromise with them. Structurally he opens this space by extending the chronological separation, only hinted at before, between the era of compliance and that of provisional agreement. He complied *then* because he was trained to like a dog; but since he is now, as he implies, neither somebody's dog nor society's puppet, he is in a position to agree or disagree — and not, one notices, on the basis of some cantankerous do-your-own-thing individualism, but rather of a nicely detached sense of where he ends and "society" begins, and of how they might get along for now.

It is customary to be wiser because older, but the cliché here is more than a cliché because Sam has learned from this conflict something rather different from what he was taught. From a process of acculturation which he describes as having been like housebreaking a dog, and which expressed "disrespect for [his] being," he has arrived at, or perhaps wrung, an ethic of "respect" for others, for himself, for his future. His ability to convert the one into the other is in large part a function of his ability to revise. For he has figured this out through writing this out, in a process that represents a step in his growth as a writer certainly and perhaps also in the kind of self-definition Friedenberg claims as the outcome of conflict and the prerequisite of "critical participation" in society.

I am not suggesting that my comments by themselves pushed Sam into revising. Much of students' willingness to do major rewriting depends, as I have argued, on the rhetorical and epistemic contexts of the course: the community of readers and writers in the class, the design and sequencing of assignments, and so on. Even with these incentives and supports, revision will not happen unless it is asked for, by name, as a regular part of the writing process.

What our written comments can do for Basic Writers is translate these incentives and demands into sets of specific opportunities for developing their thinking through revision: in our comments we can offer a consistent line of response to a central issue in the text; we can address the language the writer has already used, suggesting the implications of particular choices and opening up important questions and possibilities which are implicit in his writing; and we can recognize and affirm the kind of intellectual endeavor Sam shows in making his adolescent experience with rebellion into a way of taking on the question of paradoxical demands of individual freedom and social existence. By helping our students, in this way, to identify and interrogate the emerging meaning of their texts, by behaving, in other words, as readers of their writing the way we would like them to behave in it as writers, and by enacting in our comments how we take what they do there seriously, we in effect empower them to revise — and to use revision, as we use it, to better understand the subject which engages them and which they thereby engage.

Empowerment

Empowerment is perhaps a lot to claim for this process. Let me close, then, by suggesting one way in which Sam and Eric seem to me, in these papers anyway, to be themselves empowered by revision. It is that in revising they have been able to move against the authoritative institutional languages which threaten to structure their discourse for them. Eric had to puncture the false obviousness of phrases like "helping your neighbor" (with its automatic alliance with "feeling good" and "group effort") in order to discover how working to help others could do more for self and others than the phrase ever suggests in its routine invocations in, say, charity appeals or beauty pageants. Sam had to unravel "what my teachers which is society, said" about respect in order to learn how to begin to respect himself and how to reconcile self-respect with the fact that he "live[s] in a society." In doing this both Eric and Sam were developing theoretical ways of accounting for the politics of their situations. If, then, a student's understanding of his particular subject, and his intellectual growth in general, proceeds largely in this kind of dialectical movement, if, that is, he gets to the next stage of thinking through an issue by reflecting critically on his own, or others' prior formulations of it, then it is primarily the activity of revision which drives the process; for it is in revision that the writer is able to look again at what has been said and, with our support, to appropriate those languages he is surrounded and occupied by to his own purposes as a student.

Notes

[1] See, for example, Nancy Sommers, "Revision Strategies of Student Writers and Experienced Adult Writers," *College Composition and Communication* 31 (1980): 378–388, and Lester Faigley and Stephen Witte, "Analyzing Revision," *College Composition and Communication* 32 (1981): 400–414.

[2] See, for example, Thomas Newkirk's accounts of Anne's resistance to revision in "Barriers to Revision," *Journal of Basic Writing* 3 (Fall/Winter, 1981): 50–61.

[3] Faigley and Witte.

[4] Sommers 382.

[5] "The Epistemic Approach: Writing, Knowing and Learning," *Eight Approaches to Teaching Composition*, eds. Timothy Donovan and Ben W. McClelland (Urbana, IL: NCTE, 1980) 65–85.

[6] I am here developing a suggestion made by Susan V. Wall in "In the Writer's Eye: Learning to Teach the Rereading/Revising Process," *English Education* 14 (Feb. 1982): 9.

[7] James Moffett, *Teaching the Universe of Discourse* (Boston: Houghton, 1968) 14–59.

[8] L. S. Vygotsky, *Thought and Language* (Cambridge, MA: MIT P, 1962) 80, quoted by Ann E. Berthoff, *The Making of Meaning* (Upper Montclair, NJ: Boynton/Cook, 1981) 16.

[9] To avoid the awkwardness of "he or she," I will use the male pronoun when referring to "the writer," since it happens that the two students whose work I discuss are male.

[10] I realize that in speaking of "stages" of the composing process I run counter to the current perception of the "atonceness" (to use Ann Berthoff's term for it) of everything in the process. Prewriting, writing and rewriting are all writing, it is said, and revision is therefore "a normal constant" throughout (Donna Grout, "A Normal Constant," *Missouri English Bulletin* 41 (July 1983): 1–5). I agree with William Pixton, however, that while the view "that revision operates recursively throughout the writing process describes quite well the activities of experienced writers . . . , students trying to imitate these activities may be overwhelmed" — they simply can't *do* everything at once ("Reconciling Revision with Reality in Composition Teaching," *Missouri English Bulletin* 41 (July 1983): 20). What

they need, it seems to me, is the luxury and the space that postponing certain concerns provides. It makes better pedagogical sense, then, especially for Basic Writers, to teach first drafts, one or more revisions, and edited "final" drafts as distinct stages, and even on occasion as separate assignments.

[11] Susan V. Wall and Anthony R. Petrosky, "Freshman Writers and Revision: Results from a Survey," *Journal of Basic Writing* 3, 3 (Fall/Winter 1981): 111.

[12] The dialogue which follows is a fictional reconstruction of class discussions of this paper. It represents, I believe, the general movement, or in places the desired movement of such discussions, but without the falterings, the red herrings, the heavy silences which give them their particular dramatic tension. If we all, teacher and students, do rather better here than we ordinarily do, it is because I wanted to suggest what we can occasionally do for one another through this kind of writers' conversation.

[13] Moffett 23.

[14] This assignment, like the series on "Working" as a whole, was a collaboration between my coteacher, Susan Wall, and me.

[15] *Sisterhood Is Powerful*, ed. Robin Morgan (New York: Random, 1970) 86–100.

[16] A version of the final section of this chapter appeared in the special issue on revision of the *Missouri English Bulletin* 41 (July 1983) under the title "Response and Responsibility." It is printed here with the permission of the Missouri Association of Teachers of English. The special issue, "Revising," is available from NCTE Publications, Urbana, Illinois.

[17] Other teachers, I know, would give their responses in individual student conferences, and I have taught some Basic Writers who could "hear" a response in no other way. I would argue, though — quite apart from the merits of conferencing — that most students benefit from the experience of "reading" teacher comments — that is, of interpreting them, imagining what prompted them, and above all seeing them as questions to be addressed, rather than, say, objections to be answered or disturbances to be eliminated.

[18] I learned to pay attention to a change of mind "signalled by the emergence of new metaphors" from Susan V. Wall, "Revision in a Rhetorical Context: Case Studies of First Year College Writers," diss. U of Pittsburgh, 1982, 64.

7.

Acts of Wonderment

Fixing Mistakes and Correcting Errors

GLYNDA HULL

The teaching of editing can best begin, I've come to think, with acts of wonderment. By wonderment, I mean the appre hension and appreciation of another's way of thinking; a kind of insight, often sudden, at times marvelous, that allows one to see from another's vantage; an epiphany, if you will. We will show how it is possible for teachers to know this wonderment, by learning to see errors from the perspective of their students. And, we will show how such wonderment is possible for students, as they come to see errors from their teachers' points of view.

Prolegomenon

Here are five addition problems and a child's erroneous solutions to them. By studying these solutions, it is possible to discover the child's algorithm for addition, his systematic albeit erroneous procedure for getting the sum of two numbers. In other words, if we can figure out how it is logically possible for the child to add 33 and 99 but get 24, and if the same procedure can account for his incorrect answers to the other problems, then we have found a way to view arithmetic as does the child:

33	1091	8	28	90
+99	+ 60	+34	+70	+ 6
24	17	15	17	15

His procedure for adding, it turns out, is simply to disregard columns and to treat each digit as separate. He might, in the first problem, have proceeded by adding $3 + 3 + 9 + 9$, or in the second, by adding $0 + 6 + 1 + 9 + 0 + 1$. His answers — though passing strange — are understandable and predictable, given his *modus operandi.*[1]

One can imagine the difference this kind of discovery would make in the mind of a teacher, if she otherwise would view her pupil's solutions just as evidence of her failure to teach or his failure to learn or to follow directions or to pay attention. All of a sudden, she is instead able to see addition as her student sees it and to recognize a kind of logic in his answers. She has moved from viewing his errors as merely wrong to considering them as evidence of the way he understands math. She is, of a moment, able to appreciate as well as to apprehend, and this, I think, is the stuff of wonderment. One can also imagine the difference that such an epiphany has the potential to make to a student — given, of course, that the teacher's interpretation of the erroneous procedure is actually correct, and given as well that she can find a way to represent her discovery to him.

In recent years, with Mina Shaughnessy's example to give us heart, those who teach beginning adult writers have come to realize that errors in syntax and punctuation and grammar and spelling can be systematic — they are violations of language conventions, it is true, but they are violations that often exhibit a pattern and possess a logic. And so, realizing this, we've been eager to pass along what we know to our students, to make it possible for them to recognize the logic and pattern of their own errors and to see where their rules and procedures depart from conventional ones. Yet, as we shall see, this kind of wonderment doesn't come cheap. It isn't always apparent how to view the errors in a student's text from the student's point of view. And there is yet a bigger leap to be dared when we turn from constructing a meaning for the errors that we see in a text to teaching a student to see and to edit them.

Yet, it's worth the daring. Errors in syntax and punctuation and grammar and spelling are a big part of the problem accompanying basic reading and writing students as they negotiate a composition course. They make a great number of these errors — twenty or twenty-five mistakes per 300-word essay not being unusual — and if they see how frequently these errors appear in their writing, they are apt to be daunted by their apparent innumerability. The numbers speak to teachers too, although they are apt to be more taken aback by the seeming strangeness of the errors, a kind of extremity that pushes hard against the boundaries of convention and results not only in the common and expected homophonic confusion of *their* for *there*, but the jarring and fantastic amalgamation of *impurtichular* for *in particular*. Students don't know precisely why such errors appear so strange to readers, not having anything to measure by, though they are very sensitive to the surprise and uneasiness which greets their writing, and this sensitivity can range from disgruntlement to a debilitating kind of self-consciousness.

It's important, then, to find a way to deal with error in writing, a way to help teachers and a way to help students. That's what I try to offer, first by illustrating the problems that teachers face, with reference to a single case study, in seeing errors from a student's perspective, and then by discussing more generally what such a shift in perspective might mean in terms of classroom instruction.

Acts of Editing

I once observed a writing teacher, in the midst of a conference with a student, hold a pencil horizontally and then shift it so that its point was directed toward the student. "You see," the teacher said, "you can look at a pencil this way (and he held the pencil horizontally, its length in view), or you can look at it this way (and he turned the pencil so that its apex rather than its plane was visible)." Given its context, I imagine this demonstration was meant to suggest how it is possible to take a different perspective on something, to view an idea or phenomenon as a particle, a wave, or a field, as Young, Becker, and Pike would say; to turn an idea about in one's mind as one could turn a pencil about in one's fingers, looking first at it from this vantage and seeing it one way and then from another vantage and seeing it anew.

If mental twirling were as easy as its physical counterpart, we might have an easier time at error analysis, which, after all, requires that we engage in an analogous kind of perspective shifting as we invent new ways of seeing the errors in a text and find other ways of labeling them than is our custom. Perhaps the factor that contributes most to this difficulty is what psychologists would call the "knowledge base" of a writing teacher. Having detected and identified and labeled myriad errors in students' texts and in our own, having developed (or appropriated from grammar books) a taxonomy for those errors we see, having done proofreading and editing a sufficient number of times that we could, as they say, do it in our sleep or with our eyes closed, we've become expert enough that our knowledge, our expertise, can stand in the way of any perspective shifting. As experienced readers and writers, we edit differently than do inexperienced readers and writers — very, very differently. And as teachers of writing who mark errors in students' texts, we edit more differently still than do the authors of those texts.

Here is the last paragraph of an essay written by a college student in response to an assignment: "Write a paper about someone who has had a significant influence on you and the way you see your relationship to work. Then, when you've described your relationship with this person, go on to explain how your life as a worker might have been different had you never known this person." The student chose to write about his tribulations with an army sergeant, and he tries in accordance with the assignment to draw some conclusions about the effects of his experiences:

> My response to this story I feel work that SFC Robert Cooley had such a big influence in my work he always kept me busy "every" minute. Im not a Lazy person but, I could never understand him and they way he operated, I don't have any bad personnal feelings toward him, I feel sometimes he tryed to make me think Just Like hm toward work. Until this day everytine I see him, I have strange feeling that he has a "eye" on me and wants me to stay occupied "every" minute of the day.

Here is a transcript of a teacher's comments as he corrected the errors he saw in the paragraph and labeled them. His instructions were simply to change whatever was necessary in order for the paper to be correct and to explain his changes as he went along.[2]

> The beginning of the last paragraph is, is peculiar. I I think that what he meant to say was *my response to this story I feel was* and he's put *work* instead because *work* is on his mind and it comes up later in the sentence. *My response to this story I feel was that* umm, would make it better, but with that language he has I would want to change it this way: *The response to this story I feel was that*. I'm calling that all one error. It's probably caused by his using the wrong word, *work*, for *was*.
>
> Next error — got a run-on sentence again. Sentence should end after *work*. And rather than just leave that

short sentence hanging there by itself, *he always kept me busy every minute*, I think I'd rather combine the sentence and say *because he always kept me busy every minute*.

The next error would be to take the quotation marks from around *every*.

Next, there's a missing apostrophe to represent the elision of *a* on *am*.

I'm not a Lazy person, unnecessary capitalization, the *l* on *lazy*.

Unnecessary comma after the *but*. If he wants a comma at all, it should go before the *but*. I would put one before the *but* and after the *person*, for the pause there in the sentence.

He's written *they* for *the*. Take the *y* off that. Spelling mistake.

Got a comma splice at *he operated*. Change that comma to a period.

Misspelling of *personal*.

That sentence, *I don't have any personal feelings about him*, is of course totally contradicted by the sentence before and after it. In other words, I'd take it out, but again, since it's there, it's spliced by a comma to the sentence that follows, so we need a period after *him*.

Misspelling of *tried*.

Unnecessary capitalizations of *just* and *like*.

There's a letter missed out of *him*. Put the *i* back in there.

And I can't remember whether *toward* or *towards* is correct. Let's see. (whispers) I'd be inclined to say *towards*, but I'd have to look it up and see what was correct.

The last sentence, then, *until this day*, that's an introductory element that needs to be comma-ed off.

Everytine. He's run two words together there, presumably by analogy with words like *everything*. Needs to be separated.

Misspelling of *time*.

Omitted the indefinite article there — *I have a strange feeling*

. . . *that he has a*. The *a* should be *an*. I suppose technically that's the wrong form of the indefinite article.

Has an eye on me. I want to get rid of those quotation marks around *eye*. They're unnecessary. Same for *every*.

If we were to characterize the activity of editing as it is represented in this protocol, we would surely need to acknowledge the great degree to which it seems automatic, second nature, a reflex.

> He's written *they* for *the*. Take the *y* off that. Spelling mistake. Got a comma splice at *he operated*. Change that comma to a period. Misspelling of *personal*.

It seems as if this teacher needs, in most cases, only to see in order to know and to act. The sight of an error triggers a recognition of that error, and the recognition of that error triggers a knowledge of its correct form. So automatic does the process appear that to represent it in stages — detect, diagnose, correct — is almost to falsify its nature. The stages seem automated to the point of almost occurring simultaneously.

One way to account for such automaticity is simply to recall, as I did earlier, the amount of practice that teachers have in just such an activity. We've done it so often, we can do it in our sleep. But this explanation doesn't really address the character of the "knowledge base" that must underlie the activity. It doesn't give us a way to understand the nature of what is practiced. If, however, we compare these episodes with ones which don't seem so automatic, the nature of editing, as this teacher performs it, becomes clearer.

The most striking example of a nonautomatic episode is the teacher's struggle, at the very beginning of the protocol, with the unusual sentence *My response to this story I feel work that SFC Robert Cooley had such a big influence in my work. . . .* "The beginning . . . is peculiar," the teacher first observes, and then goes on to reconstruct what the writer's intentions might have been and to speculate about the reason for the mistake: *I think that what he meant to say was my response to this story, I feel, was and he's put work instead because work is on his mind and it comes up later in the sentence.* The teacher has no ready label for the troubled syntax of the sentence; that is, the error doesn't immediately trigger a grammar book category like *comma splice* or *spelling*. And because there's no category, there's no immediately apparent correction. Rather, the teacher imagines what the writer most likely wanted to say; that is, he approximates the writer's syntax by imagining his intended meaning. Thus, the teacher doesn't deal here in prefabricated labels and rules for written language conventions; he deals in meaning and intention.

What a different activity editing seems in the other episodes, where, for the most part, he edits quickly, automatically, efficiently by consulting his knowledge of the rules governing written language conventions, rules about sentence boundaries, quotation marks, apostrophes, capitalization, spelling. This strategy, a "consult-a-rule" approach, becomes transparent in the episode in which he can't quite recall the rule he wants:

> I can't remember whether *toward* or *towards* is correct. Let's see. (whispers) I'd be inclined to say *towards*, but I'd have to look it up and see what was correct.

Whether he is able to call up labels and rules from memory or must locate them in a handbook, editing for this teacher seems an activity which, to borrow a term from computer science, is "table-driven." That is, to access a given rule, one need only access the error that goes with it; they co-occur, chart-like. Only in unusual circumstances, such as when an error doesn't match any given rule, will a different strategy be used, such as attending to meaning or to the way a sentence sounds. I am suggesting, then, that for this experienced teacher/writer/reader, the activity of editing is mostly rule-governed as opposed to mostly meaning-driven.

Here is the transcript of part of another protocol, one in which the student author of the paragraph given above attempts to edit his paper, to find all of the mistakes in it that he can. The other speaker in the protocol is a tutor.

> S: (reading aloud) *My response to this story I feel.* Okay, I could put put a comma there, couldn't I? . . . *I feel comma,* maybe.
>
> T: . . . I think you need to put in another word, like *My response to this story* blank *that.* What would you put?
>
> S: Okay, when I done that, I put myself in this story now, because I'm talking about this guy over here. Okay, I could maybe put *I realize. My response to this story I realize that,* you know.
>
> T: . . . The trouble is that you need something else in there besides the phrase *my response to this story* even if you do have a comma. . . . Okay, without looking at your paper, how would you finish the sentence, *My response to this story is that?*
>
> S: *Sergeant First Class* . . . Okay. So I put *is that?*
>
> T: Yes, you could put, *My response to this story is that* and then finish it however you want to. . . .

S: (reading aloud) *He always kept me on the, he always kept me busy every minute,* I should put *every minute of the day.* (pauses and writes) *I'm not saying, I'm not a lazy person but I could never understand him and the way he operated.* Okay, ummm. (Pauses and then continues). Okay, ummm, I'm on *I don't. I don't have any bad personal feelings toward him although* (he writes the word *although*) *I feel sometimes he tried to make me think just like him toward work. Until this day every time I see him, I have a strange feeling that he has a eye on me and wants me to stay occupied every minute of the day.*

T: Go back to the last paragraph. You've got *My response to the story is that I feel work that SFC Cooley had such a . . .* Wait now, how are you gonna fix that? *My response to the story is that I feel . . .*

S: *. . . I feel that SFC Cooley had such a big influence in my work. . . .*

T: Okay. *My response to the story is that I feel that SFC Cooley had such a big influence in my work he always kept me busy every minute.*

S: *every minute of the day.*

T: Oh, I'm sorry. *every minute of the day.* If you had to break that into two sentences — you've got it as one sentence now — you've got *My* up there, that starts it, and it ends with *day.* If you were gonna break it into two sentences, where would you break it?

S: Maybe, uh, maybe right after *work.*

T: That's right. In fact, you've got to break it there.

S: Yeah, because I'm talking about myself and then him, okay.

T: All right. *My response to this story is that SFC Cooley had such a big influence on my work.* Period.

S: Yeah? Okay.

T: You were gonna put a comma there?

S: Yeah, I was. Uhh, could you?

T: Well, let's talk about that. . . . When you've got two sentences, you can't have just a comma between them. You could have one sentence and a period and start the next one with a capital letter. Okay. But you can't have two sentences separated with a comma unless you have some other word, like *but* or *although* or *and.*

Okay? Now, let's go on down a little bit. *I'm not a lazy person but I could never understand him and they way, the way he operated, I don't have any bad personal feelings toward him although I feel sometimes . . .* You've got a bunch of sentences there. All right, now let's start back with *I'm not a lazy person* and you tell me where that sentence ends.

S: Ummm, okay, right after *operated* I have a comma there.

T: Yeah, is that the end of the sentence? Tell me why you've got a comma there instead of a period?

S: Okay, umm, the first part, I'm talking about myself, and then I'm talking about him, about my feelings toward him, but it should have been a period there, huh?

T: Yeah, after *operated.* That rule you have about putting commas when you change subjects, when you're talking about yourself and then you're talking about somebody else and you put a comma? That won't work a lot of the time. . . .

S: I see.

There isn't much that is automatic about the student's editing in this protocol, except, perhaps, his propensity not to notice some of his errors and to correct others of them unconsciously as he reads aloud. On his own, he makes one correction: he inserts an *although* between two sentences that are spliced together with a comma — *I don't have any bad personal feelings toward him although I feel sometimes he tried to make me think just like him toward work.* It's not clear, however, that he recognizes the error that he's corrected. On the contrary, it's probable that he doesn't, since he fails to correct any of his other comma splices. It seems more likely that he adds the *although* out of an attention to how the sentence sounds or perhaps to what it means. He tries two other overt corrections: he wants to add a comma after the phrase *My response to this story I feel,* and he changes *he always kept me busy every minute* to *he always kept me busy every minute of the day.* The former attempt doesn't correct the sentence's error, and the latter doesn't qualify as a correction, for *every minute* would do, one might argue, just as well as *every minute of the day*; the change doesn't, then, address an error at all, but a matter of style or meaning. The errors that he corrects as he reads aloud, but doesn't acknowledge as corrections, are syntactic anomalies. He supplies a left-out word: *I have a strange feeling* for *I have a strange feeling*; he exchanges *they* for *the* in *they way he operated*; and he pronounces *tine* as *time* in *every time.*

So, the point is that most of the sentence-level errors that are salient for the teacher are not salient for the student. The student doesn't notice most of the errors that the teacher detected and diagnosed and labeled so automatically, and he isn't aware that he has corrected others. Unlike the teacher, he doesn't operate upon the text by means of a well-honed set of rules for written language conventions. In fact, the one rule that he is most intent upon applying isn't a convention in the usual sense at all; that is, it isn't an agreed-upon social custom for setting forth language in written form. Rather, it is an idiosyncratic rule for punctuating discourse that is driven by a concern for semantics.

The rule makes its appearance early. Like the teacher, the student stops at the beginning of the paragraph to puzzle over a construction, but he attends to a different aspect of it than does the teacher. He doesn't appear to notice anything peculiar about the way the phrase *My response to this story* is juxtaposed to *I feel*, nor does he comment on the strange collocation *I feel work that SFC Robert Cooley had such a big influence in my work*. Rather, he wants to add a comma, "maybe," he says, after *I feel*. And his explanation for this comma doesn't have anything to do with setting off introductory phrases or interjections or compound sentences or items in a series or any of the other familiar rules for punctuating. Rather, it is born of the fact that, as the student explains, "I put myself in the story" first and "now I'm talking about this guy over here." Later he uses the same rule to correct (with the tutor's prompting) a run-on sentence. He wants to put a comma between *SFC Cooley had such a big influence in my work* and *he always kept me busy every minute of the day* "because I'm talking about myself and then him." And later he defends a comma between *I could never understand him and the way he operated* and *I don't have any bad personal feelings toward him* because "I'm talking about myself, and then I'm talking about him, about my feelings toward him."

What we see here is a buggy rule for the use of commas between sentences — a rule that apparently has no basis in conventional handbook rules for the use of commas. This writer has imagined for himself, rather ingeniously, a brand of punctuation to set off changes in topic. His rule has its basis in semantics, in meaning. Indeed, it could be argued that the other changes that he initiates show a concern that has more to do with nuances of meaning — the addition of *of the day* to *every minute* and the addition of *although* — than with arbitrary print code conventions. What I want to argue is that this writer not only knows fewer rules and sees fewer errors than does the teacher, but he also approaches editing by means of a very different strategy: instead of applying rules in accordance with conventions for inscribing language, he is more likely to edit by attending to meaning and to justify his choices and his rules with reference to a message or an intentionality.

I don't, however, intend to argue that the act of editing as represented in these protocols can be generalized to other experienced and inexperienced readers and writers (although I think to some extent that it can). The point I am content to make here is that teachers, when they ask their students to edit, can expect inexperienced writers and readers to approach the task very differently than would teachers; so differently, in fact, that for one to understand the approach of the other, there needs to be a conscious kind of shift in perspective, in customary ways of viewing errors and the activity of detecting and correcting them.

Acts of Analysis

John Gardner, in recalling influences on his writing, claimed that medieval ideas and attitudes gave him a means of "triangulating, a place to stand," a framework, it would seem, for looking at issues in the present world.[3] What has long been needed for the study of error in writing is a place to stand in order to look anew at the old phenomenon, a different interpretive scheme for reexamining the familiar and rediscovering its interest. That place has been provided, partially at least, by inquiry into the sources of errors in texts, by "error analysis." The assumption of error analysis is that writers or language learners make errors for a variety of reasons — interference from a spoken dialect, for example, or the overgeneralization of a rule — and that patterns of error and the sources of these patterns can be inferred from a close reading of texts or language samples.[4] If we think about errors in terms of their sources, the reasoning goes, we can view them as procedural bugs, and we can infer the procedures that seem likely to have produced them. And once one knows why a particular pattern occurs, the nature of a particular bug, it follows that we should know better how to teach to it.

In terms of composition pedagogy, this new perspective has most clearly meant teachers paying careful attention to errors in students' essays, and particularly to repeated instances of errors, in order to imagine what about the composition of the essays or sentences in them has resulted in error patterns. When the teacher in the protocol given above speculated that the writer "put *work* instead [of *was*] because *work* is on his mind and it comes up later in the sentence," that teacher shows us the quintessence of error analysis. That is, he located the source of this error; in this case, he interpreted the error as residing in the difficulties inherent in sentence production, when the mind rushes forward and the hand, a poor and uncertain scribe, struggles to keep pace, writing *work* but intending *was.*

Of course, one might imagine other, alternative explanations for the error. We might borrow a label from Mina Shaughnessy and see in this error evidence of a blurred pattern, where the writer starts out with one sentence, *My response to this story*, gets derailed and starts another, *I feel work*, and then discards part of that sentence as well to begin a third pattern, which he finishes: *I feel that SFC Robert Cooley had such a big influence in my work.* This interpretation locates the source of the error in the difficulty the writer has in getting started and views the incomplete patterns as a record of his attempts — attempts that might never be put on paper had this writer been more experienced in trying out patterns in his head before writing them down.

Or perhaps the error is tied to something outside the writer's own linguistic repertoire. It does seem peculiar for him to begin with *my response to this story* when the story he is responding to is his own. Perhaps the syntactic disjuncture is a sign that he is trying on language that is not completely his; maybe he's taken a phrase, *my response to this story*, from the language of an assignment but has failed to make it his own syntactically. If this is so, the source of the error might lie in something larger than the difficulty of producing a sentence; it might lie in the writer's attempt to approximate academic-sounding language.

Or perhaps the source of the error lies in patterns of speech. One author who has a sharp ear for dialogue had a character in one of his novels say, *"See, my sister what she did she run a grits mill."* [5] The phrase *what she did* seems to stand in relation to *she run a grits mill* in much the same way as *my response to this story* stands in relation to *SFC Robert Cooley has such a big influence in my work.* The first phrase acts as a harbinger of the second. Viewed this way, the error becomes an example of how the rhythms and patterns peculiar to speech can find their way to the page.

And there may be other ways to account for the error as well, other interpretations as likely as the ones imagined here. In their article on math bugs, Brown and Burton take great care to illustrate how tricky it is to diagnose such errors accurately. There may, for example, be several ways to account for a student's answer to a given problem, several explanations or buggy rules that will produce the same erroneous sum. Nor do math bugs lie still and wait for us to examine them. It is not uncommon for a student to change his erroneous procedures midstream, in the act of working a problem, if those procedures no longer serve a purpose. Brown and Burton mention the case where a child formats his problem erroneously; that is, he might "left justify" 185 minus 13 by writing the 13 under the 18 instead of the 85, which in turn allows him to get the answer 55. But when he happens upon a problem that this procedure won't allow, like 185 minus 75, where 75 can't be subtracted from 18, he may invent another way to proceed, such as subtracting the smaller digit from the larger regardless of which is on top, and thereby get for his answer 635.

What is needed, then, is a way to narrow the possibilities, and one way to do this is to broaden the sample size, to look not only at the error in question, but at other instances in that student's writing of what appears to be the same error pattern, and to see which explanation (if any) seems to account for the group. Below is such a sample, drawn from the student's work across a term:

1. My response to this story I feel work that SFC Robert Cooley had such a big influence in my work he always kept me busy "every" minute.
2. My response from this story I felt that she was pressured by her own peirs who never understood Ruth's Viewpoint.
3. My first impression toward Victor Bean I felt he was all right, but as work proceeded I got to know him and his emotions toward younger people.
4. My future employment, I want to advance myself in the clerical or business field, because I feel their will be openings and advancement, high paying salary.
5. My first impression, I felt he was a pretty decent guy who Liked to work but also Liked to kid around sometimes.
6. Upon my Autobiography about work, I feel everywhere you go there's always a snotty workaholic, or Mr. Know it all, in every aspect of employment.

7. Finishing the story about Ruth James, she was the type of person who believed in herself and never Liked to be pressured by her peers.
8. Learning from the experience I had working with children you have to have patience and understanding toward their feelings.
9. Reading the story about Teresa Torres Cardenas, she wanted to fulfill her dreams.
10. Recieving a new supervisor he was easy going but he also Likes to work not as much as the other Seargent.

These examples show the writer regularly employing a kind of "topic/comment" structure. That is, he juxtaposes a topic to a comment on that topic without benefit of syntactic joining: *My first impression, I felt he was a pretty decent guy* rather than *My first impression was that he was a pretty decent guy; Recieving a new supervisor he was easy going* rather than *When I received a new supervisor, I found him easy going; My future employment, I want to advance myself in the clerical or business field* rather than *In future jobs I want to advance myself in the clerical or business field.* I am reminded of Old English poets and their appositional style, where themes are announced and then elaborated.

I am most amazed by how regularly, and with what consistency, this writer employs his topic/comment structure. Not only did he use the same syntactic constructions, the noun phrase beginning with *my* or a gerund announcing an activity, he also used them at particular places in his essays. Eight of the ten appeared as the first sentence in a paragraph, and six of the ten appeared as the first sentence in the first or last paragraph of an essay. It appears, then, that these topic/comment constructions serve in this writer's discourse to mark the boundaries of broader ideas or movements, a shift, for example, from telling a story to interpreting its significance — the move, one should note, that was specified in the assignment. Thus, I see these errors as examples of this writer imagining a means of shaping a discourse, of constructing sentences not for the sake of sentences but for the sake of a larger meaning. I see them as this writer finding a way to bring the activity of writing, of meaning making, under his own power. How clever of him, I think to myself, how ingenious.

The interpretation, based as it is on several instances of the error, seems so clear to me; the meaning that I have constructed for the error, so satisfactory. I am almost sufficiently enchanted to believe that it will be easy to represent this discovery to the student. But there's the rub.

Acts of Teaching and Learning

The assumption behind error analysis is that once we can locate the cause of a particular kind of error, then we're in a better position to teach a student to correct it. It is not, however, altogether obvious what to do about an error, even after one has managed to understand its nature. Brown and Burton suppose that for some students and some math errors, one might only need to explain the bug in order for a student to understand and to fix it. (This approach may be appealing by virtue of its directness and simplicity, but it perhaps underestimates the difficulty inherent in the activity of explaining procedures.) Brown and Burton also suggest that a teacher might need to construct a set of problems that will allow a student to discover his own errors himself. Or perhaps a teacher needs to demonstrate symbolic procedures in terms of physical procedures — by using blocks, for example, to model the concepts of tens and ones.

In the case of the topic/comment error, we presumably must find a way to make a student aware of the discrepancy between his quirky way of writing sentences to introduce a topic and more conventional ways. Here is one tutor's attempt to do that:

> T: Look at the very first sentence of your essay, and tell me if it sounds odd or peculiar to you at all.
>
> S: (reads aloud) *Reading the story about Teresa Torres Cardenas, she wanted to fulfill her dreams.* (chuckles) Okay, what I'm saying is, I'm saying that I've read the story, *Reading the story . . .*
>
> T: Yeah, it's the way this first phrase you've got is tacked onto the rest of the sentence.
>
> S: Okay, could I say *Reading this story about Teresa Torres Cardenas, she wanted to fulfill her dreams*? I could put *this.*
>
> T: You could put *this*, but that's not going to fix the problem. What readers expect when they hear this, *Reading the story about Teresa Torres Cardenas*, they expect a particular word to come after that. Who's doing the reading?
>
> S: They are, the teachers.

T: Who? You wrote this, though; you did the reading, right? This is your interpretation of the story, your response. So when you hear this, you expect a person to come next. *I, I saw that she wanted to fulfill her dreams.* You see. . . .

S: I see, I really understand. What you say is that *reading the story about Teresa Torres Cardenas may have?* . . .

T: Try *may have* and see.

S: OK, *may have* . . . Okay . . . no, no, no, no.

T: Right! Keep experimenting. See what you can come up with.

S: *Reading the story about Teresa Torres Cardenas* . . . I could put *I felt that she wanted.* So you always want to put your personal opinion next to that?

T: You don't have to. There are other ways to say that, but because of the way you started the sentence by saying *Reading the story about Teresa Cardenas,* a reader expects you to say *I saw that* or for you to put yourself in there. . . . Let me show you some more sentences like that. How would you finish this sentence: *Eating a bagel this morning* . . . ?

S: . . . *I felt that is was a nasty bagel.* But I don't want to use *bagel* twice.

T: We could say *I felt it didn't taste good.* But the point is when giving an action like this like *eating a bagel* or *reading a story* and the action comes at the beginning like this, you need somebody in the sentence doing it. It doesn't have to be yourself. You could say, *Eating a bagel this morning, Fred got choked.*

S: So you always going to put somebody in there?

T: Well, it's not that you always do, but in that situation, where you start out with words like *eating a bagel* or *reading a story* or *jogging down the road* — in that situation you follow it by putting somebody in it. Now, let's think of another way to begin this paper.

S: (pulling another essay from his folder) Here's another paper. I began it by saying *I enjoy volunteer work very much.*

T: That's fine. There are lots of ways to start a paper, just like there are lots of ways to write any sentence. That's a fine beginning.

S: I couldn't really put that in there, *I enjoyed the story.*

T: You don't want to start with *I,* is that what you're saying?

S: I want to put my personal opinion in there, but I don't really care. What I'm really saying is, I don't like the story at all. (laughing) So that's how come I don't enjoy it.

T: Okay, so why not put *I didn't enjoy* or *this is a lousy story*?

S: I don't want to do that!

T: Why not?

S: Okay, Susan [his teacher] said to really express your opinion, but I don't really want to do that, though.

T: You don't always have to say you like the story when you didn't like it. You really don't.

S: Well, some particular stories I don't really like.

T: Well, maybe that would give you something to write about. Let's come back to the paper and find another way to say that sentence. Start it with her name. If you start it with her name, how would you finish it?

S: *Teresa Torres Cardenas . . . was a part of the Cardenas family.*

T: Stick with this sentence right here.

S: *Teresa Torres Cardenas, she wanted to fulfill her dreams.* That sounds pretty good.

T: Would you say it like that, *Teresa Torres Cardenas, she wanted*?

S: *I felt that she wanted to fulfill her dreams.*

It can be difficult at times to find a way to talk meaningfully about errors to students. In this example, the topic/comment error doesn't sound strange to the student, and when asked to hear it as strange or somehow wrong, he can only imagine that perhaps *this* should be substituted for *the*. When the tutor tries to work with the student's comment that *I'm saying that I've read the story* by suggesting that there is no one in the sentence who's doing the reading — a restatement of the old dangling modifier problem — she makes no headway, as evidenced by the conversation about eating a bagel. All the student can conclude is that *you always going to put somebody in there.* When the student turns to another paper which begins differently, he confuses the structural error that the tutor is addressing with semantics; he can't begin the paper in question with *I enjoy* because he didn't enjoy the story, he explains, and anyway, he thinks it inappropriate to admit in an essay that he didn't enjoy something he'd been assigned to read. The tutor's final attempt to get the student to imagine another way of beginning his paper is a marginal success. His first inclination is to write an entirely different sentence, and his next attempt contains another kind of error, which he miscorrects.

It is remarkable, I think, how unswervingly the student and tutor talk past one another. They do so, in large part, because they are truly talking about different things. The tutor brings to her reading a particular kind of understanding of texts, where it makes sense to pay attention to the structural logic of sentences, and she tries to explain the errors in terms of that understanding. And in so doing, she loses the student, who just isn't able to participate in her discussion, not yet being a party to her notions of error and editing. He, on the other hand, seems to have his own agenda for improving his text, an agenda which turns upon a concern, not so much for how individual sentences are put together, but for what is appropriate semantically and stylistically. Given the abyss they have to negotiate, I don't think it's altogether surprising that the tutor and student aren't able to accomplish a great deal in their session together.

The question remains of how it's possible for a teacher to teach a student to edit; to teach him, that is, how to approximate what it is that we do when we edit, how to see the errors in a text in such a way as to be able to imagine conventional corrections for them. I don't think it's often possible to do this explicitly, by giving a student explanations for errors, unless a student shares a teacher's language for describing sentences — a condition that is uncommon among inexperienced readers and writers. It's also unrealistic to think, in the space of one semester in a writing class or even two, that teachers can create this shared language through instruction in grammar and usage.

What can be done in the way of teaching students to edit is illustrated in the following protocol. This conversation between a student and his tutor is a continuation of the protocol given above in which the student reveals his idiosyncratic rule for using commas as end-stop punctuation. The tutor has just explained that the student's rule about using commas instead of periods when there's a shift in the topic of a sentence "won't work a lot of the time." And the student has replied, "I see."

T: Let's look back to the first page of your essay. You've got *I was introduced to my supervisor Sergeant First Class Robert Cooley*, then a comma, right?
S: Uh huh, yes, that's a comma.
T: That's another one of those places where a sentence ends.

S: Okay, so I should have put a period.

T: Yes. Read over it and see if you see what I'm talking about.

S: *I was introduced to my supervisor Sergeant First Class Cooley.* . . . See, cause I'm talking about *my*, I'm talking about how I was introduced, and then I'm talking about my impression.

T: Yeah, even though you're talking about yourself still, you've still got two sentences there, and you'll want to separate them with a period.

S: Okay. Well, if I did put a comma there, would that be wrong?

T: Yeah, it would be wrong unless you put something else with that comma like an *and* or a *but*. Now, let's keep on talking about separating sentences. Go to the sentence that begins *I was introduced to* and read all the way to the period and tell me where you need a comma.

S: (reading) *I was introduced to my three co-workers and they showed me what their duties consisted of.* Okay, after *co-workers.*

T: Right. How'd you know?

S: Because it had an *and* there.

T: That's right, but it's not just because there's an *and* there but because there are two whole sentences and an *and.* You could say *apples and oranges* and you wouldn't need a comma. You just need a comma with *and* when you join up two whole sentences. Now let's go down to the next paragraph. Explain your reason for the commas.

S: (reading) *As the day proceeded my supervisor expected so much work out of me that I couldn't rest for a minute*, comma, *he kept me busy "every" minute of the day* period.

T: I don't understand why you put a comma after *minute.*

S: Could it be a period?

T: Yeah, but so that I can understand your way of using commas, tell me why you think there should be a comma there.

S: That's a mistake right there.

T: Well, OK. Look now at the sentence beginning *he always.* Check and see if you need a period anywhere.

S: (reading) *He always wanted his section to be first in everything, such as the AGI inspection this inspection is the biggest one of all because it would make a good impression on the higher authorities above him.* Whew. It just goes on and on. Okay, I have a comma after *everything*, but we just put that there. Okay, I could put one right after *all*. Because I'm just telling how it would make a good impression on the guy.

T: I think you need to keep the *all* as part of the sentence. Go back and look again.

S: After *AGI inspection*?

T: Exactly right. Where does the sentence end that begins *After the AGI inspection*?

S: (reads) *After the AGI inspection, he got the seal of approval for his section, he would reward us with beer, pop, and other types of food, but this reward still kept me on the defensive side because I knew sooner or later he would say "back to work."* After *side*. Let me see, no, after *work*.

T: That sentence needs to be split into two sentences, and I bet you can tell me where.

S: Okay, I have a comma right after *section* . . . I have a comma right after *food*.

T: And you have a *but*, and that's okay because it's joining two sentences.

S: What about right after *side*? No, I couldn't put it there because . . . I mean because the rest of the sentence wouldn't sound too good.

T: Go back to the beginning and look again.

S: Okay. I don't see where else.

T: Right after *section*.

S: I have a comma there.

T: But it won't work there. You tell me why.

S: (laughs) Maybe because I'm talking about my section, and then in the next part I'm talking about how he rewarded us.

T: You've got two sentences there joined by a comma, and what you need is a period. So, some of the places that you're putting a comma to end a sentence, you need to put a period.

S: I'll really have to watch myself.

T: Go on to the next paragraph.

S: (reads) *I remember one incident that happened two months ago while I was typing a letter, I was introduced to two members of my section I showed them my duties and asked some questions about themselves, then all of sudden my supervisor pops out of nowhere and asks what I'm doing, I told him what I was doing.*

T: All right, and that's all one sentence?

S: Oh. . . . Whew! I see. But I have a couple of commas in there.

T: But remember a comma doesn't mean the end of a sentence.

S: Okay, what about right after *letter*?

T: Excellent. You need to put a period there. Now go on.

S: Period after *themselves*.

T: Good.

S: (reading) *Then the two members of my section . . .* Okay, I should put a period there.

T: Excellent, Now you're catching on.

S: (chuckling)

(The tutor and student correct a few more sentences.)

T: I think we've done enough for today. But before you leave, I'd like you to write down a rule about what you've learned on how to use commas and periods.

S: Let's see, umm (beginning to write in his notebook), *put commas where they belong, and put periods where they belong.*

The success of this tutorial has to do with the student's gradually being able to perceive the pattern of an error. He finally sees enough instances of the error and gets sufficient feedback on his attempts to correct it that he is able to think about punctuating sentences in his tutor's terms rather than his own. In this instance, as in many others, the crucial pedagogical strategy is to make it possible for a student to recognize error patterns and to consider alternative constructions. The best way that I know of to do this is to make the patterns as salient as possible by grouping all errors of a general kind together in order to represent them as instances of the same problem.

I am suggesting, then, that the teaching of editing will ideally proceed through conferences — conferences similar to the last protocol where a teacher directed a student's attention to several instances of one kind of error, allowed him to propose corrections, and offered feedback on his attempts. The feedback need not (should not) consist of elaborate explanations couched in grammatical jargon. Sometimes students just don't know enough grammatical terminology to make use of the explanation. Sometimes they appear to understand and they believe truly that they do understand, but in actuality their notion of a "complete sentence" or a "comma splice" is incomplete or erroneous or is otherwise different from their teacher's, though it goes by the same name. In such cases, teachers and students will talk past each other and seldom realize it, and students won't do any better at correcting errors.

Sometimes, having recognized how limited or inaccurate is that knowledge that a student is able to articulate about English grammar, we are tempted to start at the beginning, to teach rudiments like the identification of parts of speech, in hopes of building a common vocabulary for our discussions of error. And sometimes it is necessary to step aside from a student's paper to discuss verbs in the abstract in order to say why some verbs can end in *ed* while others can't. What should be avoided is anything approaching a full-scale or formal introduction to rules of grammar and usage. Such instruction, as it moves steadily away from a student's own writing to the pages of a handbook or to workbook exercises, will inevitably become, in a student's perception, distant; it will be viewed apart from those problems he must struggle with in his own essays.

In lieu of formal and extensive instruction in grammar and usage, we've set aside class time (usually while students are reading or working in their journals) to have conversations with students about individual problems in their recent papers, conversations in which a teacher, suspecting (for example) that a student doesn't pronounce certain endings and therefore doesn't write them, calls attention to this fact ("you hear *has ask* even though the actual form is *has asked*; you sometimes leave the endings off of *ask* and other verbs in your writing") and directs the student as he searches for particular instances of that particular error in the paper ("here in this paragraph you've left off some *ed*'s; can you figure out where?"). This also works particularly well for syntax and sentence boundary errors, where students are simply told that there is something wrong with some sentences, or with the way the endings of some sentences are marked, and then set the task of choosing the problem areas and rewriting sentences or reworking punctuation. It isn't essential, in other words, that a student know how we describe and analyze syntax in order to make decisions about "good" and "bad" sentences and how they might be reworked. What is essential is that he begin to work as an editor, looking at sentences *as* sentences and revising syntactic patterns or reformulating rules for the use of commas, periods and semicolons. This is not to say that students will get everything right on the first pass. In fact, this is seldom the case. The student won't be working randomly, however, and the exercise as an editor will enable him to see his idiosyncratic systems and to revise them when told that the decisions he is making are just not always right. Sometimes the

amount of direct instruction in grammatical concepts that a
teacher must supply is greatly reduced by a student's ability to
imagine, by force of repeated example, what might be wrong in
a sentence and how a problem might be corrected. And if this
is the case, so much the better, for the nettlesome problem of
how to introduce grammatical terminology is thereby finessed.
The student has either named the problem for himself or the
name has emerged in the dialogue between teacher and student.

This procedure need not be limited to private conferences,
however. Another way to make it possible for students to recognize error patterns and to begin to work on their technique as
editors is for a teacher to highlight sections of a paper that contain instances of one kind of error with a marker or with check
marks in a paper's margin (highlighting perhaps two lines, perhaps a paragraph — depending on the student and the date in
the semester). This is often done when a paper has gone through
revision and it is no longer time for the teacher to respond with
marginal comments as a reader — when it is time, that is, for
students to edit rather than revise a paper. The students, then,
work on their own, inductively, to determine what the error
might be and how they might correct it. Initially, this procedure
works best during a writing class, after a teacher has returned
papers, for students can then be given time to search the high-
lighted areas and to correct the errors with some guidance. Students generally need help at the outset, until they get a sense of
the kinds of errors they typically make, and until they become
more skilled at the unusual form of reading required for the job
of editing.

Through these procedures students begin to learn the difficult process of search and recognition that characterizes the
work of an editor. They learn to direct that search through their
own emerging sense of the dominant patterns of error in their
own writing, and they learn to develop (and to trust) their own
resources in imagining the form to offer as a correction. A correct form, then, is something they must learn to imagine, not
something that lies beyond them (perhaps in a handbook), and
a mistake is something they can find, not a glitch hidden in
their text, a text whose varied surface they are never empowered
to read.

Some instruction can, of course, be provided *en masse*, although I find myself decreasing annually the number of things
about error and editing that I try to teach to a class as a whole.
While some students confuse word boundaries (*impurtichular*,
a student will write, along with *everytime*), others never or

rarely do, and instruction geared to the one group is wasted on (and sometimes confusing to) the other. Generally, I've found it safest to limit group instruction to those things that the majority of students don't do in their writing, rather than those things that they do incorrectly (which require both learning and unlearning). For example, inexperienced writers don't typically use quotation marks, so how to punctuate direct quotations is something that can be taught efficiently and well to an entire class. The same is true for punctuating with semicolons, though this mark is far more troublesome, dealing, as it can, with sentence boundaries. The other sort of group instruction that it's helpful to provide is information, not on particular mistakes themselves, but on strategies for detecting and correcting them. We all have heard and recommended the old saws of "read your paper from the bottom up" and "read your paper aloud." To help students attend to patterns, it's also helpful for them to keep their own lists of the particular sorts of errors they tend to make, and to proofread their papers several times, looking for only one kind of error at each pass. All of these activities can be modeled in class, using a sample student paper.

Because of the great variability among students in the kinds of errors that they make, it's hard to codify a sequence for the teaching of editing, where a teacher could be assured that it's best to begin her conversations about editing with homophone errors and then to proceed to sentence boundaries and then to punctuation mistakes. It is almost as difficult to say with any certitude precisely when in a semester these conversations should begin, although most Basic Reading and Writing students have severe enough troubles with error that to delay instruction on editing more than a month or six weeks into the term is to threaten their chances of finishing the course and being able to produce a relatively error-free essay. Generally, I have students focus first on those errors that seem most troublesome to them individually, those that are likely to persist, and it is possible to determine which those are by means of an editing protocol, as illustrated before. With those students for whom error isn't a big deal, who make the expected mistakes with some frequency, it's possible to postpone instruction until midterm. With those students for whom error is a significant problem, who make many and various errors and can't detect and correct most of them, I begin work on editing as early in the term as possible — that is, as soon as I think that students are clear on the distinction between editing errors and revising the thought of a paper. (The distinction isn't only useful as a means of encouraging students to revise; it also helps them to sort out and categorize the kinds of problems they'll need to deal with at different stages of their writing.) I make the distinction by having students engage first in revision and then, some weeks later, add editing as a separate stage in the preparation of their papers.

Epilogue

When I ask teachers to find and label the errors in students' texts, I am often surprised at the range of their responses. Not only do they show some idiosyncrasy in what they identify as an error (some blackballing as unacceptable the same constructions that others pass over and still others praise), but they also demonstrate a variance in their willingness (or perhaps ability) to imagine errors from the point of view of the author, to accomplish that shift of perspective that will allow them to stand wistful and admiring before a new understanding of a student's linguistic ingenuity. I hear one teacher puzzling over (yet engaged by) the error I've called a topic/comment mistake, hear him speculate: *I'm pretty sure it wasn't just a careless misspelling, [for] the word* work *is going to come up later in the sentence and he's just thinking ahead and it just popped in here. It was triggered by the* w, *I guess.* And I am taken aback when I hear another teacher unable to move beyond her bafflement that the sentence doesn't make sense.

David Bartholomae has noted how peculiar it is that we readers who can account for deviations from expected conventions in literary texts, and account for them in "elaborate and sympathetic ways," find it so difficult to "shift this habit of attention for supposedly 'elevated' modes of expression to the verbal wrestlings of our students."[6] He thinks of error analysis, then, as involving an act of interpretation, as depending, like readings of literary texts, upon what a reader chooses to assume about an author's intentions. Error analysis begins, he says, "with the double perspective of text and reconstructed text and seeks to explain the difference between the two on the basis of whatever can be inferred about the meaning of the text and the process of creating it."[7] (And herein analogies to math bugs fail, for there can be no doubt about a math text as it should be reconstructed.)

I've begun to think there is a kind of progression that leads to the habit of mind that makes it possible to engage in error analysis, or view errors imaginatively, with wonderment. On the one extreme, there is the tendency to see a text only in terms of our own reading of it, to correct an error as if we were the author: "This doesn't make sense, or this doesn't sound right, and it should read this way" — the kind of stance that has traditionally been ascribed to teachers of English. Then there's a kind of intermediate stage where a teacher is able to think in terms of a student's intentions, to remember that the error represents a writer attempting something, but is unable to imagine what that something could be. One teacher observed, as she studied the topic/comment error: *the student really has several different complete sentences, or potentially complete sentences, and uh, he vaguely is trying to get them in relationship to each other, but he isn't able to do that.* And then there are teachers who are able to venture beyond description to reconstruct a scenario for the production of a deviant sentence that transforms it, makes it understandable and natural.

I'm still puzzled, though, still waiting to learn, what the process of perspective shifting is like for inexperienced readers and writers. I think I have some sense of it, or at least I persist in thinking that their change of view, the alteration of their rule systems and editing strategies in favor of what they perceive to be more conventional ones, is analogous to the perspective shifting that teachers must engage in to understand the production of errors in their students' texts. That is, it consists of a comparison between a text and another's intended text (this time, the intended text of convention), and a blessed understanding of how and why they differ. It's a slower process for students, though, more arduous, and one less likely to end with a sudden epiphany and a shout of eureka — not because students aren't excited by the prospect of learning to control errors in their texts, for most are, believing as they do that sentence-level correctness is important, a route to power — but because their realizations about error and written language conventions are for a long time murky and uncertain and unarticulated. In the last protocol, the student finally begins to "catch on," his tutor says, at last begins to relinquish his notion about using commas as end-stop punctuation in favor of his tutor's system. He does so after repeated trials and feedback. But his summation of what he has learned, his statement of an algorithm for guiding the placement of commas and periods, his new rule, is an astonishing show of how few landmarks there are for him in this new territory. "Put commas where they belong," he says with all the solemnity befitting a ritual, "and put periods where they belong."

Usually, however, there is evidence to imply that a process is occurring. When inexperienced readers and writers first begin to edit their writing for correctness' sake, they begin at one extreme, one end of a progression. They order the activity by measuring what they see on the page against their notions of what a text should resemble. And these notions have their origins in many things: bits and pieces of rules and advice, perhaps misappropriated from English classes of the past, transformed now into dictum (don't use the same word twice in a sentence); a vague and often doubted sense of what sounds good and all right as opposed to what grates on the ear and sounds funny or silly or somehow inappropriate (you can't write *to two houses* because that, well, that just doesn't sound right); and an overarching attention to message, to content, to the communication of a particular meaning that promotes additions of phrases or exchanges of words while it obscures matters of correctness.

Then there's a middle stage of learning to edit that's a kind of purgatory, where a student has neither exchanged or modified his old notions of editing nor become comfortable enough with new ones to rely on them regularly or accurately. He might claim to understand one instance of an error, but be unable to see its kinship with another of the same type in his next paragraph. It is during this stage that students are still amazed when they apprehend that, yes, there really are two different words, *your* and *you're*, and they shake their heads and marvel.

Then there's a later stage still when students, if told a sentence contains an error, can generally spot and correct it. By this time, they've developed a sense of the patterns of error in their own writing and know to be on the lookout for missing *ed*'s and sentences beginning with *ing* words, a signal, they have learned, that the sentence might not stand alone. Students are most amazed now by the fact that they miss so many errors that they see so clearly once a teacher has said they are there. They shake their heads and say, "I can't believe I missed that."

And, if things turn out well, if the semester is sufficiently long and everyone is sufficiently methodical and patient, an inexperienced reader and writer will become an experienced one, and he will have developed an editing procedure and an eye for errors that allow him to produce, through editing, sentences that are correct. He will, then, having shifted his perspective through repeated acts of apprehension and appreciation of another's way of thinking, view errors and texts quite differently.[8]

Notes

[1] The examples of math bugs come from an article by John Seely Brown and Richard R. Burton, "Diagnostic Models for Procedural Bugs in Basic Mathematical Skills," *Cognitive Science* 2 (1978): 155-92.

[2] This protocol is part of some research begun with a colleague from the University of Pittsburgh, Elaine O. Lees.

[3] "Cartoons," *In Praise of What Persists*, ed. Stephen Berg (New York: Harper, 1983) 131.

[4] See, for discussion of error analysis as it is practiced in research on English as a second language, Jack C. Richards, ed., *Error Analysis: Perspectives on Second Language Acquisition* (London: Longman, 1977).

[5] Elmore Leonard, *LaBrava* (New York: Avon, 1983) 154.

[6] Review of *Errors and Expectations*, in *Linguistics, Stylistics, and the Teaching of Composition*, ed. Donald McQuade (Akron, OH: L & S P, 1979) 215. This essay is revised and reprinted in *The Terrain of Language*, ed. Donald McQuade (Carbondale: Southern Illinois UP, in press.)

[7] "The Study of Error," *College Composition and Communication* 31 (1980): 265.

[8] Preparation of this manuscript was supported by the Learning Research and Development Center, which is supported in part by the National Institute of Education.